LLEWELLYN'S

2016

Magical Almanac

Featuring
Peg Aloi, Stephanie Rose Bird,
Blake Octavian Blair, Boudica, Calantierniel,
Dallas Jennifer Cobb, Monica Crosson,
Autumn Damiana, Raven Digitalis, Emyme,
Michael Furie, Shawna Galvin, Ember Grant,
Hannah E. Johnston, James Kambos, Najah Lightfoot,
Lupa, Melanie Marquis, Mickie Mueller,
Diana Rajchel, Suzanne Ress,
Lynn Smythe, Cassius Sparrow,
Charlynn Walls, Tess Whitehurst,
Charlie Rainbow Wolf, and Natalie Zaman

Llewellyn's 2016
Magical Almanac

ISBN 978-0-7387-3405-7. Copyright © 2015 by Llewellyn. All rights reserved. Printed in the United States. Llewellyn is a registered trademark of Llewellyn Worldwide Ltd.

Editor/Designer: Ed Day

Cover Illustration: © Tammy Shane

Calendar Pages Design: Michael Fallon

Calendar Pages Illustrations: © Fiona King

Interior Illustrations © Meraylah Allwood: pages 28, 30, 88, 91, 93, 211, 213, 285, 289; © Carol Coogan: pages 35, 38, 97, 101, 253, 256, 259, 298, 302, 306; © Chris Down: pages 52, 55, 110, 113, 114, 236, 239, 242, 291, 293, 294; © Kathleen Edwards: pages 59, 60, 64, 117, 121, 122, 244, 247, 250, 309, 312; © Dan Goodfellow: pages 21, 25, 83, 85, 204, 207, 273, 277; © Wen Hsu: pages 13, 73, 76, 79, 81, 131, 132, 135, 203, 262, 265, 268, 271, 321, 323; © Mickie Mueller: pages 15, 18, 43, 46, 49, 107, 227, 230, 233, 279, 282, 327, 331; © Amber Zoellner: pages 66, 68, 70, 125, 126, 129, 315, 317.

Clip Art Illustrations: Dover Publications

Special thanks to Amber Wolfe for the use of daily color and incense correspondences. For more detailed information, please see *Personal Alchemy* by Amber Wolfe.

You can order Llewellyn annuals and books from *New Worlds*, Llewellyn's catalog. To request a free copy of the catalog, call toll-free 1-877-NEW-WRLD or visit our website: www.llewellyn.com.

Astrological data compiled and programmed by Rique Pottenger. Based on the earlier work of Neil F. Michelsen.

Llewellyn Worldwide Ltd.
2143 Wooddale Drive
Woodbury, MN 55125

About the Authors

PEG ALOI is a freelance writer and media studies scholar. She has written on diverse subjects ranging from color symbolism in film to aromatherapy to women's sexual health. Her blog *The Witching Hour* (at Patheos) explores popular media related to witchcraft, paganism, and the occult.

STEPHANIE ROSE BIRD is an Eclectic Pagan practicing hoodoo, green witchcraft, and shamanism. Deeply into meditation and yoga, she is a creative visionary. She's had five books published: *Big Book of Soul: The Ultimate Guide to the African American Spirit*; *A Healing Grove: African Tree Remedies and Rituals for the Body and Spirit*; *Light, Bright, Damn Near White: Biracial and Triracial Culture in America*; and *Sticks, Stones, Roots and Bones: Hoodoo, Mojo & Conjuring with Herbs*; and *Four Seasons of Mojo: An Herbal Guide to Natural Living*. Her debut novel, *No Barren Life*, a work of literary fantasy, will be published in 2015.

BLAKE OCTAVIAN BLAIR is an Eclectic Pagan, ordained minister, shamanic practitioner, writer, Usui Reiki Master-Teacher, tarot reader, and musical artist. Blake blends various mystical traditions from the East and West along with a reverence for the natural world into his own brand of modern Neopaganism and magick. Blake holds a degree in English and Religion from the University of Florida. An avid reader, crafter, and practicing vegetarian, Blake lives with his beloved husband, an aquarium full of fish, and an indoor jungle of houseplants. www.blakeoctavianblair.com

BOUDICA is best known for her professional reviews of books on paganism. She and her husband ran the *Wiccan/Pagan Times* website until retiring it to pursue other ventures. She also ran Zodiac Bistro, a repository of articles, commentaries, and reviews. A supporter of building Pagan community, she has worked in covens

and also has a solitary practice. She also presents at events and holds public workshops in the Northeast, and now runs an online bookstore and reads tarot cards for clients. Boudica lives in Bucks County, Pennsylvania, with her husband of many years and her cats.

CALANTIRNIEL has been published in nearly two dozen Llewellyn annuals since 2007, and has practiced many forms of natural spirituality for two decades. She is a professional astrologer, herbalist, tarot card reader, dowser, energy healer, ULC reverend, and flower essence creator/practitioner. Her flagship skill is an uncanny sense for precise event-timing. After a decade in western Montana, she is now back in San Diego, California, working toward dual USA/Irish citizenship to more fully connect with her ancestors. She is also a co-founder of *Tië Eldaliéva*, meaning the Elven Path, a spiritual practice based on the Elves' viewpoint in JRR Tolkien's Middle-Earth stories. Visit www.astroherbalist.com or www.elvenspirituality.com.

DALLAS JENNIFER COBB practices gratitude magic, giving thanks for her magical life, happy and healthy family, meaningful and flexible work, and deliciously joyous life. She is accomplishing her deepest desires. She lives with her daughter, in paradise—a waterfront village in rural Ontario, where she swims and runs, chanting: *Thank you*. Contact her at jennifer.cobb@live.com.

MONICA CROSSON is a Master Gardener who lives in the beautiful Pacific Northwest happily digging in the dirt and tending her raspberries with her husband, three kids, four goats, two dogs, three cats, a dozen chickens, and Rosetta the donkey. She has been a practicing witch for twenty years and is a member of Blue Moon Coven. Monica writes fiction for young adults and is the author of *Summer Sage*. Visit her website at www.monicacrosson.com.

AUTUMN DAMIANA is a writer, artist, crafter, and amateur photographer, and has been a mostly solitary eclectic Witch for fourteen years. She is passionate about eco-friendly living and writes about

this and her day-to-day walk on the Pagan path in her blog "Sacred Survival in a Mundane World" at http://autumndamiana.blogspot .com/. When not writing or making art, you can find her outside enjoying nature or investigating local history in her hometown of San Jose, California. Contact her at autumndamiana@gmail.com.

RAVEN DIGITALIS is the author of *Shadow Magick Compendium, Planetary Spells & Rituals,* and *Goth Craft,* all from Llewellyn. He is a Neopagan Priest, cofounder of an Eastern Hellenistic non-profit community temple called Opus Aima Obscuræ (OAO). Also trained in Georgian Witchcraft and Buddhist philosophy, Raven has been an earth-based practitioner since 1999, a Priest since 2003, a Freemason since 2012, and an empath all of his life. He holds a degree in anthropology and is also a professional tarot reader, DJ, small-scale farmer, and animal rights advocate. For more, visit www.ravendigitalis.com, www .myspace.com/oakraven, www.facebook.com/ravendigitalisauthor.

EMYME is a solitary practitioner who resides in a multigenerational, multicat household in southern New Jersey. Hobbies that renew her are gardening, sewing and crafts, and home care and repair. Emyme has self-published a children's book about mending families after divorce and remarriage. She is an avid diarist; dabbles in poetry; creates her own blessings, incantations, and spells; and is writing a series of fantasy fiction stories. Her personal mantra is: Curiosity, Objectivity, Quality, Integrity. catsmeow24@verizon.net.

MICHAEL FURIE (Northern California) is the author of *Spellcasting for Beginners* and *Supermarket Magic,* both published by Llewellyn Worldwide, and has been a practicing Witch for over twenty years. An American Witch, he practices in the Irish tradition and is a priest of the Cailleach. Visit him online at www.michaelfurie.com.

SHAWNA GALVIN is an alumnus of the University of Southern Maine's Stonecoast inaugural class of 2004. Her novel, *The Ghost In*

You, and a collection of poetry and essays, *Mimi's Alchemy: A Grandmother's Magic,* were released in 2014. Her short stories, articles, flash fiction, and poetry have appeared in *Words & Images*; USM's *Free Press*; *Virtual Writer*; *Postcard Shorts*; poems in *Voice of the Bards* and *Retail Woes* through Local Gems Press; and several flash fiction and short fiction stories with Pill Hill Press. Her work is also due to appear in upcoming Llewellyn almanacs, Horrified Press, and Static Movement publications. A freelance editor who has edited short stories for Brutal as Hell, she is embarking on a spooky publishing journey at Macabre Maine.

EMBER GRANT is the author of two books, *Magical Candle Crafting* and *The Book of Crystal Spells,* and she has been writing for the Llewellyn annuals since 2003. She enjoys nature photography, gardening, and making candles, soap, cards, and jewelry. Visit her at embergrant.com.

HANNAH E. JOHNSTON is a witch, mother, and musician. She has researched and written about young people and Pagan witchcraft for over a decade and is the author of *Children of the Green: Raising our Kids in Pagan Traditions.* For more information, visit her website at www.hejohnston.com.

JAMES KAMBOS is a writer and artist. He enjoys researching and writing about folk magic traditions of Appalachia. He holds a degree in history from Ohio University. Southern Ohio is where he calls home.

NAJAH LIGHTFOOT is a Priestess of the Goddess. She is a Witchvox Sponsor, a Lucky Mojo Certified Practitioner, and an active member of the Denver Pagan community. Najah is dedicated to keeping the Old Ways while living in these modern times. She enjoys movies, good food, and practicing the art of Shao-lin Kung Fu. She can be found online at www.craftandconjure.com, www.facebook.com /priestessnajah, and www.twitter.com/priestess_najah.

LUPA is a Pagan author, artist, and amateur naturalist living in Portland, Oregon. She has written several books on nature spirituality, including *Plant and Fungus Totems: Connect with Spirits of Field, Forest, and Garden* (Llewellyn, 2014), and is a prolific artist working with hides, bones, and other organic and recycled materials. When she's not creating awesome things in her home, Lupa may be found exploring the Oregon wilderness. She may be found online at http://www.thegreenwolf.com.

MELANIE MARQUIS is the author of *A Witch's World of Magick* and *The Witch's Bag of Tricks.* She's the founder of United Witches global coven and a local coordinator for the Pagan Pride Project in Denver, Colorado, where she currently resides. She is also a tarot reader, folk artist, freelance editor, and literary agent. Connect with her online at www.melaniemarquis.com or www.facebook.com /melaniemarquisauthor.

MICKIE MUELLER is an award-winning and critically acclaimed artist of fantasy, fairy, and myth. She is an ordained Pagan minister and has studied natural magic, fairy magic, and Celtic tradition. She is also a Reiki healing master/teacher in the Usui Shiki Royoho tradition. She works primarily in a mix of colored pencil and watercolor infused with corresponding magical herbs. Mickie is the illustrator of *The Well Worn Path* and *The Hidden Path* decks, the writer/ illustrator of *The Voice of the Trees: A Celtic Divination Oracle,* as well as the illustrator of *Mystical Cats Tarot.* www.mickiemuellerart.com

DIANA RAJCHEL is a third-degree Wiccan priestess in the Shadowmoon tradition. She fills Pagan infrastructure gaps with services to people of all spiritualties relating to life, death, birth, and peace of mind. Author of *Divorcing a Real Witch* and books on the sabbats Mabon and Samhain, she has written on topics relating to paganism and the occult since 1999. Rajchel is also an experienced tarot reader, has a lively interest in how American folk

magic like hoodoo can apply to modern life, and is fascinated by modern urbanism and how magical lifestyles fit with it. At present she lives in the San Francisco Bay area with her partner.

SUZANNE RESS has been writing for many years. She published her first novel, *The Trial of Goody Gilbert*, in 2012, and has since completed two more. She is an accomplished self-taught gardener, beekeeper, silversmith, and mosaic artist. She lives in the woods at the foot of the Alps with her husband, daughter, four horses, three dogs, four hens, millions of bees, and an ever-changing assortment of wild creatures.

LYNN SMYTHE is a natural witch living in south Florida on 1¼ acres of land devoted to herbs, vegetables, and butterfly gardening. She is a freelance writer and the founder of six diva-themed blogs including the Backyard Diva, www.backyard-diva.com. When she wins the lottery, she plans to retire to a remote sanctuary in the far western regions of North Carolina.

CASSIUS SPARROW is a Hellenic Polytheist and witch, tarot reader, author, and garden enthusiast. He is a devotee of both Hermes and Dionysos, and a practicing polytheist for over ten years. He currently lives on the Gulf Coast of Florida with his darling wife. In his free time, he can be found writing, baking, or working in his herb garden. Contact him at cassiussparrow@gmail.com.

CHARLYNN WALLS resides with her family in central Missouri. She holds a B.A. in anthropology where her emphasis area was in archaeology. She is an active member of the St. Louis Pagan community and is a part of a local area coven. Driven toward community service, she served as the programming coordinator for the St. Louis Pagan Picnic for the past ten years. She is now cohosting a monthly discussion group in the St. Louis area with Ellen Dugan. Charlynn teaches by presenting at various local festivals on a variety of topics. She continues to pursue her writing through articles

for *Witches and Pagans Magazine, Llewellyn's Magical Almanac, Witches' Companion, Spell-A-Day Almanac*, and her blog *Sage Offerings*.

An award-winning author, feng shui consultant, and intuitive counselor, **TESS WHITEHURST** presents ancient, sacred, and highly empowering wisdom in an extremely friendly and accessible way. She's written six books that have been translated into nine languages, and her articles have appeared in such places as *Writer's Digest, Whole Life Times*, and *Law of Attraction* magazine. She's appeared on morning news shows on both Fox and NBC, and her feng shui work was featured on the Bravo TV show *Flipping Out*. Tess lives with her long-time boyfriend, Ted Bruner, and their magical black cat, Solo, in a cozy, incense-scented, twinkle-light-lit apartment in Venice Beach, California. Visit her at www.tesswhitehurst.com.

CHARLIE RAINBOW WOLF is happiest when she's creating something, especially if it can be made from items that others have cast aside. She is passionate about writing, and deeply intrigued by astrology, tarot, runes, and other divination oracles. Knitting and pottery are her favorite hobbies, although she happily confesses that she's easily distracted by all the wonderful things that life has to offer. Charlie is an advocate of organic gardening and cooking, and lives in the Midwest with her husband and her special needs Great Danes. www.charlierainbow.com.

NATALIE ZAMAN is the coauthor of the *Graven Images Oracle* deck (Galde Press), and the YA novels *Sirenz* and *Sirenz Back in Fashion* (Flux) and *Blonde Ops*. Her work has appeared in *FATE, SageWoman*, and *newWitch* magazines, and she writes the feature "Wandering Witch" for *Witches and Pagans*. For more, visit http://nataliezaman .com or http://broomstix.blogspot.com, a collection of crafts, stories, ritual, and art for Pagan families.

Table of Contents

Earth Magic............................13

Nature's Pajama Party:
The Winter World of Wildlife ....
    by Lupa 14

Chalk Magick by Melanie Marquis 21

Rituals of Death in Southeast Asia
    by Raven Digitalis........................26

Root to Crown: Cultivating a Chakra Garden
    by Natalie Zaman.........................34

The Elements in Your Kids
    by Hannah E. Johnston....................43

Spiritual Practice via Archeological Discovery
    by Charlynn Walls 51

Copper Energy Wands
    by Charlie Rainbow Wolf....................58

Evolutionary Ancestor Spirits by Lupa 66

Our Magical Pets
    by Autumn Damiana 73

Air Magic............................81

Mighty Bubbles!
    by Melanie Marquis 82

Heart Gifts: Energetic and Spiritual Exchange
    by Blake Octavian Blair 88

Casting a Circle with the Archangels
of the Four Directions
    by Tess Whitehurst 96

Careful What You Wish For
  by *Calantirniel* 106

Witch in a Pinch:
Celebrating Sabbats or Esbats
without Formal Ritual
  by *Michael Furie* 110

What To Do When Magic Fails
  by *Diana Rajchel* 117

Everyday Color Magic
  by *Peg Aloi* 124

Appalachian Bottle Tree Magic
  by *James Kambos* 131

Almanac Section 137
  Date, Day, Festivals and Holidays, Moon Sign,
  Lunar Phase, Color and Incense of the Day
  2016 Sabbats and Full Moons 142

Fire Magic 203
The Wild Hunt
  by *Charlynn Walls* 204

Urban Crossroads: Magick in the City
  by *Cassius Sparrow* 210

The Magic of Twin Souls
  by *Shawna Galvin* 216

Concentrated Candle Magic:
A Surprising Method
  by *Mickie Mueller* 226

Predators in the Pagan Community
  by *Boudica* 235

Polyamory and Paganism
    by *Autumn Damiana* 244

Envisioning Magic
    by *Dallas Jennifer Cobb* 252

Photos for Magical Manifestation
    by *Suzanne Ress* 262

Water Magic 271

Simple Shell Magic
    by *Ember Grant* 272

Enchant Your Beauty Routine
with DIY Products
    by *Mickie Mueller* 279

Spring Cleaning—Hoodoo Style
    by *Najah Lightfoot* 285

A World of Magick Mirrors
    by *Stephanie Rose Bird* 291

River Song
    by *Monica Crosson* 298

Old Man Krampus
    by *Emyme* 309

Unlock Your Inner Spirituality with
the Magical Power of Water
    by *Lynn Smythe* 314

The Hidden Moon:
Magical Workings for the Void-of-Course Periods
    by *Diana Rajchel* 320

Gem Elixirs
    by *Charlie Rainbow Wolf* 326

Earth Magic

Nature's Pajama Party: The Winter World of Wildlife

by Lupa

I was talking to a fellow hiker a while back, discussing the merits (and drawbacks) of winter hiking. She maintained that she didn't care for it and preferred summer excursions, saying, "There's nothing happening when it's cold, and everything's dead or sleeping anyway!"

I can understand why someone may feel that way, at least in places that don't stay warm year-round. Here in Portland, Oregon, while our winters aren't as harsh as in northern climes, they are quieter than summertime. Most birds migrate south, deciduous plants shed their leaves and quiet down, and small animals either die off or hide away in warm places to wait out the cold.

But it would be inaccurate to say that nothing is happening! We just have to look a little more closely to find out what's going on in our natural neighborhoods. And the best way to do that is to go out into the cold and experience it directly. (If for whatever reason this isn't possible for you, just spend some time looking out a window and making your observations from indoors as best as you can.)

This isn't just about going for a walk to get some exercise. Instead, you're going to be carefully noticing everything that's going on around you, from the ground to the sky. You may have to use your imagination a bit for things that you can't necessarily see but know are there anyway, such as hibernating animals or incoming weather systems. They're also a part of the story.

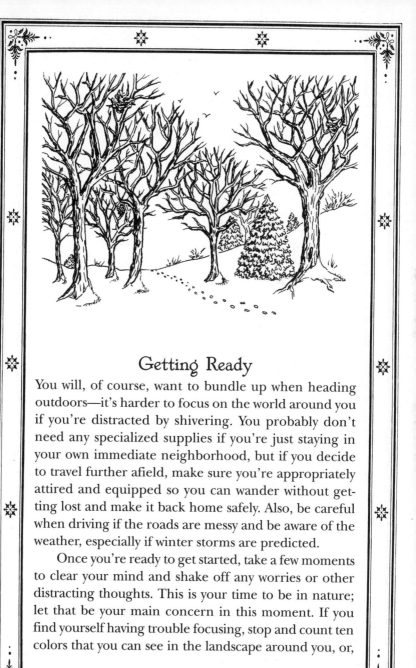

Getting Ready

You will, of course, want to bundle up when heading outdoors—it's harder to focus on the world around you if you're distracted by shivering. You probably don't need any specialized supplies if you're just staying in your own immediate neighborhood, but if you decide to travel further afield, make sure you're appropriately attired and equipped so you can wander without getting lost and make it back home safely. Also, be careful when driving if the roads are messy and be aware of the weather, especially if winter storms are predicted.

Once you're ready to get started, take a few moments to clear your mind and shake off any worries or other distracting thoughts. This is your time to be in nature; let that be your main concern in this moment. If you find yourself having trouble focusing, stop and count ten colors that you can see in the landscape around you, or, alternately, count ten breaths, focusing on how the air feels going in through your nose or mouth, down your throat and into your lungs, and then back out again.

Then, say the following, either out loud or silently within:

I greet the Land around me, and all that live upon it.
I greet the Sky above me, and all it carries.
I open up this conversation with you, in this quiet time,
And I promise to listen as best as I can
With my ears and my eyes and my heart open,
And with all my senses attuned to you.
Let us not be fair-weather friends,
But let me know you also now,
In this quietest of times.

Now you can start your nature walk. There's no specific direction you have to go in; let yourself be drawn into your environment, though take note of where you're going so you can find your way back. As you walk, be aware of every detail from the feel of the ground under your feet to the color of the sky. You might even try pretending this is your very first time exploring the Earth, as though you came into existence just this morning or traveled here from another world. Let the things you would normally take for granted appear new and fresh.

If you're having trouble knowing what to look for, here are some ideas:

Who's Awake?

Although winter is a quieter time, there are still beings who are up and moving about. You might see some of them while you're out. Keep your eyes peeled for birds in particular, though depending on where you are you might catch a glimpse of mammals as well (reptiles and amphibians are in hibernation, of course). I've even seen the occasional insect on an unusually warm day in January.

Just because you don't see the animals themselves doesn't mean you can't find signs of them. If there's snow on the ground, check for animal tracks. Or if it's above freezing, look for patches of mud that might show signs of animal activity. You may even find bits of shed fur or feathers, especially if it's very early or late in the season. And keep an eye on the plants that are left, as herbivores such as rabbits or deer may have left signs of their browsing and grazing.

Take some time to appreciate the toughness and ingenuity of animals that must survive in this cold weather without the benefit of central heating and pizza delivery to make things easier. Consider the adaptations they've made over millions of years, from thick fur and fat to their food-seeking savvy. And be grateful for the warmth and shelter and food you have waiting for you when you return home.

Who's Asleep?

Winter is a time of dormancy for a lot of species, which is why it may seem so quiet. Plants and fungi slow down greatly at this time of year, though conifers and others still photosynthesize and cycle water through their tissues. Occasionally if the temperature rises enough, some plants may produce flowers too early, which are then damaged by a later cold snap; the more cautious plants avoid wasting the energy and resources on flowers that freeze. Many animals, including reptiles, amphibians, and some mammals also hibernate. Some sleep the entire winter through while others may get up periodically to find food, especially if the weather warms up for

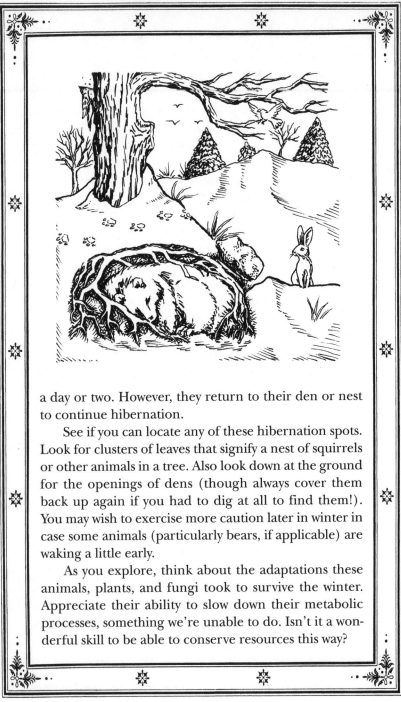

a day or two. However, they return to their den or nest to continue hibernation.

See if you can locate any of these hibernation spots. Look for clusters of leaves that signify a nest of squirrels or other animals in a tree. Also look down at the ground for the openings of dens (though always cover them back up again if you had to dig at all to find them!). You may wish to exercise more caution later in winter in case some animals (particularly bears, if applicable) are waking a little early.

As you explore, think about the adaptations these animals, plants, and fungi took to survive the winter. Appreciate their ability to slow down their metabolic processes, something we're unable to do. Isn't it a wonderful skill to be able to conserve resources this way?

How's the Weather?

No matter what we biological beings are up to, we still must consider the weather. Every day of every year, the complex interplay between the atmosphere and the surface of the Earth affects where precipitation forms and falls, how strong the wind blows and in what direction, and how much sunlight each place gets.

It's probably cold where you are—but is it colder or warmer than usual? Is the sky cloudy or clear, and is there precipitation? Think about the effects this is having on the land and its inhabitants. Remember the signs, weeks or months ago, that hinted at the changes to come, such as the Sun moving farther away and setting sooner each evening, and the average daily temperature slowly sinking from week to week. Do you remember when the first snow or first frost took place this winter?

Take a moment to appreciate the tilt of the Earth on its axis that contributes to our seasons each year. Be grateful for the atmosphere that helps insulate us from more drastic shifts in temperature, and keeps conditions livable for us.

Where's the Water (And What's It Doing?)

We often don't consider the rain and snow that falls outside of how much it affects us, especially if we're inconvenienced by it. It also may seem unnecessary for so much water to soak into the ground when there's not enough heat to dry things up as in summer. But all year long, living beings rely on this precious resource.

Trees still keep drawing water through their roots and lose it through respiration; if not enough water accumulates during winter, they can dry out and begin to die. And those animals that are up and awake still need to drink. However, water may not always be accessible; it may be frozen in a thick layer of ice over a lake, or soaked into deep, cold mud. Some animals may eat snow, but their bodies waste precious heat and energy to melt it. If you were an animal outside, where might you go to find water to drink?

Water can affect the land, too, in sometimes dramatic ways. Water that accumulates in the cracks in stones may expand when it freezes and cause the rock to crack; even large cliff faces may shear off in this way. See if you can find any places where ice has caused such damage, even if it's to human-made structures.

These are just starting points; you'll likely discover other details about the winter world not mentioned here. And that's great! The more you notice, the more you'll find that winter is hardly a boring time. After all, nature never really does sleep, even during the supposed "long winter nap."

Chalk Magick

by Melanie Marquis

When you think of the most powerful tools that can be utilized for magick, chalk is probably not the first item that comes to mind. Wands—yes, cauldrons—certainly, but little old ordinary chalk? Not so much. Despite its versatility, uniqueness, and handiness, chalk is often overlooked and underrated as a magickal tool. It can be used to cast spells and create potent works of image magick, and can even be used to create your own sacred ritual space. Chalk is convenient, something we can carry around and make use of whenever the need for magick arises. The possibilities are endless once you become familiar with the special qualities and capabilities of chalk magick.

Chalk and Its Magickal Properties

Chalk comes in many forms and varieties, each with its own unique magickal properties. The chalk we're most familiar with from our schools days—blackboard chalk or sidewalk chalk—is generally made from gypsum or calcium sulfate dihydrate. It's typically found in caves, salt beds, or areas where lakes or seas have evaporated. Because of the gypsum content, blackboard chalk is great for achieving clarity, activating psychic powers, and aiding communication between dimensions. Another type of chalk is called natural chalk, which is a form of limestone that has a high concentration of calcite, or calcium carbonate. It has its origins underwater, forming as the shells of tiny marine creatures settled on the ocean floor became compacted together and hardened into rock over the course of millions of years, giving this type of chalk a strong affinity with the water element. It's excellent for increasing energy, encouraging creativity, easing transitions, and boosting protection. There's also tailor's chalk, which is made of talc, also known as magnesium silicate. Tailor's chalk is especially useful in spellwork to bring peace and harmony to disjointed or chaotic situations. Yet another type of chalk made from magnesium carbonate is used by gymnasts and rock climbers to improve grip by preventing their hands from becoming slippery. Rock climbers' chalk is great for spells intended to stabilize, calm, or strengthen.

Magickal Chalk-Making

You might even consider making your own magickal chalk so you can create different sizes, shapes, and colors. The first step is to select a mold in which to dry your chalk into its hardened final form. You can use paper cups, empty toilet paper rolls, empty milk cartons, or even pie tins for the molds. Consider square-shaped molds to create chalk to use in spells intended to bring limits, ends, and structure, while round shapes are great for spells meant to improve and ease the free flow of energy. Specialty shapes like hearts, moons, and clovers can also be useful; just match the shape to the spellwork at hand. Also, consider its size. Small-sized chalk is handy for on-the-go magick, while a giant-sized chunk of chalk opens up a whole new level of fun and possibility.

Once you've selected your molds, simply line them with waxed paper so that the chalk will be easy to remove once it dries. Next, in a separate container, mix together two parts plaster of Paris for every one part water. For instance, I've found it's good to start by mixing two cups plaster of Paris with one cup of water. Make sure the water is slightly warm so that the plaster of paris will more readily dissolve. Next, add small amounts of washable tempera paint to produce the desired colors just right for your magick spell. About two tablespoons paint for every two cups of plaster of Paris is a nice starting place; you can add a little more if you want a richer, brighter color. Try creating red or pink chalk for love magick, green chalk for prosperity spells, blue chalk for happiness charms or good-luck spells, purple chalk to induce passion or increase psychism, black chalk for defensive magick, and orange chalk for a boost of additional strength or energy.

If you want to jazz up your chalk creations to make them even more suitable for a specific spellworking, consider adding a few drops of essential oil or a small amount of dried and powdered herbs to make the chalk more in tune with your magickal aims. Try rose or jasmine oil to give the chalk a romantic vibration, cinnamon to amplify magickal power, or powdered nutmeg to produce an ideal chalk for protective magick as well as for psychic or dream work, shamanistic spells, and as a tool for inducing mediumship.

Pour the well-blended chalk mix into the molds before it begins to harden, then leave it in a warm, ventilated area for a few days until it completely dries. Carefully remove the chalk from the molds, and it's ready for use.

Chalk's Many Magickal Virtues

One of the virtues of chalk that makes this specialized magickal tool so handy is the fact that it's temporary. Chalk provides us with the means to carry out our spellworkings in ways ordinarily impossible, allowing us the opportunity to place magickal symbols on public sidewalks, buildings, and elsewhere with only minimal fear of being cast as a graffiti bandit. Try mapping out a route of magickal symbols in your town, creating special markers for your friends to discover and decipher, or simply creating images of what you would like to see more of in your town. For instance, if people tend to be grumpy, try drawing little happy faces or sun symbols all over the town with your magickal chalk. Chalk can also be used to temporarily mark ritual tools to imbue them with additional vibrations conducive to specific magickal workings. If you're casting a spell for protection, for instance, you might use chalk to adorn your wand, chalice, or any other tool with pentacles, eye glyphs, crosses, or other protective symbols.

You can even use chalk to create a magick circle or sacred space in which to cast spells and perform rituals. Simply draw a large circle on pavement or concrete using your special chalk or create a perimeter around a more natural, outdoorsy area by drawing magickal glyphs on trees, boulders, smaller rocks, and fallen wood.

Go Big!

Another of chalk's special abilities is that it enables the spell-caster to create giant, colorful works of image magick in larger-than-life proportions. With some chalk and an empty parking lot or driveway, you can bring to life a whole new landscape especially designed to manifest your magickal goals. If, for instance, you want to cast a spell to help you with your career ambitions, you might use chalk to draw a vast hallway complete with doors marking milestones you plan to achieve along your journey to success. As you stroll along your hallway to success, "open" each door by drawing a big check mark over it, visualizing as you do so the completion of each goal. For a spell to bring prosperity to an impoverished community, you might draw a gigantic image to represent the town and its people, complete with hearty, abundant crops, sound infrastructure, smiling faces, full bellies, and other details depicting the improvements you want to manifest.

Dissolve Your Worries Chalk Spell

Hold a piece of chalk in your hands and search your heart for any nagging or draining worries or anxieties you might be harboring. If you find any, let these feelings course through your body and direct that energy into the piece of chalk. You can do this by visualizing the worry as a dark shadow or simply feeling the energy as it moves through your body and directing it with conscious intention to move out of your body and into the chalk. Now place this piece of chalk in a container of hot water and allow it to dissolve completely. Adding salt to the water will rapidly speed up the process, while using straight vinegar instead of the water creates a nice bubbling effect that is fun to watch. Your spell complete, pour out the liquid containing the dissolved chalk, and expect that the worries on which you focused your magick will quickly begin to disperse.

∾

Versatile and convenient, temporary yet powerful, chalk deserves greater recognition as an awesome and effective magickal tool. It might not look as fancy as a wand, and it might not sparkle like crystal, but in a pinch, chalk works. Experimenting with the many ways we can utilize chalk in our magick, we gain new abilities and insights we can incorporate into our personal practice. Challenge yourself to create new methods of making and using chalk magickally, but most of all, have fun with it—it *is* only chalk, after all!

Rituals of Death in Southeast Asia

by Raven Digitalis

*"Identifying ourselves with the body
is putting the cart before the horse
and is why we stumble in life."*
—Ramana Maharishi

L ife is a fragile experience. Merely knowing that death is inevitable is not enough in terms of fostering our human relationship with the Great Unknown. Death and dying is something that Americans, and indeed most Westerners, have an odd relationship with. As the infirm and elderly are pushed aside to nursing homes and hospitals, we don't encounter the energy of death or dying on a regular basis unless it's related to our profession.

Many people in cultures outside of North America have formed a sort of personal relationship with death either as a spiritual energy, as an actual deity, or as a secular fact of life. For we multicultural magical folk in the West, it can be immeasurably helpful to examine other cultures' relationships with profound forces such as death. For the sake of this article, we'll hop over to Southeast Asia and look at some of their rites, rituals, and beliefs concerning this ultimate force of reality. Southeast Asia includes Indonesia, Lao Peoples' Democratic Republic (Laos), Thailand, Malaysia, Singapore, Cambodia, Vietnam, Myanmar (formerly Burma), the Philippines, East Timor, and Brunei.

Secondary Burial

One of the most distinct features of Southeast Asian mortuary practice is secondary ("double") burial. Most Southeast Asian traditions practice this for specific cultural and social reasons.

Borneo

One of the most notable regions to practice secondary burial is Borneo, located in Indonesia. Borneo is the third largest island in the world and is known for its lush rain forests. It might be the most anthropologically researched region of Southeast Asia in terms of death views and rituals, much of which is due to anthropologist and University of Virginia professor Peter Metcalf's groundbreaking ethnographic research in the 1970s. Metcalf's research focused greatly on the Berawan, a small tribe consisting of four communities in north-central Borneo. The only detailed research prior to this was conducted by Robert Hertz, whose research in the early 1900s focused on the sociology of their religion, in particular how it was reflected in Berawan funerary rites.

Members of the Berawan tribe sometimes perform secondary burial when a member of superior rank dies. The secondary burial rites are largely an extended version of the much more common "single burials," which conduct similar behaviors in a single ritual. A secondary burial has four stages. The first stage in the Berawan secondary burial rites lasts between two and ten days, which includes rites to honor the person immediately after death. Specific songs and rituals are performed, and offerings of food and tobacco are given to the dead by putting food in the corpse's mouth and a cigarette in its fingers. On the first night after death, no one in the deceased's house is allowed to sleep, and lamp vigils are maintained to protect against potentially harmful spirits.

The second stage is that of initial storage. In this, the deceased's family stores the corpse in a container (a large earthenware vessel or a tree trunk coffin) either in the longhouse or on a platform in the graveyard. This can last between eight months and many years, depending on when the family is able to afford the secondary burial. During this period, the soul is viewed as being in a liminal state between the realm of the living and the realm of the dead. For the bereaved, a certain fear sets in. It's believed that a wandering malignant spirit may, at this point, reanimate the corpse as a zombie. However, as the body decomposes, it becomes a less appealing shell for a spirit to enter.

The third stage of the Berawan mortuary ritual, called *nulang* (a term related to "bones"), consists of moving the dead from the graveyard site (if the remains were placed there) and into a

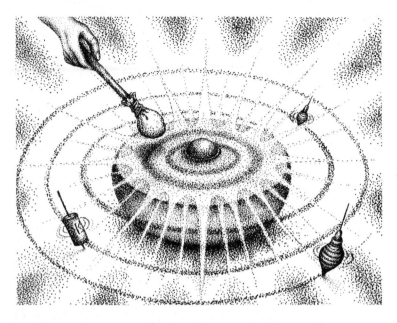

longhouse. Sometimes during this stage, family members remove the corpse and clean the bones. Guests are called to observe the cadaver before its secondary burial. This is the official funeral ceremony. When friends, family, and village members come together, they make noise that can be heard long and far. Special funerary songs are sung as the deceased finally and officially "dies" socially. Instruments are used to mark transition and acknowledge the reality of change. Making noise through vocal intonation and the use of instruments is a characteristic of numerous tribes' rites of passage (or "status change"), be it birth, passage into adulthood, weddings, or death. In the Berawan ceremony, people play gongs of all types, and a special deep-bass funeral drum is played through the day and night. Outside, children spin tops; not only is this a game, but the whirring sound of the tops emulates what the Berawan call the "language of the ghosts." Adults also play games, everyone socializes, and the passing of the loved one is celebrated.

When the observations have come to a close, the body is usually placed in a nicer glazed jar and is moved to a local mausoleum. At this point, the spirit is seen as officially having entered the land of the dead, completely and successfully released from its earthly bonds.

Other Indonesian Tribes

The Berawan aren't the only Indonesian tribe to practice secondary burial. The Ma'anyan, also of Borneo, practice a variation of this. When a person dies, they are temporarily stored in an underground coffin. Over a number of years, corpses accumulate in the graveyard. Differing from the Berawan, a massive funeral ceremony is performed for all the accumulated deceased simultaneously. In this, the coffins are excavated and burned (cremated) in succession, usually a dozen at a time. After the festival, which can last for weeks, the bones and ashes are collected and finally stored together in the cemetery.

The island of Bali is Indonesia's largest tourist destination and contains the country's greatest number of Hindus. The Vedas say that the most spiritually aligned way to dispose of the dead is through cremation, as the soul can most easily be released from the body. Most Balinese families cannot afford cremation, unfortunately, and are left to bury their dead in simple graves without coffins. For the elite, bodies of the dead are first kept in an area of the family's house or, in the case of prestigious rulers, displayed in a pavilion on palace grounds for at least forty-two days. At a later date, an elaborate public ceremony ensues, the body is burned, and its ashes scattered to the sea.

In Sulawesi (formerly Celebes) in Indonesia, the Toraja retrieve the stored dead from a designated area every few years, wrap the remains in cloth, and store them in a cave with ancestors past. During the time before this secondary rite, a local slave of the Toraja is assigned to care for village corpses in a hut some miles from the village. The slaves who watch the Toraja bodies during the liminal period are to respect the bodies by wiping away secretions of decomposition and ensuring that the bodies aren't stolen by "black magicians." These dread sorcerers are recognized across regions of Asia and elsewhere, and are usually (and unfortunately) called "witches" in anthropological studies for lack of a better social translation.

Thailand

Social status is a huge factor in how a corpse will be treated. The wealthy are able to afford more elaborate burial ceremonies than a commoner. This occurs across most cultures, but Thailand is a prime example of traditional treatment of the royal dead. When

a Thai king dies, his body is washed and dressed in fine clothes for public display on a bier. Following this brief presentation, the body is put in a large urn made of gold, which is stored on an ornate catafalque in the palace for at least one hundred days. During this time, offerings of food are left by the urn for the king's spirit, and the fluids of decomposition are collected in a separate golden vase. During this liminal period, a massive funeral pyre is erected. The breathtakingly elaborate pyre stands hundreds of feet tall, adorned with traditional Thai conical peaks representing Mount Meru (Sumeru), a mythologized mountain sacred to local Hindus and Buddhists alike. When the time comes, the remains of the king are brought to the pyre and the flesh is ritualistically removed from the bones. The new king respectfully washes the bones with scented water, anoints them with perfumes, and wraps them in a white cloth, which is then placed in a sandalwood box. The whole structure is alighted and cremation of the bones lasts from sundown that night to the following morning.

East Timor

The Southeast Asian island Timor is divided into two regions, West Timor and East Timor. Whereas West Timor is part of Indonesia, East Timor became the first independent country of the twenty-first century with the assistance of the United Nations in 2002. In her 1977 thesis, Harvard's Elizabeth Traube described the Mambai people of East Timor, including their funerary rites. She observed that when a person dies, the body is moved to the house of its patrilineal (agnatic) descent group, where it is dressed in appropriate attire for the summoned close kin to observe. After a few days, once the stench of decomposition really sets in, the body is buried in the dancing ground. After this initial burial process, the bodies may become partially unearthed or disturbed when they are later reburied, but the Mambai don't view this as a bad thing. The remains of relatives are never intentionally tampered with after their initial burial; instead, a number of sympathetic magical rituals emulating a secondary burial are performed during the Sensu Stricto: the Mambai festival of the dead. Burial/dancing sites are usually found in the center of each village, which emphasizes the Mambai peoples' contrast to other villages. For most other tribal cultures, burial sites tend to be found outside of a village's perimeter rather than of within. For the Mambai, venerable treatment of the dead is a pinnacle of their culture. Still, some onlookers may see the Mambai view of the cadaver as questionable because they see nothing taboo about the corpse being disturbed or manipulated during the process of secondary burial; they do not believe this is disruptive to the soul. The body is viewed as a temporary frame or shell and is distinctly different from the person's actual spiritual essence. The perceived insignificance of the corpse itself after burial is unique in this case as compared to Southeast Asia as a whole.

Headhunting

When ninteenth-century travelers and explorers journeyed Southeast Asia, fearful accounts of headhunting (or "headtaking") surfaced. This exotic practice was immediately seen as uncivilized and savage, obviously the result of angry natives with a lust for blood. Like most early perceptions of foreign activity, this view was a bit ethnocentric. Ethnocentrism refers to other cultures being judged from the subjective standpoint of the observer's cultural norms—which are often notions of superiority.

In various regions of Southeast Asia, warring tribes used to take heads of the slain as wartime trophies. In most cases, such as with the Toraja of Sulawesi, the taking of one enemy's head was sufficient. This was undergone as an act of magic to weaken the opponent's vitality. A great amount of life force is viewed as being present in the head, which can be taken by severing it. For the Ilongot of Luzon in the Philippines, heads were severed and thrown in the air during wartime, left where they landed on the earth instead of being taken back to the village. This symbolized the finale of the killing and was seen as a practice that would lift the weight of sorrow from the killer's heart.

At the same time, the taking of an enemy's power isn't always the reason for headhunting. Tribes across Borneo cite a variety of reasons for displaying heads such as making offerings to the gods, preventing sickness, warding off evil spirits (including Christian missionaries), promoting crop growth, or marking initiation. Common practices among many Southeast Asian tribes include a ritual commemoration for the person whose head was taken, and animal sacrifices to mark the victory. Celebratory feasts including dance, divination, and spirit possession (invocation) often followed the taking of a head, as was the case with the Buaya people of northern Luzon in the Philippines. Cannibalism, however, has never been documented as existing alongside headhunting in any Southeast Asian society. Currently, headhunting is universally prohibited. As a substitute, some tribes use a coconut or another similarly sized item in place of the head.

Cannibalism

When the topic of human cannibalism is mentioned, we tend to think of brutal savagery, murder, and a variety of less-than-pretty images. Understandably, the thought of a person eating another person doesn't sit well with most of us. Like most taboo subjects, especially those almost entirely foreign to us, cannibalism has been blown out of proportion.

Very rarely do people perform cannibalism out of hunger alone—or just for the fun of it. The act is almost always symbolic and spiritual, representing things such as social communion, the absorption of an enemy's prowess, the releasing of a soul by recycling the physical body, or the reintegration of a person's spirit back into a group. Some tribes practice endocannibalism, which is the most common form. (Exocannibalism, the eating of a stranger or unrelated person, usually due to an issue of revenge with an enemy, is quite rare.) The prefix endo- means "within," and in this case refers to a particular group of people consuming the flesh of someone who belonged to the same group before death (either by kinship or tribal status). This is a funerary rite. Endocannibalism energetically ensures that the ancestor's essence remains within the group, strengthening their descendants. As a part of mortuary ritual in many parts of Indonesia, the secreted liquids of a decomposing body—which are thought to contain extreme life essence—are often mixed with rice and consumed within a tribe, especially across Indonesia.

The South Fore tribe of Papua New Guinea used to practice endocannibalism. When a person in the tribe died, the maternal kin were responsible for dismembering the corpse by removing the brain, excising internal organs, and stripping muscle from bone. In the 1960s, a neurological disease called kuru peaked in Papua New Guinea. Kuru had easily identifiable symptoms, but the way in which it spread was unclear until Western researchers isolated cannibalism as the cause. When New Guinea stopped practicing cannibalism, the spread of the disease also came to a halt.

A Matter of Perspective

These Southeast Asian examples of death and funerary rites are but a handful of the multitude of examples of death-related rituals across Asia and across the globe. While most people are only aware of the rites of passage within their own cultures—not only of death, but of birth, marriage, adulthood, and other significant moments of life—it becomes so very necessary for we individuals of magical, mystical, and esoteric persuasions to study rituals that are foreign to our own. Western cultures have incredibly deep, rich histories, but the same can be said about Eastern cultures. While we in the West may find ourselves mainly exposed to Western spirituality and history, exploring outside of our confines can help us become more knowledgeable and complete spiritual practitioners.

Root to Crown:
Cultivating a Chakra Garden

by Natalie Zaman

A Living Ritual, A Sacred Space

We are all connected:
Animal and element.
Person and plant.
Star and Stone.

Life is energy, and while we walk this planet, we are custodians of a small piece of that power. I believe that one of our purposes is to connect to our fellow beings, to share our life force, and to remember that while we are individuals, we are also part of a larger entity. To help make that connection, there is nothing like a working relationship.

Gardens are collaborations between humans and nature, and the creation of nature-centric spaces for spiritual purposes is not a new idea. The medieval cloistered garden with its carefully planned geometric layout was a place of meditation and retreat. The Zen garden's swirling lines and minimal components make it an ideal place to ground and center. The pattern and rhythm of these sacred spaces are an aesthetic not unlike ritual—one that is always evolving because it incorporates living elements.

Ayurveda, the belief that everything in the universe is interconnected, allows that there are plants, stones, symbols, and colors associated with each chakra (power centers in the body that regulate energy flow). While the chakras themselves are not physical, they are located over major organs, and not surprisingly, can have physical effects when obstructed or unbalanced—something all of us have experienced.

Work with nature to create a chakra garden. A living ritual and a project of practical magic, the perpetual sharing and cycling of energy in a sacred space can help you open your personal power centers and reconnect to the Divine. Continuing the circle beyond the garden gate, you can harvest the plants to make magical tools for future workings.

It is an experiment worth trying.

Know, Sow, and Grow

Before cultivating your sacred space, you should have some basic knowledge about each chakra as well as an idea of what you'd like to make from the harvest. Use these suggestions as a guide as you plan your chakra garden. The important thing is for it to be a reflection of your spirit.

Plant directly in the earth if you have the space; however, using pots allows for more flexibility. Potted plants can be moved inside or out to achieve ideal growing conditions and rearranged or isolated for prayer and intention. There are many herbs, flowers, roots, and barks that correspond to the essence of each chakra and its body area, or its color (if using pots, coordinate the colors of your containers to match the chakras). Some herbs such as mugwort and lavender are associated with multiple chakras and are universally beneficial.

Don't be discouraged if a plant dies. Return it to compost and begin again, perhaps with something different. All living beings are unique. Be patient. It might take some trial and error to find the plants that resonate best with your energy.

Muladhara, the Root Chakra

Know. Located at the base of the spine, the root chakra rules the lower part of the body. All the chakras are interconnected, but all are based here. This is the foundation. When your root chakra is balanced you feel stable and grounded.

Sow. Root vegetables and earthy, woodsy herbs such as hawthorn, wood betony, and sage correspond to the grounding nature of the root chakra. Muladhara is red; make a colorful offering with roses, red cedar, and sandalwood.

Grow: A Sage Smudge Stick. Used in many cultures for grounding and clearing negativity, sage is widely available and easy to grow. Dry the leaves after you harvest them, then gather a neat handful and bind them end to end with a cotton cord to form a tight bundle. Light it, then fan the smoke over the root chakra. As you breathe in sage's earthy scent, visualize the center as an orb of red light. Continue to smudge until the light is clear and bright.

Swadhisthana, the Sacral Chakra

Know. Closely linked to creativity and relationships, the sacral chakra is located from the lower abdomen to the navel and governs the body's reproductive centers. When your sacral chakra is clear, you connect easily with others and are comfortable with your choices and creative power.

Sow. Seeds are the beginnings of creation. Vanilla pods, sesame seeds, and caraway seeds will fuel the sacral chakra. Swadhisthana is orange. A colorful offering can be made with calendula, tiger lilies, or a bowl of crushed turmeric. (Using preharvested plants for this work reflects the elements of a Zen rock garden. Combinations of growing and harvested plants can create an environment just as powerful as one where all is "alive.")

Grow: A Kolam to Reconnect. To balance the sacral chakra, create a *kolam* (Indian powder painting) of its symbol, the six-petaled lotus. Form a cone with a piece of paper, leaving a small opening at the tip. Fill it with crushed turmeric. Using the cone as you would a pencil or pen, gently shake out the powder to form the symbol. The traditional place to do this ritual is on the pavement in front of your home. To align yourself with the purposes of the sacral chakra, chant aloud or to yourself as you draw:

I create, I connect.

Take your time tracing the symbol, but don't worry about making it perfect; focus on your intentions and the chakra. Leave the kolam to make a connection to nature; wind, rain, and animals will do their part taking up the grains of turmeric to bind your energy to theirs. As you become more confident with this ritual form, consider executing more complex designs with different herbs and colors to make further connections.

Manipura, the Solar Plexus

Know. The solar plexus is located between the navel and sternum. Physically, it rules the spleen, pancreas, stomach, and liver—the digestive system. When your Solar Plexus is balanced, you feel a healthy sense of self-esteem, self-acceptance, and personal power.

Sow. Stomach-settling herbs like chamomile, ginger, cinnamon, and fennel are good for cleansing the solar plexus. Manipura is yellow and can be represented by daylilies, daffodils, goldenrod, and yarrow.

Grow: Tummy Taming Tea. As you brew a soothing cup of tea made with chamomile leaves and flowers and honey, speak a mantra of the solar plexus:

I accept myself as I am.
I am empowered.

Visualize your solar plexus as you drink. With every sip, picture it growing brighter like the Sun.

Anahata, the Heart Chakra

Know. Physically, the heart chakra regulates the heart and lungs as well as the blood and the circulatory system. It also governs feelings associated with the heart such as love, anger, fear, and hope. When your heart chakra is open, you let go of anger easily, love largely, and forgive readily.

Sow. The color of Anahata is green, a healing color. Medical studies have shown that eating green foods—especially vitamin-packed, leafy green veggies like spinach, kale, and collards—helps prevent heart disease, high blood pressure, and

cancer. Herbs that strengthen the blood, such as garlic, will also strengthen the heart chakra.

Grow: Soup For The Soul. The preparation of food can be a spiritual act, and nothing is so magically comforting as cooking and eating a pot of homemade soup. The next time you prepare soup from scratch, toss in a sachet of energy-infused parsley and thyme from your chakra garden along with a heart-strengthening spell:

> *Parsley for happiness,*
> *Thyme to heal and love,*
> *My heart to yours*
> *As below, so above!*

Eat and share the soup to strengthen the heart chakra, and be open to love and forgiveness.

Vishuddha, the Throat Chakra

Know. Located in the neck, the throat chakra rules communication. Vishuddha is sky blue, a wonderful color for self-expression. On a clear, cloudless day, you can see far into the distance; when your throat chakra is balanced, you express your ideas clearly and honestly.

Sow. Peppermint, clove, and lemon balm will soothe and coat the throat and stimulate its energy center. The pale blue petals of cornflowers, nigella, and borage will make more colorful offerings to the throat chakra.

Grow: A Balm To Heal. Make lemonade from scratch with the juice of six lemons, spring water, sweetener to your taste and a half dozen each of crushed peppermint and lemon balm leaves. The herbs will add a bit of bite to the lemonade and a spark to the throat chakra. As you blend the ingredients, infuse the lemonade with the essence of the energy center:

> *My words, the Sun,*
> *My voice the sky,*
> *Crisp and clear,*
> *Honest am I.*

Serve over ice to imbibe this brew's refreshing properties.

Ajna, the Brow Chakra

Know. Also known as "the third eye," the brow chakra governs concentration, intuition, and visualization. It is located in the middle of the forehead between the eyes, its power focused on the organs of the senses. When your brow chakra is clear you are bright and sharp.

Sow. Mind-focusing herbs such as rosemary, clary sage, and mugwort can represent the brow chakra. Ajna is indigo— a color and a plant that can be processed to make ink and dye for magical workings.

Grow: Indelible Ink. In *The Mists of Avalon*, when the character of Morgaine is made a priestess, a crescent moon is tattooed onto her forehead with woad, the blue ink of ancient days. To make magical indigo ink or dye, place your indigo leaves in a pot (one you don't use for preparing food) and cover them with water. Bring them to a gentle simmer, then keep the water hot for about two hours. Remove the pot from the heat, strain the leaves, then stir in a little baking soda. (Sixteen ounces of leaves requires about two tablespoons of baking soda). As the mixture cools, transfer it from one container to another to oxidize it (this step deepens the blue color). When cooled completely, the liquid can be used as a dye or as an ink to record dreams, insights, and spells the old-fashioned way with a quill pen.

Sahasrara, the Crown Chakra

Know. Situated over the brain, the crown chakra governs our connection to the Divine and reaching higher states of consciousness. When your crown chakra is open you feel a sense of peace and contentment, knowing you rest in the arms of the universe.

Sow. Lavender is an appropriate offering to Sahasrara, but morning glory with its purple flowers and heaven-reaching vine truly embodies the spirit of the crown.

Grow: Crowning Glory. Cultivate morning glories until you have a good length of vine with several flowers. You may need to use a small trellis to keep the plants from tangling with each other. Carefully remove the vine and cut enough length so that you can wrap it around your head at least once. As you tie the ends together to form a crown, chant:

I am crowned with the God and Goddess.
I am connected to the universe.
Show me your wisdom.

If you make a crown for someone else, place it on her head. If the person is not present, place it as a wreath on your altar with her photo or name in the center.

The Shape of Things to Come

Once you've chosen your plants and what tools you will create with them, you need to decide if you want to create a garden that incorporates all of the chakras or focus on one energy center at a time. I created a container garden and worked with the heart chakra on its own before adding any of the others.

Clearing a surface to use as an altar, I placed two pots in the empty space, one each for the parsley and thyme I uprooted from my outdoor garden. As I repotted each plant, I visualized it surrounded by an orb of green light before giving it a few words of encouragement with a growing incantation:

What is planted today
Flourishes and grows
With earth, air, water, and sun
Anahata* flows.
My heart* opens.

*or whichever chakra you are working with

To help direct more energy, you can place crystals in a pattern around the pots or in the earth around your plants. There are specific stones associated with each chakra, but you can always use quartz crystals, which are all-purpose in directing energy. Alternate the points to and away from the plant as the energy is being cycled and shared. If you incorporate stones into your chakra garden, use your intuition and favorite reference to decide which ones to use and how to lay them out.

Assembling your plants in a sacred shape will add another layer of intention and meaning to your work. Often the chakras are depicted in an ascending vertical line, starting with the root, each energy center feeding into the next up through the crown. *Chakra* is the Sanskrit word for "wheel." If you cultivate plants for all of the Chakras at the same time, consider placing them in a circle. With no beginning and no end, the cycling of energy will be constant.

For daily meditation and clearing, spend time with (or in) your garden. Take a few breaths to ground and center, then focus on each plant one at a time. Visualize a core of light in the center of each plant; picture the light in the color of the chakra that plant represents. To share and cycle the energy, see the light move toward you, then circle back and forth between yourself and the plant. If the light looks or feels muddy or dull to you, keep the exchange going until the light is bright and clear. Be sure to give a word of gratitude when you're finished, and when you harvest. It doesn't have to be elaborate; a simple thank you is brilliant.

Go forth and bloom!

For Further Study

Cunningham, Scott. *Cunningham's Encyclopedia of Magical Herbs.* Woodbury, MN: Llewellyn Publications, 1985.

Cunningham, Scott. *Magical Herbalism.* Woodbury, MN: Llewellyn Publications, 1983.

Dillard, James. *Crystal Grid Secrets.* Bloomington, IN: Balboa Press, 2013.

Moon, Hibiscus. *Crystal Grids: How And Why They Work.* Create Space Independent Publishing Platform, 2011.

The Elements in Your Kids

by Hannah E. Johnston

Our children come into the world with their spirit already formed, with a blueprint of their unique qualities, gifts, and challenges. As they grow, they are raised and nurtured in ways that foster certain attributes and limit or ignore others. For many Pagan parents, educators, and caregivers looking to understand our children with more depth, the elements give us a familiar framework for considering our children's natures. In respecting children's individual needs, we consider their natural talents and tendencies and can gain great insight into their needs when we frame these in meaningful ways, such as through the elements.

Earth, air, fire, water. The sacred spiritual elements that support all life in most Western Pagan traditions. The fifth, spirit (Goddess and God), is found in all living things, and all of us carry the spark of the Divine within us.

By considering the elemental matrix within our children, we can begin to pinpoint their elemental makeup. By doing so, we can find ways to actively change emerging destructive patterns and to grow in compassion and understanding for their individual struggles, thus allowing the fifth element to shine through.

Below, I offer some basic tenets of the four elements and how to apply that to understanding the personality of our young folk. This is not to say that someone is purely one element—they rarely are. You may find that your child has a combination of elemental traits in their fundamental nature, so what you are looking for are your child's tendencies, patterns of behavior, strengths, and challenges. Your child may go through phases where the elements are out of balance or the child is struggling with an element in their life. Ideally, we would have all the elements in perfect balance—and reach enlightenment!

Earth

Most children are earth-focused for the first five years of life. Life in this phase revolves around the body—sleep, food, comfort, and family. Earth kids are solidly built and very physically present. These children have stamina and are cautious—they are not the kids racing around the playground, they are the ones standing watching or building with any material at hand, sticks, Legos, blocks. They often learn to walk and toilet-train without a hitch (but a little later than most) and easily establish sleep patterns. They are naturally children of routine and habit, quiet at times and comfort seeking. They may appear strong-minded and stubborn and prefer the company of one or two other children whom they have come to know. These children love to be outdoors and really need to be outside come rain or shine—they are the hardiest children!

Earth-focused kids thrive in the countryside rather than the city. The city can be a very stressful place to an earth child, as they hate to be rushed and crowded. They also dislike big groups—expect them to balk at the prospect of birthday parties. As they grow, these are kids who like hiking, helping to put the garbage out, and getting dirty. And they are excellent cooks. Their nature is patient, but when their rhythm is disrupted they may become explosive, which can often be bewildering as their mild manner is usually so reliable. Verbal communication is challenging—expecting an earth child to tell you how they feel can be frustrating.

In terms of academic achievement, they work hard but are rarely the high fliers. They find community-based work highly fulfilling, and for those who have more air in the mix, work in technology (hardware) and the sciences can prove rewarding. For those who have earth/fire natures, local politics and grass-roots community organizations are valuable outlets. Get them connected early, as they have a strong sense of justice and a firm moral aptitude. Frequently an attachment object is fiercely guarded and self-comfort is a central skill for these kids to learn. Disruption, instability, and uncertainty are immensely unnerving to children with earth natures. They may appear stoic even when change can be profoundly disturbing to them. Illness is a significant manifestation of imbalance for earth kids as they are usually so hale and hearty. When this happens, they need comfort, not just medicine. Earth children need clarity, a lot of physical space, and time. Emotionally they are highly loyal—family, clan, and community are intensely important to them.

Air

Air children are the ones who will learn to talk before other babies and they are the most easily distractible children. Tall and thin, air kids tend to live in the realm of thought. They are good with abstracts and patterns; they will look for them and can become a little fixated with them. They are drawn to literacy and numeracy early, but are also highly artistic by nature. Visual and musical expressions are extremely valuable outlets to air kids, and they may need a lot of time to explore these forms. For many, air children seem to be model kids; clever, talkative, attractive, but simultaneously they can be emotionally distant. Nondemonstrative and fickle, they may find friendships hard to maintain and although well liked, they often have only the emotional energy for one or two good friends. Reason and objectivity are their modes of problem solving, but building empathy and compassion is a harder journey.

They often have their eye on the big picture rather than details, so can appear dreamy when in fact they are working out a complex idea. Their bodies are a source of both joy and anxiety, often simultaneously. They may be picky eaters, refuse medicine, and have phantom pains. They don't always sleep well and may suffer from nightmares and disrupted sleep. They strongly need rhythm and consistency in their home environment for them to feel secure and happy, as they cannot always generate such consistency within. These children dream big and have a great drive to experience new cultures, places, and people. They do well in conventional school structures. Air/fire children are intellectually inquisitive and competitive, and will excel in languages and pattern-based subjects such as math, science, and sociology. Air/

earth children (an unusual and complicated mixture) can be quite hidden and solitary. Draw them out by exploring history through expressive means—reenactment societies like Living History, traditional music, and folk dance are good. An air teen will be fascinated with technology, but may spend far too much time locked away on a computer. You may need to find ways of unplugging them and getting them to join you and stay in the present. Board games, card games (especially those that involve money), and a regular debate night are ways of ensuring they remain connected to family life.

Air kids with their big-picture perspective are motivated by righting the world's wrongs and often feel worldly injustice more keenly than they experience emotion in their personal relationships. These kids need a cause!

Fire

Fire is the prevalent quality in Western culture, so many of our children will strongly display these traits. Fire kids are generally energetic, outgoing, and gregarious. Quick on their feet and quick in their moods and tempers, fire kids are always on the go. These kids love to sing and dance! They are theatrical by nature and may appear to be the center of any group. They are naturally charismatic but not always benign leaders! Fire kids love people, they love parties, and where there isn't one, life feels like one around fire kids. They frequently enjoy competitive sports because they thrive on both competition and the energy of crowds. (The kinds of sport will depend on what other elements are present.)

These kids are strongly influenced by mainstream culture and may find it hard to be an outsider. If you are an unconventional parent, you may have to work hard to give these kids enough to allow them to thrive. Fire kids are strongly motivated by goals. A chart for good behavior or a hill to summit, a play performance or a football game, they thrive on attainment. The downside to this is that they often perceive themselves only in terms of how well they are achieving. This means that a fire child's confidence is often strongly connected to their outward abilities. Their need for goals can also crush them. This can be particularly difficult for young adults in the fire phase of their lives when self-esteem is unfortunately too often focused on externals such as fashion, friends, and academic achievement. Strong team-based activities that help them build lasting relationships can be crucial.

Fire kids are the risk takers; they love danger. For fire/earth kids, long-term goals and adventures are really valuable ways of tempering their drive—saving money to go on a long trip, or building a complex Lego city, or playing a game of chess over a series of weeks are all ways to engage these kids. A fire/water kid will love playing psychic projection games with you, and keeping a tally of who is getting the most answers right! A young fire/air kid will find an air meditation a real challenge, but will love dressing up as a bird, but be specific—air kids will need to know the kind of bird in order to "be the bird."

These are the kids we worry about when they get to teen years because they can be thrill seekers. This isn't your fault, nor is it theirs, but needs to be channelled into pursuits and activities that respond to this need.

Water

Water children are often pale and physically soft—their skin is soft, their joints flexible, and their body reflects how they are feeling. Water children are interested in relationships above all else. By nature, they are intuitive and highly emotional in all aspects of their lives, which can be difficult for adults around them, as they seem to possess the most irrational, flighty, and inconsistent nature. Yet these children are strongly empathic; they find ways of understanding people that as adults we should value. They are natural bridge builders between people, which makes them valuable friends. Relationships are intensely important and water children seem to do their best when they work cooperatively.

What motivates and touches these kids are things that speak to or of the depth of human experience. Art, healing,

and the realm of the spiritual and devotional come naturally to water children. Unfortunately, children with water talents are rarely prized in Western culture—we have no monks who will come to our village and choose the most devotional children for training, we have no apprenticeships that start in childhood for the healing arts. Many of our institutions fail these children. They appear to be dreamers and although well liked by adults and children, they can be frustrating as they seek pleasure, beauty, and play above regimens, homework, and obligation. They can become self-indulgent if not given other ways to express their nature, and their empathy can tip over into hypochondria, overindulgence, and depression. Water children strongly need a purpose and they need things to take care of. These children should always have pets or work at an animal sanctuary or a zoo. They are motivated by causes that seek to resolve pain and conflict as they loathe these elements in their own lives. They can become passionate and sacrifice all their energy to organizations that seek to protect and shelter the vulnerable. A preteen water child will need a lot of grounding and centering exercises. They will love to learn to dowse, but would find going for a hike a tiresome pursuit. If you tell her she needs to dowse to find ley or energy lines, you may have a chance of having her cooperation, however! Older water children may appear remote or very emotional. They are likely to become "emo" kids and have a propensity for frequently changing their identity and style—don't be alarmed if they are a punk one month and then preppy the next. This is a way for them to find their place. These children are the least physically robust and as such, their health can be used as a barometer for their emotional well-being. Like air kids, water kids need the rhythms of home to be constant and consistent. They also strongly respond to a consistent emotional life at home. Water/fire kids will love to play—acting and musical theatre, for example. They are also the most sports-minded of the water blends and may love swimming, yoga, and softer martial arts such as aikido or budo, all of which can be excellent strength and stamina builders.

~

Our children come with a myriad of elemental dispositions and tendencies. We can use the frame of the elements to encourage them to reach beyond their comfort zone, to problem solve, and to help them find balance in their lives. No matter which elements your child comes into the world with and develops as s/he grows, our young folks have much to teach us about the nature of the world's sacred elemental patterns, just as we can show them how the elements move in divine ways within all life on Mother Earth. Whatever the matrix of your beautiful children, they are all faces of the divine and a seed of the future. Thus, as guardians of our future, we can honor them and the flows of energy they move within.

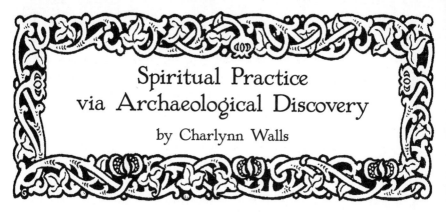

Spiritual Practice via Archaeological Discovery

by Charlynn Walls

Our spiritual heritage stems from the historical past, but it is so much more than so many words dancing across the page. It provides a specific part of where we come from and what resonates within us. But how many of us take the time to delve deeper and learn more about a specific culture or particular practice that was once prevalent? What calls out to us to learn and expand our minds in pursuit of our spiritual path?

When we challenge ourselves to step outside our comfort zone and explore all there is, we open ourselves up to the potential inside each of us to make more than a superficial connection. There is the possibility of deeper magickal practice based on visible evidence within the archaeological record—to literally reach out and connect with a piece of the history that encompasses the time of ancient peoples.

What Is Archaeology?

Modern movies such as *Indiana Jones* and *The Mummy* depict the archaeologist as an idealistic fortune-hunter who faces danger at every turn. While there are some dangerous places, it is usually much less romantic. Often the biggest adversaries while in the field are sun, heat, and insects. Archaeology is a discipline that seeks to understand the past and relay it in a context that modern people can relate to.

In the United States, archaeology is considered one of four branches of anthropology. It focuses on studying the human past through excavating the remnants of material culture. Material culture is what has been left behind by past cultures and can include artifacts, architecture, and what remains of the cultural landscape. It is a discipline heavily rooted in science, but one that also seeks to understand the societal and cultural impact.

The first archaeological process is exploration or the field survey. During this phase, the team investigates an area that has the potential to yield material culture involving the research question at hand. Dig sites generally build upon previous knowledge in hopes of physical confirmation. After finding the site and reviewing the evidence collected, a determination is made on whether there will be an excavation. Not every site can be excavated, so in those instances, ground-penetrating radar, aerial photos, and soil samples may be collected for future research.

When a site is determined to be viable based on accessibility and the probability of finding relevant preserved materials without disrupting hallowed cultural remains, the next phase is excavation. This is when the actual digging into the past occurs. The site is usually cordoned off into one-meter squares. This can

be after the site is clean scraped, meaning that the land is taken down to a flat area beyond the distance that plowing can affect the surface. Once that has been completed, the archaeologists and volunteers begin the sometimes arduous task of systematically going down through the layers of soil. They watch for changes in soil composition and color along with any artifacts.

The provenance, or where the artifact is located, is carefully measured and recorded. Photographs are taken and maps of the location are carefully created by the excavation team. This systematic preservation of this information is important because there is no way to put an artifact back in the soil exactly the way it was removed. Because this data is the only thing future archaeologists will be able to refer to and interpret when examining new findings, there is great value in the proper recording of the data.

The artifacts, soil samples, maps, and other field data are recorded daily and sent back to the laboratory. When weather prohibits working in the field or when the excavation phase is complete, the next task is analyzing the information. A single site can yield thousands of artifacts. They all have to be carefully cleaned, examined, and catalogued. Once that process is complete, then the analysis of the site's contents can begin.

Analysis of the artifacts begins with a spatial comparison of what was found. In other words, they compare where objects of a certain type were found in relationship to one another. Distance apart is a factor, but so is which layer of soil the artifacts were found in. Another part of analyzing the data is comparing discoveries at this site to findings at other similar sites. Do they contain the same types of artifacts? Is there a similar spatial distribution? Also, of those artifacts collected, is there a cultural or spiritual component, or are they used in a more practical daily application?

Interpretation is the final component to the archaeological process. Only after all of the other steps have come to fruition can one begin to compare what was found to what we have come to accept as truth about a region or culture. Sometimes the information obtained confirms long-held beliefs, and sometimes it shakes us out of our complacency.

When we remain open to the possibilities, our spiritual practice can remain fluid. With that fluidity, we are then able to continue to evolve our magickal and spiritual practices because we are not steadfastly holding to a belief or practice that may come into question.

Past Spiritual Practices: What Can We Learn?

So, what is there to learn about past spiritual practices, and how can we interpret that from the archaeological data? Though we are often aware of our past, we often hold on to assumptions that are no longer true. By examining the current data and theories based on recent evidence, we can adapt our spiritual practices based on factual evidence.

Many times, Wiccans and Pagans wax philosophical about our spiritual origins being nested in the ancient past without much physical evidence to support it. Most assumptions have been built on the mythological anecdotes found within texts that explore a specific cultural pantheon. However, adding concrete evidence as a part of that dialogue provides emphasis and gives the belief structure much more weight because of the tangible nature of artifacts.

Research and excavations are being done on all of the major cultures that Wiccans and Pagans identify with. Granted, some of the findings are only published in stuffy academic journals, but there is a wealth of information out there if you are willing to do the research and delve a little deeper. While not everyone is going for a reconstructionist view of their spirituality, the archaeological perspective can certainly enhance one's current practice by giving an insight that may strongly resonate with a person, even if they do not share all of the proclivities of that particular spiritual practice.

Case History

One of the more accessible periodicals to the layperson is *Archaeology Magazine*, and one with a distinctly Pagan flair is *The Pomegranate*. These publications are updated on a regular basis and feature contributors who are noted individuals in the scientific community.

Provided below are instances where magic was directly referenced in *Archaeology Magazine* and *Live Science*. The November/December 2008 issue of *Archaeology* had a discussion of a property that was excavated in Cornwall, England. The artifacts recovered from the pits have included flint fragments, white feath-

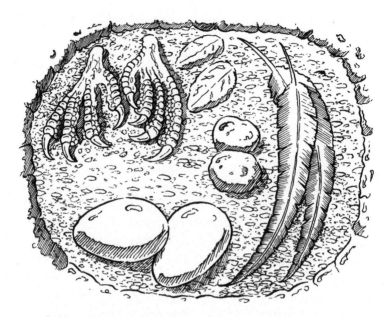

ers and skin from a swan, stones, claws of other birds, and eggs. Those collected from a pool of spring-fed water on the property have yielded heather branches, nail clippings, hair, straight pins, and part of a cauldron.

Ravillious (2008) quotes archaeologist Jaqui Wood regarding her take on some findings on her property: "My theory is that maybe if you got married and didn't become pregnant in the first year, you might make an offering to St. Bride in a feather pit." These findings would certainly provide some great insight into Celtic practices and could provide a foundational basis for similar practice by those who follow a Celtic or British Traditional Witchcraft pathway.

A much more recent find documented in January 2014 in *Live Science* has detailed the contents of a Roman Empire ritual deposit in Turkey. The excavation turned up a nearly intact clay pot that contained some interesting contents, which included an intact eggshell, a coin, a bronze needle, and nails. These items were found buried beneath a building in Sardis. It was placed on top of a previous structure that was decimated by an earthquake. The thought on this ritual deposit is that it was a ritual charm designed to help protect the new structure from future earthquakes.

Nails and needles have often been added to witch bottles as protective talismans. The addition of the coin and egg are thought to ward off evil and pay homage to Zeus, whose visage was captured on one side of the coin in order to elicit his help in stopping the shaking and provide strength to the earth on which the new building was constructed. Considering the find and that it was Roman in nature, those following a Hellenic pathway could apply this to what they are already practicing.

Redefining Your Spiritual Practice

How do we then redefine our spiritual practices? We take a look at our past and not just as a historical document or artifact, but more as an extension of our spiritual practice; it becomes a living thing. It is a testament to those ancestors and practitioners. We continue to honor them through our own practice, and we may even learn a thing or two along the way.

With the finds at the Cornwall, England, site, there seemed to be a particular affinity for fertility magicks, a topic that still gets a fair amount of attention. What ways were the people of Cornwall working that could provide a modern-day insight? The use of the feather-lined pit could be a great jumping-off point. If you were looking to become pregnant or were conducting the ritual for a friend, you could create your own small pit and fill it with feathers, which would form the basis for a very snug nest. There are online sources for feathers that are humanely collected (though please note that collecting feathers of certain birds is against the law). Once you have the bottom of the pit lined with feathers, you could add to that an egg that symbolizes the possibility of life. In addition, you could add stones or herbs that would promote fertility. Once you had everything you wanted to include, you would then cover the pit with another protective layer of feathers, much like a womb, and then cover it with earth.

Consider the application of protection magick based on the discovery in Sardis, Turkey. How would you create a similar magickal application? You could create your own vessel out of clay. From there, you could collect items that are considered protective. You could start with the items that are similar to what you have researched and then add in your own touches. Instead of a visage of Zeus you could include another image of a god/goddess you connect with, such as Poseidon if you live near the ocean, or Hera if you are looking to protect your own home and family.

The possibilities are truly endless. Best of all, those that are based on previous practices reconnect you to an older magick.

Conclusions

History gives us an idea of what ancient peoples have done as a vital part of their cultural and spiritual practices. Archaeology provides the tangible evidence for the cultural and spiritual traditions of our predecessors. It is this direct link to the past that gives a unique understanding of older ritual practices.

As modern magickal practitioners we have a responsibility to learn as much as possible from the past. Through the knowledge of what was practiced before we can adapt it toward future ritual usages and form a link between past and present. Doing so enhances our current practice, provides more stability for our current spirituality, and continues the endless cycle of magick, which enriches it for future generations.

References

Gannon, Megan. "Ancient People Fought Demons and Disasters with Eggs." *Live Science,* January 14, 2014, m.livescience.com/42504-disaster-preventing-eggs-sardis.html.

Ravillious, Kate. (2008). "Witches of Cornwall." *Archaeology Magazine* 61, no. 6 (November/December 2008). http://archive.archaeology.org/0811/etc/witches.html.

Copper Energy Wands

by Charlie Rainbow Wolf

Magic wands are nothing new, and a quick search through a metaphysical shop will provide a wide variety of them, from wood to crystal to metal. I've been making wands and staves for over twenty years, and my favorite ones of all are those made from a hollow copper pipe with a quartz crystal mounted on the end. Working with the soft metal and the clarity of the stone just seems magical in and of itself, long before the wand is actually charged and used.

Of course, wands can be made from other metals and stones, but copper and quartz just feel right to me. For one, the quartz is so unique; I use the unpolished stones to emphasize the natural character of the crystal points. It may not look as neat and flashy as polished stones, but there's something about working with the raw energy of the quartz.

The Wand

I like the energy of copper for these wands and staves. Copper is a soft metal (number 29 on the atomic table), and has been used for centuries as a building material. Copper is also a trace mineral in our bodies. Magically, copper is a conductor of healing and love. It is used in ritual to help to conduct the energies and is worn as a symbol of protection. Copper can also bring balance, as it is a Venusian metal.

Copper piping, available at any builder's merchants or home-improvement store, is fairly inexpensive and available in different sizes. My absolute favorite copper to use, though, is a piece that has been removed from plumbing. This copper may not look as pretty and shiny, but it's already had water flowing through it, and water is an important life force. This seems to bring the wand to life much faster than one made of

brand-new copper. And if you know a plumber, it may also be cheaper!

It doesn't really matter what size copper is used. I've got staves that are over an inch wide and taller than I am, and I have wands that are no bigger around than a pencil and no longer than my hand. I haven't noticed a big difference in their efficiency, although your experience may be different.

To start, I'd recommend getting a length of standard copper tubing, somewhere around a half-inch thick. The most efficient way is to buy a long piece and cut it into several shorter lengths. If you are going to do that, be sure to buy end caps that fit your width of copper pipe. It's also possible to get short lengths of copper that have one end already sealed. I've worked with those, too; they seem to have a nice "whoosh" feel to them when used as a healing wand. Play around in the plumbing section a bit, and choose a width that feels good in your hand. Don't worry about its length. Use your intuition and go with what feels right and fits your budget.

The Stone

As I mentioned previously, I like working with quartz the best, although other stones can be substituted for the capstone. Rose quartz makes a great addition for a healing wand to promote love and harmony, while amethyst is very appropriate for a wand that is going to be used for spiritual growth or for a staff that is going to be used in ritual or ceremony. I prefer quartz because there is a form to fit nearly every purpose imaginable. It's easy to obtain, fairly inexpensive, and no two stones are the same. Katrina Raphael talks about the different terminations of quartz in her book series, The Crystal Trilogy. To get the most out of your energy wand, choose a stone that is in keeping with its purpose.

Channeling crystals do just that; they channel energy and information to the person using them. There is a seven-sided face, front and center of the stone; and another smaller three-sided face on the opposite side. These stones help you connect with the collective unconscious. In doing that, they help you to find your authentic empowerment and your place in the grand scheme of things.

Isis crystals, or **Goddess crystals**, are shaped very much like the channeling crystals, although they have five, rather than seven, sides to their front face. As their name suggests, these are very feminine stones that help you to get in touch with your own feminine side, as well as that of the Divine

Mother. This is a wonderful stone to add to a wand that is going to be used for healing—whether on an individual level or in a group setting.

Transmitter crystals can be recognized by the formation of their natural points. These crystals have a smaller triangle at the front of the stone, with two seven-sided shapes either side of it. These stones are great for projecting your intent out into the cosmos. They help you understand what you want, and they assist you in leaving a thought-form of energy to manifest when the time is right.

Window crystals have a large and equally balanced diamond shape, front and center of the stone. You'll know you have a real window crystal when the shape is symmetrical and allows you to look into the stone itself. Window crystals not only show you the inside of the stones, they can reveal much about your own inner self too. These are excellent stones when doing shadow-self work.

Time-link crystals look very similar to windows but are quite different upon closer inspection. Whereas the diamond in a window is symmetrical and at the front of the stone, a time-link window will slant to the side of the stone. The parallelogram will slant either to the right or to the left. Slanting to the left will assist in allowing your energies to travel back in time to do healing or repair work to release old baggage and lay aside old wounds. The links that slant to the right will help you to project your energy forward in time. This will allow you to take steps toward creating the future that you want to live, one that is up until now only a possibility.

Laser wand crystals are among my favorite quartz points with which to work. Although, like any quartz points, they can come in different sizes, most of them are tiny dynamos of power, and they focus energy with compelling precision. These may not be the most stunning stones to look at, but to those who vibrate on their frequency, they're addictive and beautiful. They are long and slender, with small terminations. I like using lasers the best in small healing wands, where a burst of accurate and focused energy is needed.

Double-terminated crystals are quartz points that have a termination (natural points) on both ends. These stones have the ability to draw energy in and also release it simultaneously. I like them nearly as much as I do the lasers when making wands, because I seem to be able to actually feel the power coming into the quartz point, and exiting the other end, filling the hollow wand with that resonance. These wands make exceptional healing tools.

~

There is a whole world of quartz out there waiting for you to explore and find just the right one for your purpose. It doesn't really matter how it is terminated; what matters most is that you resonate with it, and you feel it is the stone that you want to adorn your wand. Once you have chosen that, you're ready to begin.

The Finishing Touches

You now have your copper and your capstone, but you're going to want to dress your wand. I recommend wrapping it in leather or some kind of hide. If you are a vegan, then faux leather will suffice, or even velvet. It needs to feel comfortable to your skin, and you'll probably want it to look nice too.

Hides and fabric can be purchased from retail outlets, but I'm all about reusing things. My first wands and staves were made on a budget; I used copper piping that I obtained at scrap value from a plumber and old leather coats on clearance at a thrift store. I can't stress enough that there's really no one way that has to be used. Do what works for you. It's your intent that is the most important.

You may also want to decorate your wand. A friend of mine used to do beautiful peyote beadwork to adorn hers. Leather thonging can be tied around the wand to help hold the wrap in place with the ends decorated with meaningful beads or charms. The items and the colors are entirely up to you; choose those that resonate with your own energy and with the wand's purpose.

Constructing the Wand

You're also going to need a hacksaw, some simple glue, a pair of needle-nosed pliers, a small hammer, and possibly some sinew or strong thread. Gather any herbs or other items you want to include in the hollow copper of the wand. Be sure to take the appropriate safety precautions. Hacksaws can give you a nasty cut, and copper filings can get into your skin as splinters.

Start by gluing the end cap onto your copper if you need to do so. Let the glue dry a bit, and then use the hacksaw to cut an "x" shape in the other end. This is where the stone is going to go. Take your time with this. The hacksaw will have a mind of its own, and that's okay—to a certain extent. What you're doing here is making it easier to fit the copper piping around the base of your crystal point. It's easier for your first wands if you choose a point that is roughly the same diameter as your copper piping—another great reason why I like using lasers! Cut your copper so that the stone fits into it nicely. The cut needs to be at least one-third the length of the stone, although I prefer to sink mine more than half their length, which seems to make for a more secure fit.

Using the needle-nose pliers, gently splay the copper where you've cut it, and fit the base of your crystal into the end of the wand. This will be trial and error. You may find that the stone fits one way better than the other; let it go how it wants to go. When it looks and feels balanced and comfortable, gently tap the copper into place around the stone with the hammer. At this point, you can add glue to help the stone set. Some people insist that this should not be done, but I've never had an issue with it. The glue is around the stone, not on the terminations. If you would prefer not to use glue, then wrap a bit of sinew or strong thread around it to hold it in place.

Dress the Wand

The next step is to dress your wand. I've always dressed mine by cutting long lengths of leather or hide about an inch thick, and spiral wrapping them around the wand. Gently overlap them as you work your way to the top. Use glue to prevent slipping if need be. Pay particular attention to the finish of the wrap around the capstone. To make it look neat and tidy, you might want to taper the ends. Also make sure that the wrap is helping hold the capstone firmly in place—you don't want to go through all the effort of making your wand just to have the stone fall out! The wrap can also be sewn around the wand, and I've seen some amazing wands made this way, but it's not a method I've employed.

You're probably going to be keen to dress your wand and make it your own, but try to be patient. Give everything a time to set up before starting to work with it again, particularly if you have not used glue in the construction. A bit of patience now could save you a lot of headaches later. Dress your wand however you wish. Look on the Internet for some ideas—there are truly some beautiful wands and staves out there.

Usage

So, you have this wonderful item in your hands now. You've made it from start to finish, choosing the stone, obtaining the copper, putting it all together, and decorating it. Now it's time to learn to use it. There's really no wrong or right way to

do this, either. The magic isn't in the wand, it's in you—but the wand will come to life when you use it.

First, let's take a look at the actual wand. It's just an inanimate object with no moving parts. So, how can it work? It all has to do with particles of matter. Everything is made up of matter: this book, that chair, the wand, even you. Matter is energy, and energy is always moving and changing. When you start to use your wand, you're taking a conscious part in that change, using the energy of your thoughts. You make a decision, and the energy goes one way; you change your mind, and the energy goes another way. When you involve your wand in the thought process, you blend your energy with that of the wand, and your thoughts create the intent for what you're going to do. (This is why I like having separate wands for different purposes.) Using thoughts to project intent is nothing new. People have been using that for centuries in meditation, prayer, positive thinking, affirmations, and other such practices.

The intensity of the energy that builds up in the rod depends more on the emotional intensity of the person using—or charging—it, rather than the size of the wand (although the big copper staves can look really cool). Think of it as putting your prayer or your desire into the wand, and using that as the energy to charge it. Then, when you're ready, point the wand where you want to discharge the energy, and mentally set it free. That's it—easy, yes?

～

Like anything else, practice makes perfect. The more you work with your wand, the more you will bond with it and it with you, so that you can use it quickly and efficiently. Working with a copper energy wand is fun and exciting, and you can expect to see subtle—but nonetheless awesome—results with just a bit of practice. Always remember that the magic is in you, not in the wand. Like any other tool, care for it diligently and use it with responsibility, and you will find that it can fast become a wonderful ally.

Evolutionary Ancestor Spirits

by Lupa

When you think of your ancestors, you likely imagine a long line of human beings from your family's cultures stretching out behind you. You might especially focus on those who predated Christianity, hearkening to pagan roots far into the mists of prehistory. And for many of us, these ancient people feel like they lived an impossibly long time ago. But they're actually our very youngest relatives; we have much older ancestors than that.

Homo sapiens sapiens, the subspecies that includes all of modern humankind, evolved as a distinct species about 200,000 years ago; that's but a breath of time in the history of life on this planet. The first living beings appeared 3.8 *billion* years ago, and the roots of our family tree stretch all the way back to that point. Yet we almost always neglect to honor these ancestors along with our more recent kin, and I'd like to invite them back into our rites and shrines.

There are, of course, challenges. Unlike our human ancestors, we can't point to specific cultures and populations and say, "I came from these people." We don't have a complete fossil record of every one of our ancestors, and we don't even know the exact progression of our direct human and other primate predecessors. There's not even a specific point at which a particular mother primate gave birth to the very first modern *Homo sapiens sapiens*—there's no "first human" we can point to. Evolution is a gradual process that acts in tiny changes from generation to generation.

But we do know the general progression of evolution that led from the first unicellular life forms to the modern human. We know approximately when the first multicellular life forms showed up, and when those that would become the animal kingdom first split off from the earliest plant ancestors and then later diverged from what would become fungi. Although we don't know which species of early vertebrate fish first developed a primitive backbone and eventually gave rise to every animal with a skeleton, we know it existed in the Cambrian seas more than 500 million years ago. And while we don't know every species that led to us, we can trace the evolutionary progression of our ancestors from fish to amphibians to reptiles to mammals, and then later to the first primates. We still debate which hominid species are our direct predecessors and which ones are just ancient cousins, but we know that at some point all hominids shared a common ancestor. "Mitochondrial Eve" is the name given to the oldest common ancestor of all modern humans; we only know that she lived somewhere between 100,000 and 200,000 years ago, but we can acknowledge her just the same. And so it is with all of our nonhuman ancestors.

Genealogy Turned Up to Eleven

We contact our ancestors through sacred acts and rites. We build shrines to them, make offerings to them, and revere them from generation to generation. While ancestor worship may no longer be the mainstream practice it once was, many people have pictures of family members long past hanging in their homes, and some even talk to the people in these photos (though they may not admit it).

It's easy to feel connected to the beloved dead we're most closely related to, especially those we knew in life. It's tougher to feel some connection to a tiny fish barely the size of our finger that lived hundreds of millions of years ago, or to have a picture of Uncle Tetrapod next to Aunt Mabel.

A lot of that stems from a lack of familiarity. We can't travel back in time to meet our evolutionary ancestors (though, believe me, plenty of scientists wish we could!). What we can do is research what scientists have discovered about these ancients and get to know them a bit better. There are plenty of books and other resources on the evolution of life on Earth; there are three in particular I'd recommend as starting points:

The Origin of Species by Charles Darwin established the scientific theory of evolution. While it may be considered a bit of a dry read by modern standards, and evolutionary science has progressed in the 150 years since its publication, it's a gold mine about the basics of evolution.

The Ancestor's Tale: A Pilgrimage to the Dawn of Evolution by Richard Dawkins is an excellent book for tracing our evolutionary family tree back to the beginning of life. While it's not a species-by-species path to our oldest ancestors, Dawkins does highlight some species that marked important shifts and changes that evolved as life ebbed and flowed over the eons.

The Walking With... Series by the British Broadcasting Company: This is a series of documentaries created in the late twentieth and early twenty-first centuries using computer animation to re-create a whole host of prehistoric creatures. *Walking With Dinosaurs* is the best-known series, but others cover animals that came before and after the enormous reptiles, as well as the evolution of humans and our relatives. The documentaries have some inaccuracies (such as showing one animal evolving into another without evidence of a direct link), and the behavior of many of the species discussed is speculative, based on the behavior of similar animals today. Still, as a general look at how life has changed and adapted over millions of years, the documentaries are a good, entertaining introduction.

The Eldest Ancestor on the Mantel

Once you've familiarized yourself with at least the basics of our ancient family tree, it's up to you to decide how you want to honor your evolutionary ancestors.

You may have found that certain beings were particularly of interest as you did your research. These may not necessarily be direct ancestors; for example, one of my plant totems is *Cooksonia caledonica*, the totem of one of the very first plants on dry land. Obviously I'm not a plant, and animals and plants branched off from each other as separate kingdoms long before *Cooksonia* popped out of the water. But she and I have had good conversations nonetheless, and I've learned good things from her.

If none of the evolutionary ancestors stepped forward as you researched, you may wish to more openly invite them into your life. You can use the following meditation as it is, or modify it for your needs.

Evolutionary Ancester Meditation

First, prepare a quiet place where you can be comfortable and undisturbed for at least an hour, with whatever sounds, smells, and sensory enhancements you prefer. Give yourself a few minutes to settle in and leave behind the cares of everyday life.

Now, focus on the tip of the index finger of your dominant hand. Bring your focus in tighter and tighter until you're visualizing a single skin cell on the tip. Imagine that you're sinking into that cell and then traveling through it to the nucleus. Inside the nucleus, you find a strand of DNA, which stretches into a spiraling staircase, with you entering at the very top of it. At the center of the staircase, traveling up all the way down its length, is a cord—should you need to return to the top of the staircase quickly, all you have to do is grasp the cord, and it will pull you back up safely.

Start to walk down the staircase; you notice that instead of walls, the staircase passes by a solid line of doors, one right after another, edge to edge. If you feel yourself particularly interested in one of these doors, open it up.

Inside each door is a different moment in time. If you open a door, you might find yourself on a sunny morning in the Cretaceous period surrounded by seed ferns and an array of giant reptiles and tiny mammals and proto-birds. Or you could end up on a beach during the Cambrian, and dive into the water to explore some of the strangest creatures ever to live on this planet. You might even enter a door into the dawn of life itself—warm shallow seas with tiny unicellular life forms not yet differentiated into individual kingdoms.

There is no rush. Explore as you will. You may find that certain ancestors approach you, for these are the spiritual versions of Earth as they were at different times, and they are where the ancestors reside. There's no script; let the conversa-

tions happen naturally. If you aren't sure what to say, greet the ancestors and ask them why they've met you there. Some may merely be curious; others might want to talk in more depth.

Once you're done in one place, you can head back to the staircase. You may wish to explore more places, or you might want to just head back up the stairs and finish your meditation so you can contemplate a single experience.

~

After you've completed the meditation, spend some time reflecting on what happened. Who did you talk to, and where did you meet them? What did they have to say, and why did they approach you? Did they introduce you to other ancestors? Are there places where you didn't meet any ancestors, but that you feel you need to go back to? Or places you didn't have a chance to get to but that you're curious about?

You may wish to write in a journal or otherwise record the results of the meditation and reflection to document it. You may find that earlier meditations and work with the ancestors ties in with later experiences in interesting ways, or that your relationships with the ancestors deepen over time.

The evolutionary ancestors may make requests of you during meditations and other communication with them, like setting up a small shrine to them or doing more research on the time they lived in. You are never obligated to fulfill any request you aren't comfortable with; I've known people who felt they absolutely had to buy an expensive fossil or similar item for their shrine because the ancestors demanded it, even though it meant rent wouldn't be paid that month. It's okay to be spiritual; it's unnecessary to be a martyr.

On Being Good Ancestors

There is one lesson from the evolutionary ancestors that I do feel we should all take to heart: it is not enough to call upon our ancestors now, but to be good ancestors for the generations to come. Earth has seen five mass extinctions in which the majority of life on the planet was extinguished; these were likely caused by everything from global climate change to the famous asteroid that did in the dinosaurs. However, it is theorized that we are at the beginning of a sixth mass extinction—one brought about by our own actions. Scientists estimate that extinction is happening up to a thousand times faster than normal; instead of losing a half dozen species a year, we're losing dozens a *day*. Many of these species have never been cataloged by science.

An asteroid doesn't know what damage it causes when it crashes into a planet full of life. Neither does the atmosphere when it collects too much carbon and causes the planet to heat up. But we know what we're doing, and thankfully more of us than ever are trying to turn the tide away from extinction and other environmental disasters.

In my work with the evolutionary ancestors, the message has been clear: we have inherited a planet that has survived many disasters, and the beings that survived could only hunker down and scrape by until conditions got better. Because we have the opportunity to stave off this latest extinction event, it is our responsibility as the ancestors of the future to do so. When life thousands or millions of years from now looks up at the stars and asks us what to do in times of need, what will we tell them? Do we tell them that we squandered the available resources and cheated those who came after us? Or will we be able to tell a story of how we saved the world and the living beings we shared it with from destruction? Maybe we can tell the story of the mass extinction that was stopped.

But it takes us acting now, for the good of the planet, for the good of other beings today, and for the good of those who will come after us. We need to act now to make the future better, not just for our human children or their children, but for those who will be here long after we as a species have gone extinct. For the line of ancestors is billions of years old, and if we can avoid complete annihilation of life on Earth, it will continue for billions of years to come.

Our Magical Pets

by Autumn Damiana

Some people believe that spirits decide where and when to be born on Earth as babies, so that they effectively "choose" who they will be with during their lifetimes. The same might be said of pets, who are also born into our lives or come via other mysterious pathways because they are destined to be with us. Take, for example, my own situation: I would say I'm a hardcore "cat person," but I recently adopted a puppy that, to my surprise, grew into a striking resemblance of Anubis, a god I've been devoted to since my teen years. It could be coincidence, but it doesn't feel that way—it feels like Anubis wishes to share a closer relationship with me. Maybe he feels neglected since I found paganism and have discovered an affinity to other gods? Maybe in entrusting me with one of his kin, he is calling me back into his service?

The special bond we share with our pets is as real as the one we share with our human family members and friends, spirit allies, and our deities, and deserves some attention, especially in a magical household. From a Pagan perspective, our pets can also be our familiars, a representation of our totems, our magical allies, and even a connection to gods, goddesses, and the Divine. If you are a Pagan with a love of animals, you will most likely keep pets, and if you keep pets, you probably not only love them but honor and revere them as well. You would also probably like to include them in your practices. Here are a few ideas how to do just that.

Pets as Familiars or Magical Allies

Although the theory of the "witch's familiar" is partly based on fictional ideas about witches that were made popular during the Inquisition, the animal familiar is a concept with some basis in fact and that has been further defined by modern witchcraft. Considering that almost all Pagan folk consider their pets as family, it's not surprising that they would want to bring their pets into rituals or forge a bond with them as magical allies. However, while a pet may be the embodiment of a totem animal, totems are typically symbolic or spiritual in nature while a familiar exists in the physical realm and as such has its own physical, mental, and spiritual needs.

To meet these needs, do not automatically assume your pet wants to work with you on a magical level. Before attempting to bring your pet into ritual, spellwork, divination, or any other magical endeavor, you should have a stable, trusting, intuitive relationship. You should also have the courtesy to "ask" the animal first. Start by building up a psychic rapport with your pet. This can be done a variety of ways. For one, share small amounts of food and/or water with your pet out of your own plate, bowl, or cup after you have partaken, so they ingest your essence. (Use caution, as water/food additives and specific edibles can be toxic.) Meditate with your pet, journey with your pet in the spirit realm, or attempt to shapeshift into the same species as your pet. In all three instances, you must focus on the animal and tune in to its senses, attempting to see, hear, smell, feel, taste, and ultimately experience the world as it does. Then, slowly meld your human reality into the encounter to create a bond. Animals are highly psychic and can sense a deliberate attempt to connect with them. You can also do Reiki, crystal therapy, or even chant over your pet or your pet's food/water/toys/etc. to further the connection. You will know your pet is psychically linked and wants to do magical work with you when the animal responds to your moods instinctively, visits you in your dreams or on the astral plane, or is drawn to you when you do ritual, divination, or spellcasting.

Once you get to this point, feel free to include your pet in your magical workings. Because animals are naturally drawn to positive energy, they might be curious about your spiritual practice, mystical activities, and everything else associated with these. However, there are some situations and conditions that require caution:

Circle: Most Pagans believe that animals have pure spirits and can enter and exit a circle at will without disturbing it, but they need to be closely observed. We all know how jumping/flying/running pets and wagging tails can knock over candles, burning incense, cups and plates, and delicate items like glass. Some pets may react badly to large groups of people or the intense energy of a circle. And some pets may be moody, wanting to be included at some times and then sit out at others, so use your intuition.

Ritual tools: Because your tools will smell like you, have your energy, or be "psychically imprinted" by you or your workings, your pet may want to investigate them. If you are not okay with this, be sure to store them someplace safe—it's not fun to discover a chewed-up tarot deck, a broken chalice, or an altar arrangement strewn all over the room. Also keep in mind that pets have different reactions than people—your pet may scent, pee on, or otherwise mark your objects or take/hide them somewhere because they appreciate them enough to "claim" them or because they want to add their essence to yours.

Magical supplies: Your pet has senses like your own, but these may be differently tuned. Smoke, incense, essential oils, smudging blends, herbs/spices, and some foods may have scents or other qualities that are completely overpowering, and possibly deadly, to your pet. Beware especially of allergies—dogs cannot consume anything with chocolate, cats/birds/small mammals are

not tolerant of most essential oils, and reptiles/amphibians can absorb things from your skin as they are handled. Always make sure your magical environment is safe for your pet.

People: If you practice with others, make sure that each of these individuals gets introduced to your pet before a ritual under normal, nonmagical circumstances. Some pets who are typically mild-mannered or obedient may exhibit undesirable behavior when confronted with too many new experiences like raised energy, unfamiliar circle members, and new smells and sounds. A scared or confused pet can bite, scratch, and soil things or be otherwise aggressive or disruptive.

Remember, if you do see or sense that your pet is anxious, scared, overwhelmed, overexcited, or feeling threatened, take your pet to a comforting area away from your magical activity where it feels safe and can calm down!

Popular Pets and Their Correspondences

Throughout history animals have been linked to gods, goddesses, mythology, and magical symbolism. Below is a short list of some of the most typical associations in Wicca/Witchcraft. Please note that I could not find correspondences for every common pet, and that the references I have listed are general. For example, Anubis is actually a jackal-headed god, but is often associated with dogs, and I have included both Hera and the Morrigan as bird goddesses even though their sacred animals are the peacock and the raven. Do your research on the specific correspondences for your pet and see what you can find. Also feel free to substitute anything that makes more sense to you.

Dog: Anubis, Hecate, Artemis/Diana, Ares/Mars; hellhounds; werewolves; Sirius (star), Canis Major and Canis Minor (constellations); Chinese zodiac sign.

Cat: Bastet, Sekhmet, Freyja, Artemis/Diana; Maneki Neko (Japanese folktale); "nine lives"; Western zodiac sign Leo (lion); the Yule Cat (Icelandic folktale).

Rabbit: Artemis/Diana, Eostre; the moon and fertility; Trickster figure; Chinese zodiac sign; good luck amulet (rabbit's foot.)

Birds: Hera/Juno, Aphrodite/Venus, Athena/Minerva, Thoth, Ra/Horus, Isis, Maat, the Morrigan; the phoenix, the crane, the Bennu bird, the thunderbird (various world myths); Chinese Zodiac sign (rooster).

Snake: Wadjet, Quetzalcoatl, the Minoan Snake Goddess, Demeter/Ceres, Mercury/Hermes; the caduceus; sea serpents; Chinese zodiac sign; the Druids.

Reptiles/Amphibians: Heket (frog), Sobek (crocodile or lizard); the World Turtle/Turtle Island (Native American and various world myths); dragons; salamanders (fire elementals).

Fish: Poseidon/Neptune, Dagon; Western zodiac sign, Pisces; Dorado (constellation).

Livestock animals: Pan/Faunus, Dionysus/Bacchus, Western Zodiac sign Capricorn (goat); Poseidon/Neptune, Epona, Macha, Pegasus, unicorn, Western Zodiac sign Sagittarius (horse); Hathor, Hera/Juno, Zeus/Jupiter, Ares/Mars, Western Zodiac sign Taurus (cow/bull); Freyr, Demeter/Ceres (pig/boar); Western zodiac sign Aries (ram); Chinese zodiac signs (ox, horse, sheep, pig).

Other small pets: Arachne, dreamcatchers, Trickster figure in African/Native American myths (spider); Western zodiac sign Cancer (crab); Selket, Western Zodiac sign Scorpio (scorpion); Chinese zodiac sign (rat).

Choosing a Magical Pet

Getting a pet is a big decision. Obviously, all practical aspects of pet ownership—the time, space, and money your pet will require—need to be thought through and discussed with everyone in your household. You might also have special or at least different considerations to mull when going about obtaining a magical animal companion.

Often, just the decision to get a magical pet will immediately be followed by an opportunity—your friend's dog or cat has a litter, a stray will turn up in your yard, the neighbors move and need to find homes for their animals. Sometimes you need to look a little harder, such as visit the local animal shelter or pet fair, or search online. Obviously, adopting an animal is beneficial to all involved, but if a pet comes along that somehow just feels right, go with your instincts.

You can also do specific kinds of magic to bring you the right pet—you *are* looking for a magical animal, after all! I have noticed that many spells that are designed to attract a lover or friend can be easily modified to attract an animal companion. Just remember that if you are really looking for the pet that is best for you, try not to get too hung up on details. It may even be too much to visualize the specific kind of animal you want—what if you wish for a ferret, and in doing so, miss out on owning a wonderfully magical chinchilla? Another option is to ask the gods for help. You can ask your patron deity to assist you, or if you are absolutely sure you know what kind of animal you want, you can pray to that animal's totem spirit or associated deity to unite you with your pet.

Once you do have a pet, you can start the process I described above to connect with your pet psychically and hopefully work up to magical practice. Please keep in mind, however, that there is no way to guarantee that any animal you choose is going to become the magical companion you desire. So just make sure before you commit that you will be happy with your pet as an ordinary companion if this turns out to be the case.

A Few Tips and Alternatives

We worship the Goddess as Maiden/Mother/Crone and the God as Warrior/Father/Sage and relate to them as we also pass

through these stages in our lives. Our pets go through these stages too. Most pets (with a few exceptions) have much shorter life spans than humans, so although my dog is only a puppy right now, we will be the "same age" in about five years, after which she will grow into a Crone long before I do. This can be a sad thought, but it also helps me to see the Goddess manifest within her. The same can be observed in any pet, and it can be a magical experience.

Showing kindness to an animal is said to honor the deities associated with it, and pleases the gods in general. This can take the form of worship or an offering if done with intent. Try fostering an animal, volunteering at an animal shelter, or giving time and/or money to your favorite animal charity or cause. Pampering your own pet certainly qualifies too!

Can't have a pet at this time or just haven't found the right one? There are still ways to have a magical relationship with an animal. Pet-sitting or spending time with a friend's pet is one option. And who knows? Maybe the neighbor's cat that always comes sniffing around when you cast a circle is trying to tell you something! You can also frequent parks or farms, visit petting zoos, feed strays, and the like.

If you are worried that your children are really not ready for a pet (especially a magical one) you can try to work up to it. Get them pet rocks, stuffed animals, statues, and books/pictures of the desired pet. Then let them show you they can care for a virtual pet (which will "die" if you forget to care for it) or one of those toy robot pets. If this goes well, you can start with something simple, like a fish, a hermit crab, or a millipede, and later a hamster, a parakeet, or a turtle, and so on.

Sometimes it's just not possible to have the magical pet we truly desire, like a tiger or a monkey. But that doesn't mean that you can't have a magical relationship with the spirit of that animal through a more practical pet! An aquarium filled with goldfish, for example, is a great substitute for a pond full of koi, since both fish are a type of carp. Obviously a dog can be a substitute for a wolf, but how about a mynah bird instead of a raven or crow (which are both illegal to keep where I live), a seahorse instead of a horse, or even a lizard instead of a dragon! Get creative—any pet can be a magical pet!

Air Magic

Mighty Bubbles!

by Melanie Marquis

There's just something magical about bubbles. Those irridescent, air-filled orbs remind us of the beauty of simply filling space, whether it's an empty sky filled with bubbles or an empty heart filled with love and joy. If you like the idea of bringing more magick into your everyday life but struggle to find the time and motivation to do so, bubble magick might be just the thing to kick your practice into full gear. While you might be feeling too stressed or exhausted at the end of the day to pull out a whole bunch of ritual tools and perform a complex rite, blowing a few bubbles with your magickal intentions in mind is fast, easy, and relaxing. And it's a lot of fun! Blowing bubbles engages our imaginative, creative, and playful faculties. With just a little know-how, you can cast a variety of powerful magick spells with nothing more than a tiny bottle of bubbles. Here's how.

Basic Bubble Blend

Bubbles are easy to come by and inexpensive, but if you want your bubbles to pack an extra magickal punch, try making your own bubble solution. Simply mix four parts water to one part dish soap. To make your bubbles extra strong and long-lasting, add a couple tablespoons of corn syrup, sugar, or liquid glycerin to each cup of water. Stir the mixture slowly and gently so that it doesn't get too sudsy. Think of the magick you'll cast with the bubbles as you blend and be aware that you are creating more than a simple plaything—you are indeed crafting a new, effective tool for spellcasting. Once it's mixed, let your bubble solution sit for a day or so to

allow the ingredients more time to bond together. This basic recipe can be used as is, or you can switch it up and make new varieties of magickal bubbles by incorporating scents and colors.

Scented Bubbles

Using scented bubbles adds an extra touch of fun and magickal symbolism. You can purchase commercially made mixtures or add your own fragrances to produce more personalized or specialty blends. Just gently stir in a few drops of essential oils or a tablespoon or so of scented liquid soap to each cup of bubble solution. Try matching the scent to the intention of your bubble magick. If you're using bubbles for a cheering charm, for instance, consider adding watermelon or orange scent. If your bubble magick is intended to empower your goals with greater strength and energy, patchouli-scented bubbles would be a fine choice. For bubble magick with a romantic flair, experiment with strawberry, cherry, or floral scents. Breathe in the aroma of your scented bubbles to help you ground and get "in the zone" before your magickal workings.

Colorful Bubbles

You can also make tinted bubbles by mixing in a few drops of food coloring, tempura paint, or liquid watercolors for each cup of bubble solution. You can even create glow-in-the-dark bubbles by adding a tablespoon of washable, glow-in-the-dark paint to each cup of your basic bubble mix; just charge them under a bright florescent bulb, then take them outdoors and let them light up the night. Be sure to reserve your colorful bubbles for outside fun only, as they can cause stains. Try blowing tinted bubble solution on a canvas or piece of paper to create magickal works of art. You might draw a target on a piece of paper, and in the bull's eye, write a word or draw a symbol that represents your magickal goal. Blow bubbles at the paper and envision yourself achieving the goal each time the bubble hits the target. When possible, select a color for your bubbles that best harmonizes with your spell goal. Try blue or pink bubbles for love, yellow for happiness or change, orange for energy or strength, or purple for psychic power or spiritual development.

Choosing a Bubble Wand

In addition to incorporating scents and colors, you can further harmonize your bubble magick by choosing a bubble-blowing wand that best matches the intention of your spell. For example, if you're casting a spell to attract good fortune, try using a blue, gold, or green bubble wand, colors symbolic of success and good luck. You might also consider crafting your own custom-made bubble wands, creating unusual shapes using pipe cleaners. Try a heart-shaped bubble wand for a love charm or a star-shaped wand for an added boost of luck and magickal power. A hula hoop becomes a giant bubble maker. Experiment with different shapes and sizes of bubble blowers to add greater meaning to your magick.

Enchanting Your Bubbles for Magick

Be sure to align the energy of your bubbles to their magickal purpose before you begin. This is sometimes referred to as empowering, enchanting, or charging, and it can be a swift and straightforward or lengthy and involved, process. To quickly charge your bubbles to their purpose with minimal fuss, simply hold the container in your hands and think about the aim of your magick, the effect you hope the bubble charm will achieve. Envision the energies of your intentions flowing into the bubble solution. For instance, if you want to cast a charm to increase your wealth, visualize yourself surrounded by riches and conjure a feeling of prosperity in your heart,

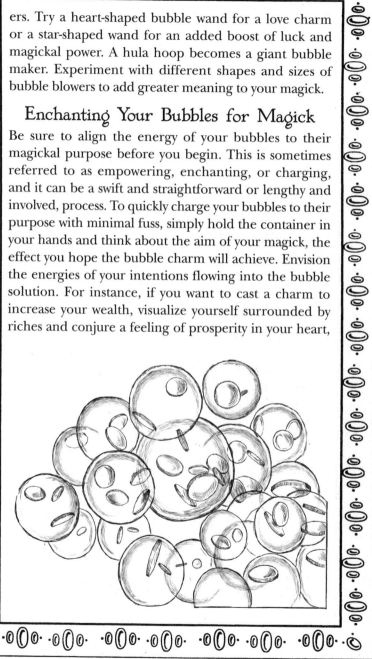

projecting these visual images and potent emotions into the bubbles.

Basic Bubble Charms

To perform a basic bubble charm for manifestation, blow a stream of bubbles upward into the sky above. As they float away and pop, envision the bubbles releasing their magick into the surrounding air to bring your wishes into manifestation. For an alternative, have a friend blow a barrage of bubbles at you. Pop as many as you can, declaring your magickal wish manifest as each bubble bursts.

To cast a basic bubble charm for increase, try using a drinking straw for a bubble blower. Blow through the straw to produce a plethora of tiny bubbles. See how many bubbles you can get into the air at once, and envision the subject of your magick increasing and multiplying in kind. If your spell is for an increase in your vegetable harvest, for instance, envision the many bubbles as many healthy, ripe vegetables swirling in the sky around you. Another method of casting a bubble charm for increase is to blow a really big bubble. Use a medium-sized bubble wand, and blow very slowly and gently to get the bubble to maximum size. As the bubble expands, think of the aim of your magick expanding as well, be it an expansion of personal skill, an increase of good fortune, or the growth of a new project.

Bubble Charm: Breeze through Obstacles

Begin by creating a custom-shaped bubble wand out of a pipe cleaner. Consider your obstacles, both external and internal, as you craft it. Starting about halfway up the length of the pipe cleaner, bend the wire at right angles to create a square shape at the top of your bubble wand. Twist the end of the pipe cleaner around the handle to secure it in place.

The next bit of preparation is to mix a batch of bubble solution especially attuned to your own personal power. Start with the basic bubble solution, then add essential oils that harmonize with your astrological sign, a spritz of your signature perfume, or even a drop or two of your own saliva. Think about your personal charisma, ambition, tenacity, courage, or other qualities you possess as you blend these additional ingredients. Remember to stir the mixture gently so that it doesn't turn into a frothy mess. Allow your bubble solution to sit outside overnight under waxing moonlight to further empower it and ready it for magickal action. The next morning, take your bubble solution outdoors. Spend a moment enjoying the sensations of the natural world surrounding you; consider how you are a part of this natural world, and use this awareness to tap in to the earth's powerful vibrations. Allow this connection to increase your feelings of strength, skill, and capability. Dip your bubble wand into the solution and blow, envisioning yourself having successfully overcome the challenge at hand. Notice how the flexibility of the bubble enables it to move through the sharp edges and angles of the bubble wand without harm and without lasting effect on its final form as a perfectly round bubble, just as you will be able to breeze through your obstacles and emerge unscathed.

~

As you can see, bubble magick is a very versatile art. Think of some new ways to use bubble magick in your everyday life and magickal practice. Would carrying around a tiny bottle of bubbles for magick on the go be handy? How might gigantic bubbles be used in a spell? What about blowing a double-bubble? Consider the many possibilities, and let the magick of bubbles carry you onwards and upwards to new heights of magickal success!

Heart Gifts:
Energetic and Spiritual Exchange

by Blake Octavian Blair

The talents, gifts, expertise, and spiritual services that many of us offer to others as clerics, healing arts practitioners, diviners, and all permutations thereof have very real and deep value. It is logical that we want and need to acknowledge that which we receive, and it is natural to want to receive acknowledgement for the time and efforts we have given. Generally, this is done in some form of tangible payment, monetary or otherwise. While it is true that in our modern society and culture we all need money to survive, there are many occasions in which a non-monetary form of compensation is appropriate or preferable. One approach to this situation is that of the heart gift: a gift given in gratitude that is of spiritual and/or practical value to the recipient.

This isn't a new concept to magickal folks. We like and strive to maintain balance in our personal lives and with our work. Most ethical magickal folk believe in some form of reciprocity. When it comes to giving and receiving services, this holds especially true. When there is no reciprocity, it creates not only animosity as well as a feeling of being taken advantage of or that what you have given has been underappreciated or devalued. However, not completing an exchange also does a great disservice to the person who received the service. Essentially, to not ask for some type of exchange puts the recipient of the service in debt, even if only energetically, and essentially makes a beggar of them. This is a familiar lesson to those with Reiki training. In Reiki, we are taught that there should always be an exchange, a reciprocity, no matter how simple. My Reiki teacher once told me the story of her volunteering at a senior home and being offered a cookie by an elderly woman from her "meals on wheels" lunch. My teacher's initial internal reaction was to decline the offer. How could she accept this from an elderly woman in this situation? However, as the Reiki recipient offered once again, my teacher realized that by offering this cookie the woman was offering something she considered of value. The elderly woman did not want to be in debt by not giving something of value in appreciation for receiving something she valued. Not wanting to leave this kind woman feeling like a "beggar," my teacher accepted the cookie graciously.

Some people feel that to ask for or to desire some form of exchange (you could term it as "payment") for your spiritual services is a desire that comes from a place of ego. I couldn't disagree more. We simply want more than passing acknowledgment; we want to know what we have put into the world is valued. Everybody wants to feel appreciated and valued. The desire for this acknowledgement is certainly far from entering the territory of operating from a place of ego.

Heart gifts are a concept that has existed across cultures further back than I can trace. The practice has gone by many names and often there is/was no term for it. However, I feel that the term "heart gift" is a good working term and descriptor. The process of choosing the right gift should be one of heartfelt thought and be given in gratitude. When choosing a heart gift, it is not about an item's inherent monetary value, it is about the spiritual and/or practical value. Ideally, I strive to choose items that are high in both. Later, we will explore some starting places for ideas for things to give as heart gifts. While we are still on the topic of value, it is a good time to delve into the topic of situations that lend themselves to heart gifts.

Heart gifts can be an appropriate form of payment when it is hard to place a monetary value upon something, or perhaps when a practitioner specifically requests that you not give a monetary payment. Generally, before any services are rendered, all parties agree to the expected payment parameters for the exchange. Usually, if heart gifts are acceptable, the practitioner will present the option to the recipient in these preliminary discussions. Another situation that sometimes presents itself is that of a person who clearly needs a service but legitimately cannot afford to give a standard monetary payment. If a practitioner observes that someone needs the service but might decline seeking it due to budget constraints, sometimes they will choose to offer to provide the service as a sort of gift—and request a heart gift in exchange.

Gifts Versus Bartering

The heart gift scenarios I just presented are quite a bit different from bartering in a few ways. First, in bartering one tries to attempt to match a monetary value in some way. Heart gifts do not try to match monetary value—their value is measured in spiritual and practical value. As the title implies, they are gifts from the heart. (Monetary value is completely independent of spiritual or practical value.) Another way in which heart gifts differ is protocol. Sometimes the seeker or recipient approaches the practitioner for a service and the practitioner states ahead of a transaction that the payment is to be a heart gift. Sometimes a tradition states that certain rites or initiations cannot be charged for monetarily but that a heart gift is appropriate. Further, sometimes no payment is requested at all, in which case it would be appropriate to take it upon yourself to give a heart gift to responsibly complete the energetic exchange. However, unlike in bartering, I would not seek a service from a practitioner and suggest a heart gift for payment. In my opinion, that is not in good taste. This starts to enter into the territory of when heart gifts are not appropriate.

Money is a sticky topic among magickal people when it comes to rendering certain services or teachings. I am not in the camp that automatically condemns money as the official Pagan devil. I feel that money is a valid form of energetic exchange. We all work hard for our money, and it is our energy put into a tangible form. To pay in money is to pay with your energy. However, I also realize money does not grow on trees. (If you develop an enchantment that truly does grow a real live tree full of cash, please write me with it!) I can understand being in a position of needing a service but not being able to pay monetarily. I've been both the practitioner and the recipient/seeker in such situations.

If a practitioner does not present the heart gift option to you, it is for a reason, and it usually isn't a malicious or greedy one. It simply means, for whatever reason, that it is

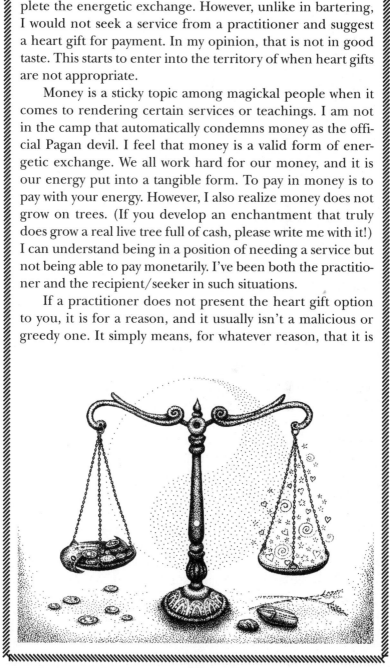

not the appropriate form of payment for the particular transaction. (If their tradition specifically forbids them to monetarily charge for something, and they do so anyway, that is their karma of a broken oath to deal with!) This leaves open monetary payment or bartering. You can always offer to barter up front when you legitimately cannot afford to pay; however, it must be of value to the practitioner and monetarily comparable in value to the service or product the person is offering. If it is not, and they don't need what you are offering, it is not wrong, greedy, or rude for them to decline. I do believe that workers are worth hiring and that things of value are worth paying for. Time, services, and expertise are valuable. If a person sticks to their guns on needing a monetary payment, consider that they need to pay their rent, bills, and buy groceries too. I know that I sure do!

What to Give

Once a heart gift is mutually agreed upon as the form of payment for services to be rendered, it is time to decide what would be a good choice of gift for the practitioner. As I mentioned earlier, we are looking at spiritual and practical value, not monetary. A two-dollar crystal can be just as appropriate a gift as a fifty-dollar statue, or a ten-dollar bag of coffee. The most important criteria when making your selections are if the gift is a good fit and of value and use to the person and that the gift be chosen and given from a heart-centered mindset. Now, let's look at some various ideas that you can use as leaping off points in your gift selection process.

Practical gifts

Spiritual supplies relevant to the practitioner's path and services they offer are a nice choice that will almost surely be received with gratitude. If you know a practitioner uses smudging in their spiritual practice and sessions, you may gift them with smudging herbs and materials. You could even create a simple handmade smudging feather for them. If they use aromatherapy, a nice small bottle of a quality essential oil would make a wonderful gift. A handmade tarot deck bag

would be a wonderful gift for a card reader! Do they engage in mantra recitation? Then how about a lovely strand of mala beads? Gifts that relate to their practice will have inherent spiritual value and their practicality makes them a double score.

Handmade Items

My mention of a handmade tarot bag as an idea brings me to another category of gifts worth considering—handmade items. Handmade items intrinsically require you to put forth energy into them, and generally if you're going to take the time and effort to create something by hand for somebody, you likely care a great deal for them. This makes it a perfect heart gift. Think of how meaningful a crocheted throw blanket, either for their personal use or to lay on top of their healing table, would be to them. Perhaps candlemaking is a skill you possess—a homemade candle with herbs and essential oils would make a wonderful gift for almost any spiritual person. Perhaps you can design and create a beaded necklace for the practitioner to wear that provides energetic protection—

always welcome for those who see many clients. A handmade gift has an extra level of practical value from a magickal standpoint in that you can infuse the gift with a specific and loving energy for the recipient as you make it via intent, concentration, and prayer.

Consumable Gifts

Another gift category to consider is consumables. What do you give the person who has everything? Sometimes a person doesn't need another athame, another tarot deck, or something that potentially will be a dust collector on a shelf. The consumables category includes magickal supplies such as candles, incense, oils, and the like. However, it also includes food. Who doesn't love tasty treats? A batch of homemade cookies, jams, and jellies made from your garden harvests, nice locally roasted coffee beans, and herbal teas are all examples of really wonderful and thoughtful potential heart gifts for your practitioner. I know that as coffee lovers in our house, you quickly win your way into our hearts with a bag of coffee from one of our favorite roasteries! (Praise be to Goddess Caffeina!) Consumable gifts are great in that they can be those slightly indulgent and decadent items one may not always spring for themselves or have the time to make themselves. Furthermore, for the person who has everything or space for nothing, they can enjoy the gift and the pleasures it has to offer without worrying about it taking up permanent space!

Thoughtful Combinations

You can think "outside the box," or rather perhaps "inside the basket," and create a lovely gift basket by pairing and combining items. Themed baskets, such as a magickal relaxation assortment, can be fun. You could include a candle of a calming scent such as lavender or vanilla, a box of chamomile tea, and a jar of homemade bath salts or a homemade bar of soap! These types of gifts, despite being abundant in size, are generally low in monetary cost and high in practical and spiritual value. The basket's components can be a combination of purchased and handmade items. Have fun with it!

~

While we make no qualms about the fact we do often charge monetarily for our services, when the occasion has been appropriate for heart gifts, my husband and I have received some wonderful heartfelt items. We have received stones and crystals, smudging materials, candles, soaps, and even a beautiful original painting by a client who is an artist. We have given our fair share of heart gifts over the years as well. We have given handmade incense cones, mojo-style spellbags, hand-beaded jewelry, quilts, homemade vegan cupcakes, and more. All of them were perfect for their specific occasions and recipients. When it comes to heart gifts, the Divine has a way of guiding the seeker to the perfect gift and seeing that the perfect gift arrives to the right practitioner and at the most perfect time. When operating from a heart-centered place there is as much joy in giving as there is in receiving. The next time an appropriate situation presents itself, I hope you can joyfully engage in the giving of heart gifts. Blessings of the heart be upon you!

Casting a Circle
with the Archangels
of the Four Directions

by Tess Whitehurst

Some traditions name three magical realms: earth, sea, and sky. A practical application of this conceptual framework might consider earth to be the physical world of rocks, trees, plants, and animals; the sea to be the fluid world of thought, emotion, intuition, and spirits; and the sky to be the bright, heavenly world of light, unseen connections, and celestial orchestration. You might say that all three realms are equally important, and that appropriate employment of each can provide a most effective synergy.

In diverse cultures and religions, the sky realm is also the realm of angels: those powerful ambassadors of the Great Spirit who can bless us with divine intervention, immaculate protection, swift assistance, and immediate, positive change.

The general wisdom is that the angelic realm is something of a hierarchy, although not in the earthly sense. Rather, if you think of the singular divine source as the sun, the angels would be like rays of the sun. While countless angels may abound as divine representatives helping humans with any number of everyday situations, the much smaller number of angels closer to the one divine source would be the more potent, universal, archetypal rays: these angels are also known as the archangels. And as you may know, some branches of magic (such as ceremonial magic) incorporate archangels as a matter of course.

Though I'm not a ceremonial magician, I quite enjoy calling on the archangels of the four directions—Raphael, Michael, Gabriel, and Uriel—as a variation on the theme of simply invoking the elements when casting a circle. And, when I choose to go this route, for the fifth element of spirit, I invoke the presence of Archangel Metatron.

If you enjoy aligning with angelic energy, you'll find that working magic in such a circle feels significantly powerful and effective. Additionally, although magical circles of all varieties are protective by nature, an archangelic magical circle has a particularly protective feeling to it... and I am talking instant, double-duty, (energetically) bulletproof protection. Consequently, when you're working protective magic, or magic to recharge your energy or boost your aura—or if you just feel like you could use a supercharged spiritual boost for any reason—an archangelic circle might be an excellent way to go.

Below, we'll talk about exactly how to cast such a circle. But first, let's meet the five archangels we call upon for the purpose, and become acquainted with their history, lore, and unique spiritual signatures.

Raphael

Direction: East
Element: Air
Name meaning: "God heals"
Colors: Green, silver
Scents: Cedar, sage

"Rapha" is the Hebrew word for "doctor" or "healer," and Raphael—also known as the Divine Healer—is in many ways the quintessence of divine healing energy. In fact, he's often the first helper I call on when I desire to summon physical healing for myself or another. After I do so, I envision and sense a very bright, emerald-green light surrounding the person who needs healing, recalibrating and strengthening her body and aura in exactly the way that is needed.

Needless to say, Raphael's healing expertise makes him an excellent helper for healers of all varieties to call on for help in their work.

Raphael is also associated with the swiftly moving energy of the planet Mercury (ruler of the exceptionally airy sign of Gemini and the health-conscious sign of Virgo), and like other beings associated with Mercury—such as Hermes Trismegistus and the Magician card of the tarot—he is aligned with the magical arts. In fact, he is said to have gifted Solomon with his magical ring, which depicted a six-pointed star.

Another attribute of Mercury that Raphael shares—also shared by his cardinal direction of east, the direction of the sunrise—is an alignment with new beginnings.

Finally, just as the element of air is instrumental in clearing space and removing negative energies, Raphael—particularly in tandem with Michael (see next entry)—can be petitioned for help with energy clearings and removing or subduing undesirable entities. (This is demonstrated in The Book of Tobit, and also by the fact that Solomon uses his magic ring for such purposes.)

Michael

Direction: South
Element: Fire
Name meaning: "Who is like god"
Colors: Royal blue, fiery red
Scents: Garlic, cinnamon

Considering how often the singular divine presence is implied to be synonymous with the pure white light of the sun, it should come as no surprise that Michael—the archangel most associated with fire and bright light—has a name that means "Who is like god."

Because he specializes in such vital magical aims as clearing, shielding, and protection (which he often performs with the help of his famed sword of light), I call on Michael every day. And like many modern spiritual practitioners, I find myself working with him more often than any other divine helper. In addition to instantly removing stagnant and unwanted energies from environments and personal energy fields, he can shield people and places with bright, fiery and/or royal blue light that is impenetrable by negativity. Although it can be helpful to clear and shield yourself and your home every day with Michael's help, being allied with him can also come in very handy in a pinch; for example, if you suddenly find yourself in a situation where you feel spiritually or physically unsafe. And nothing fancy is required to petition his assistance! Indeed, all you need to do is ask.

Similarly, in many magical traditions, Michael is called on for help with the iconic "fiery wall of protection oil," which is used to anoint candles and people for physical and spiritual protection. He's also aligned powerfully with garlic: the go-to herbal protector for many magical practitioners, with a masculine, solar energy that many find to be analogous with blindingly bright, purifying white light.

Indeed, if you've worked with Michael even a little bit, you've likely gotten a sense of his vast power to overcome spiritual challenges and instantly shift an energetic landscape to one of pure positivity. His role as patron saint of firefighters and police seems like a natural fit: he has instantly come to my aid on more than one occasion when I have felt particularly physically unsafe. One of the ways he does this is by infusing you with a sense of confidence and grounding, so that in addition to having more presence of mind (and therefore more ability to make wise moves and defend yourself effectively), you're also less victim-like in your posture, and therefore less likely to invite an attack. But that's not all: if you call on him in a pinch, he can energetically defend you and, if necessary, send physical bodyguards in the form of police, security guards, or friends who "coincidentally" appear exactly when you need them.

Gabriel

Direction: West
Element: Water
Name meaning: "God is my strength"
Colors: Deep blue, black
Scents: Ylang-ylang, copal

In many traditions, just as the east is associated with birth and new beginnings, the west is associated with death and the afterlife. In the same vein, water—the element of the west—is the fluid realm of spirit, intuition, and the unknown. It's natural, therefore, that Archangel Gabriel is not only associated with dreams and intuition, but he's also considered a psychopomp: a being who escorts spirits to the other side after their earthly transition. And he's not just any psychopomp: as author Judika Illes states, "It is considered an honor and a blessing to have Gabriel as an escort to the Beyond...Gabriel presides over a palace in the Sixth Heaven, where lucky souls get to spend eternity."

Of course, as the archangel of the water element, he's also aligned with the womb of all life; therefore, conception and birth are under his dominion. And like the Yoruban ocean goddess Yemaya, he is associated with miracles, and is considered a provider of blessings of all forms. (Also like Yemaya, some consider him a female, and while it may be somewhat moot as I am not convinced that angels have genitals and indeed they usually appear to be androgynous, he does seem to have quite a feminine energy about him, and certainly would not be offended to be referred to as a "she.")

His name, meaning "God is my strength," may not at first glance appear to be aligned with the yielding water element, but consider the Grand Canyon: if it weren't for the seemingly eternal, flowing presence of the Colorado river, the vast, sprawling seventh wonder of the world would never have been formed. Indeed, although stone is famous for its hardness, if time is considered from the standpoint of the divine, water's relentless strength easily shapes and dissolves it.

Uriel

Direction: North
Element: Earth
Name meaning: "God is light"
Colors: Brown, black, olive green
Scents: Vetiver, myrhh

As a divine emissary of the celestial realm who is also deeply aligned with the earth element and that which we perceive through our five senses, it seems utterly natural that Uriel should be the one credited with gifting humankind with the knowledge of alchemy. His name, meaning "God is light," also mirrors his alchemical associations: consider the fact that our very eyes and brains evolved in response to our planet being bathed in light. Their unique construction allows us to see different wavelengths of color, and indeed to interpret the way pure white light is bent and refracted in order to show us the diversity of the entire physical world. Modern alchemists, such as scientists and visual artists, rely on light and color for their creations, constructions, and conclusions. And perhaps our most famous and influential alchemist—Sir Isaac Newton—famously refracted light through a prism to take our human understanding of light (and its role in comprising the entire visible world) to a whole new depth.

Like Gabriel, Uriel's feminine vibe and appearance sometimes causes him to be referred to as a "she," but again, gender pronouns are a human construction and are largely irrelevant when it comes to angels (and often humans for that matter). So take your pick.

Uriel's earth alignment also makes him particularly suited to assist with weather prediction and support before, during, and after natural disasters. In fact, he is credited with warning Noah about the flood.

A lovely, bewitching angel with dark wings who often appears less like a traditional angel and more like a tall, dark faerie or elemental, Uriel is also aligned with the traditional earth element associations. Indeed, according to author Christopher Penczak in *Ascension Magick*, "Teachings on grounding, being secure in the material world, and prosperity are (in Uriel's) domain."

Metatron

Direction: Above and Below

Element: Spirit

Name meaning: Not technically clear, but known as "He who

sits beside the Divine Throne" and "The angel of the presence"

Colors: White, purple, electric blue
Scents: Kyphe, frankincense

Hermes Trismegistus's famous magical precept, "As above, so below," is characteristic of Metatron in more ways than one: first, because his energy is often compared to a pillar of fire, and he is also aligned with the Tree of Life, which reaches roots deep into the core of the earth and branches up into the cosmos (a conceptual construct present in a number of ancient cosmologies). In other words, he is seen as a powerful intermediary between heaven and earth. Second, because he is the angel most associated with hermetic wisdom such as divine alchemy and sacred geometry (although Uriel gifted humanity with it, Metatron keeps it alive in our consciousness through his otherworldly teachings and unseen support). And finally, many believe that he was once present on earth (below) as the Biblical scribe Enoch and now resides in heaven (above) as a divine scribe and keeper of the Akashic records (incidentally, a role that indicates his possible alternate identity as the Egyptian god Thoth). Naturally, all of these qualities make him the perfect archangelic representative of the element of spirit.

Metatron's energy is highly focused and organized, and calling on him can help you not only to tap into divine wisdom and creativity, but also to keep your attention on things like writing, teaching, and manifesting your divinely inspired dreams into form. This means he's an excellent ally to call on when things like time management and motivation are of the essence. (As a matter of fact, I call on him just about every single time I sit down to write.)

Archangelic Invocation

Keep in mind that as you call each angel and connect with his energy, additionally connect with his associated element: feel wind whipping around you when calling Raphael, envision a sphere of crackling fire around you when calling Michael, feel ocean waves rushing around you when calling Gabriel, connect with the deep fertile soil when calling Uriel, and envision a pillar of light or Tree of Life connecting you to earth and sky when calling Metatron.

Begin by facing east and centering your energy. Relax your body, take some deep breaths, and envision sending roots deep into the earth and branches high into the sky. When you feel adequately centered, say:

> *Sacred healer, health on high,*
> *New beginnings, morning sky,*
> *Raphael, please be here now!*

Face south. Say:

> *Fierce protector, warrior bright,*
> *Fiery ally of blinding light,*
> *Michael, please be here now!*

Face west. Say:

> *Womb of darkness, river long,*
> *Ocean waves divinely strong,*
> *Gabriel, please be here now!*

Face north. Say:

> *Light of all we see and touch,*
> *Earthly home we love so much,*
> *Uriel, please be here now!*

Face east again. Hold your hands (and wand, feather, etc.) up to the sky and say:

> *Pillar bright from sky to earth,*
> *Keeper of wisdom, reminder of worth,*
> *Metatron, please be here now!*

Place your hands on your heart and say:

> *Raphael is before me,*
> *Michael is to my right,*
> *Gabriel is behind me,*
> *Uriel is to my left,*

Metatron is below me, within me, and above me.
I am safe, I am protected, I am empowered.
And so the circle is complete.

When you're ready to open the circle, simply face west and say:

Thank you, Gabriel.

Face south and say:
Thank you, Michael.

Face east and say:
Thank you, Raphael.

Face north and say:
Thank you, Uriel.

Face east, raise your arms up, and say:
Thank you Metatron.

Take a deep breath, envision the energies releasing fully into the ether, and say:
The circle is open.

For Further Study

Illes, Judika. *Encyclopedia of Spirits*. New York: Harper-Collins, 2009.

Mitchell, Stephen. *Tao te Ching*. New York: Harper Perennial, 1988.

Penczak, Christopher. *Ascension Magick*. Woodbury, MN: Llewellyn Publications, 2007.

Virtue, Doreen. *Archangels and Ascended Masters*. Carlsbad, CA: Hay House, 2003.

Whitehurst, Tess. *Holistic Energy Magic: Charms and Techniques for Creating a Magical Life*. Woodbury, MN: Llewellyn Publications, 2015.

Careful What You Wish For

by Calantirniel

What magical person has not heard this warning? We hear stories all the time about unethically casting love spells onto a specific person that sometimes work—and *not* with the desired results! In the movie *The Craft*, we remember how Sarah's spell on Chris had backfired. We note that he turned darkly obsessive and stalked her, which was far worse than him not liking her at all.

I personally learned something that went a lot further than this. The universe basically told me:

Be careful what you SAY!

And this did not just apply to being in a ritual circle or doing spellwork—it is applicable whenever I am awake and speaking—what a big responsibility! My story follows.

In the mid-to-late 1990s, I lived in the Raleigh, North Carolina, region. I was newer to magic and a single mother of two school-age children with little to no support from my ex-husband, financial or otherwise. My work-life was changing rather drastically too—I often opted to work for myself rather than a safe, steady paycheck, which at one time resulted in five different sources of income!

However, I managed to win tickets to popular and underground musical events *all* the time. Astrologically, this area is near my Jupiter line, so luck did play a role. So when a particularly awesome concert was coming to town, I was bummed because there were no ticket-giveaway contests, and I really wanted to go with a friend of mine. I then realized I needed to be thankful for all the times I had won tickets for other gigs and just have faith that money would come—and it did really fast. An old customer ordered three more of my crochet hats, so I bought the pair of tickets in

advance and my friend was to pay me back at the concert. But something unexpected happened. A few days before the concert, I went into the store where I sold crochet hats and discovered that one of my creations didn't sell, but was actually stolen! The store's manager was sad she couldn't compensate me with money but instead had many T-shirts she was clearing from the store and told me to take around five of them to help me out. Most of the T-shirts were not my style, but I found a few gift items this way for other people. Then, my eyes fell upon the *only* shirt for the *very* band I wanted to see—from their first album, which I still believe is their best! I was very happy to find it, as it was the last one, so I expressed this to the new owner. I felt like it was meant to be.

My reputation for winning tickets to many concerts apparently got around, so she asked me if I won them. I laughed and told her, "Not this time, but with all the times

I have been fortunate? I would pay *twice* to see them play!" Now, even though I was just joking around, what I meant was that I would pay twice for two different performances at two different times—but the universe decided to hear this differently and consequently have some serious "fun" with me.

Upon going home, I could *not* find the tickets I purchased *anywhere*. The concert was coming and I still didn't find them. And while it was tempting to think the hot and sultry weather was affecting my thinking, I somehow knew the tickets were not lost or stolen—I knew it had something to do with my little joke!

So? In faith, I ended up buying *another* set of tickets with money I again manifested! I told Spirit when I did this that I now realized my "error" and that apparently, joking around is not the way I am supposed to do things, and that it would be amazing if I could be further compensated for the prior tickets, but I won't expect it. I went on to mention that I learned my lesson.

The hot-and-sweaty night of the concert, another friend of mine (who was at the time very pregnant) came over so my children had company while I was gone, and my bottle of rosemary essential oil broke in the living room—and when she went to open the windows to air out the place, she ended up breaking my window! Seriously mischievous energy going on! Luckily the oil smelled great and the window was easy and cheap to fix; I did it myself with a neighbor, so I didn't even need to call the landlord.

The very next day after the concert, I was cleaning my bedroom and oddly noticed my winter hat that I crocheted lying in a weird way on the side of my bed that I never really went to other than for cleaning. *Tucked inside* of the hat that was lying face-down on the floor was *what?*

The old tickets!! Argh, what was I going to do now? There were no refunds—period.

My prayer about compensation was heard though. I was "inspired" to write a letter to the promoters to tell them the story—but there was no way they would believe the truth. So I needed to carefully "craft" a more believable story that would have *no* further repercussions on me. My inspiration came when my friend who was watching the kids had to go to the hospital, only to discover she was in a serious false labor.

So I changed a couple of details with the story (i.e., that it happened the *night* of the concert, not later) and I accompanied her, and that she got out so late that I had no time to run home to other side of town to pick up my tickets, so I met my friend and bought another set. I then explained I could prove that the other set was not used since the stubs were not detached, and I could prove that, if necessary. I told them I knew they did not have to compensate me ever, but expressed that as a single mother who worked hard for the money to begin with, any efforts they could provide would be so appreciated. I double-checked the energy, and it felt good. I mailed off the letter. About a month later, I got *free* tickets in the mail to see another band! I was not interested in this band but I felt so thankful because I thought: I will just sell them! The best of luck happened when I went to the concert to sell the tickets that the show became *sold out*!! I recovered my money while at the same time giving the buyer a good deal. However, the buyer turned out to be a ticket scalper as he wasn't interested in the show either, and he was mad at me because the tickets were "free." I told him they were *not* free for me. I told him the story I told the promoter, and then he was okay with it. I went home and felt compensated.

Not only that—I learned a HUGE lesson. I need to be very careful about what I say, even if I am not in a ritual circle, since it has the power to manifest—and to do so in some pretty undesirable ways!

Witch in a Pinch:
Celebrating Sabbats or Esbats
without Formal Ritual

by Michael Furie

I bet most of us have been there; I know I have. All of the plans have been made, items have been gathered, and I feel ready to go, but for one reason or another, I'm unable to perform a sabbat or esbat ritual on the proper day due to some unforeseen circumstance. Whether it be last-minute work obligations, family visits, lack of child care (if they're too young), or any other surprise, our best laid plans can be disrupted. Certainly, rituals can be postponed a day or two, but when I was younger things like this would really bother me. I always had this nagging feeling that I was missing out, not participating in the fullness of the energy shift, and not tuning in to the energy of the countless other witches, both current and ancestral, who worked on these days as well. It might sound immature, but I just felt cheated, which subsequently kept me from being properly engaged in whatever was keeping me from ritual. Instead, I would just end up sullen and crabby, desperately waiting for the chance to get back to my holiday.

Realizing that my behavior wasn't making anything better, and determined to find a sensible solution, I came up with some ideas to bridge the gap between formal ritual and no ritual at all. Over the years, most of my practice has evolved into kitchen witchery, primarily because this has been a way to integrate my witchcraft practice with my somewhat hectic daily life. Outside of the kitchen, there are many ways to enhance our regular day, as long as we remember that magic is literally everywhere and the main shift has to occur within ourselves by means of our intent. Whether or not someone is a solitary or in the broom closet, these methods can either be used as is and no one else will even know of your witchiness, or they can be elaborated upon if desired to create more of a family-style holiday celebration.

Work with the Energy of the Day

For me at least, the most difficult occurrence is when I've had to work on a holiday. Since our sabbats aren't federally recognized, this happens from time to time. If the holiday is a sabbat and I have to be out in the sun driving or whatever, it can be an opportunity to absorb solar energy. Of course, going into a meditation or flashing an athame while driving down the road isn't the safest option, so what's a witch to do?

Use Your Breath

A method that has worked for me is steady breathing with the intention that the energy of the day is being drawn in to your entire body and held there. This can be done while walking or driving a car since it does not require very much concentration—simply set the intention in your mind and breathe. The same can be done for a full moon, though in many work situations, it might have to be done while driving home or looking out a window on a coffee break during a night shift.

Carry a Talisman

Drawing on the energy of the day (or night, depending) is an important aspect to any witch's celebration, and it needn't be limited to times of formal ritual. If, however, you would prefer to use a more structured method of capturing the energy of the holiday, try using a talisman. A simple talisman can be created the night before (or the year before, since these can be used indefinitely) either as a formal circle ritual or just by holding it and empowering it outdoors. The easiest natural talisman is to use a stone found somewhere in nature to act as a channel for and anchor of the energy of the sabbat or esbat. I'd advise against using metals if you will be going to a place with a metal detector or security; also, little bags of things tend to look suspicious, so little "good-luck charm" type items or small stones are best. This stone, once charged, can be carried in a pocket or handbag to connect you to the current of energy. To charge the stone, hold it in both hands and breathe your intention into it while visualizing an energy field surrounding the rock in a color appropriate to the holiday, such as red or green for Yule, or silver or white for a full moon. As you do this, fix within your mind the desire that the power shall remain as long as the stone exists and that it will draw in force from the universe as needed to preserve the charge. When you feel that the stone is fully energized, it can be painted or decorated in some symbolic fashion to seal the charge, and it is then ready for use. To use it, carry it with you or place it in the car or office to help tap into the energy of the holiday.

Drink It Up

At work, you can even use a coffee break to connect to the energy of the day. If you actually do have a beverage, coffee is surprisingly appropriate for a sabbat whereas tea seems more ideal for an esbat. Whatever the choice, the drink can be quietly blessed before consuming and then ingested to bring the energy of the season within. Beyond this, a coffee break (or any other free time) can be used to connect with not only the energy of the day, but also the ancestors, elements, and deities. This method needs to be planned in advance however for it to work. In modern times, we now have a wonderful

little magic rectangle that can connect to anywhere on earth in seconds; I'm speaking, of course, about the mobile phone. Far from "merely" being a phone, most of these devices have Internet capability and a built-in camera. The camera function is of the greatest importance here.

Since magic works according to the transmission of energy, light itself is a form of energy and photographs have been used in magical spells and rituals practically since the medium was invented, we can build an appropriately decorated altar for the day (with any symbols or talismans aligned with those we wish to invoke), photograph it, and reconnect with its energy whenever we wish. I used to be somewhat ambivalent about the idea of photographing altars and rituals—liking the idea of seeing different altars and rites, but also worrying that the act of digitally capturing the scene took away from the power of the ceremony. My conflict was resolved, however, when I realized that freezing the moment in time was essentially an act of preservation and a way to tap in to that ritual's energy whenever desired. I'm still quite selective of what magically related happenings I will photograph, avoiding taking pictures of very personal rituals, but I feel that since the pictures will transmit energy via their image they do make an excellent method of projecting magical intent.

Applying this to celebrating the holidays, we can create the altar, photograph it with a camera phone ahead of time, and then whenever we have the chance, say on a coffee break, open the photo, gaze at it with an open, receptive, reverent attitude and connect to its intention and energy on the actual day needed. My favorite way to do this is for Samhain. A crucial part of many practitioners' Samhain celebrations is to honor and remember their ancestors. Looking at old photographs can be a big part of this remembrance, so having copies of the chosen pictures on the phone, even by taking a snapshot of the original with the phone's camera, can be a great way to connect with loved ones who have passed on during Samhain when a formal ritual may not be possible.

The Ritual Meal

Another means of connecting with a holiday is, of course, the ritual meal. There are three possible options here: lunch, dinner in a restaurant, or dinner at home. For lunch

or dinner in a restaurant, the food can be blessed subtly; if it's a sandwich, you can hold it and send energy into it; if it's on a bowl or a plate, you can stir it a bit and send energy through the fork; the drink can be charged through the cup; and so on. Even prayers and blessings can be said silently to yourself without drawing much attention. For a quick purification before the meal, washh your hands in the restaurant bathroom with intent. Afterward, the meal can be eaten with reverence. Even though there may be mundane conversation with family or co-workers going on at the time, the sabbat feast can still continue and nourish the body, mind, and spirit.

When we are cooking the meal at home, we have more options when it comes to blessings and prayers of devotion than when we are in public. Even if we are among friends and family who are not a part of our traditions, we can still prepare the food with blessings: energy stirred into the soup, baked in the bread, grilled in the burger, or even cooked in the pizza! In my experience, when I sit down to dinner on one of my holidays with others who may not share in (or even be aware of) the significance of the day, I still like to mentally include them in my celebration. Not in a magically manipulative way, just in a change of my own perspective. I used to feel like other people were blocking me—making me take time from my holiday to participate in mundane activities—but that isn't a fair assessment. I realized that spending the holiday with others, whether they're aware of it or not, can be a wonderful addition to the day. Now, I just view the meal more akin to a Thanksgiving type of celebration, being grateful for the opportunity to spend time with loved ones and cultivating the sense of community within myself that can be found in larger Pagan gatherings.

◦

I hope that this article shows that even though we should all try and celebrate the holidays in our preferred manner when we can, altered plans and sudden obligations shouldn't stop us from finding ways to keep the power and beauty of the day close to us. That way, we may still participate in the shifting of nature's cycle even if we have to work, have unexpected visitors, lose our babysitter, or whatever the so-called obstacle may be. It is even possible to celebrate while in the hospital. The food can still be blessed and a magic circle can be visualized around the bed while lying in it. Even the energy of sunlight or moonlight shining through the window can be drawn in and used not only for celebration, but also for healing. Breathe in or visualize the energy absorbing into your body and traveling to the site of the problem.

Magic really is everywhere, and making the conscious decision to connect with the energy shift taking place is a vital factor in any holiday celebration. It is a basic process of even the most complicated of sabbat and esbat rites, the result of which is to enliven our spirits with the spark of nature and divinity. This can be done wherever we happen to be—we needn't be cloistered in the ritual circle. As Witches or Pagans, we have both the mindset and the ability to tune into the web of energy that creates all life. The bottom line is that it doesn't matter where we choose to do this, as long as the connection is achieved; we are better people for having made the effort and better Pagans for having practiced our craft.

What To Do When Magic Fails

by Diana Rajchel

Magic works! Okay, magic works except when it doesn't.

For many folk magicians, spell troubleshooting has a slight taboo on it—as though it's okay to try a little magic, as long as no one tries to perfect the art. This odd habit probably comes from a time when people considered all magic diabolical. The people who see magic work usually want to get better at it—and that's where troubleshooting comes in.

The following guidelines will help you figure out where your nonstarter spells went wrong and let you know what to do to get your intentions back off the ground.

What Time Frame Are You Using?

Hoodoo practitioners say magic works in threes: three days to see a sign, three weeks to see progress, and sometimes three years to a spell's completion. Before you start your spell, assign required results. Work an expiration date into phrasing or imagery and appoint a specific symbol, such as a rare animal, as an omen. As you do this, remember that the laws of thermodynamics are more powerful than you. Successful spells work within the constraints of nature. This law of working extends to social situations. For example, you might not be able to speed up meeting the exact right Mr. or Ms. Right, but you can use magic to achieve a mindset that makes you more receptive when compatible people approach.

Is Magic Simply Not Working?

Every so often, the valves that drip our private flows of magic get shut off for some mysterious maintenance. The notices for when this happens usually involve a sub-sub-basement in a glass case beneath a government building. Finding out what's going on takes a visit to a good, ethical astrologer. People undergoing a Saturn return or who have Mercury and/or Uranus running at awkward angles on their individual charts may find magic difficult or unavailable until these planets finish their tour.

Saturn returns in particular mark periods of cosmic trial. These act as cosmic initiations that involve removing toys and tools normally used to deal with the challenge presented during the return. For magic workers, any spell at all might refuse to get off the ground. So healing for illness, magic to find a job, magic to change luck—none can avail you during a return, and no one else can succeed in a working for you, either.

Mercury, possibly the most important planet in magical work, goes offline three times a year. While clever individuals detour Mercury retrograde through solar energy, any work on anything besides the magic worker himself or herself may only proceed very slowly. If something happens in an individual's chart where Mercury's natural energy gets blocked, there may be little to do besides wait it out.

Fate and Free Will Can Supersede Magic

For those who believe fate and free will both play roles in the universe, there may be instances such as the death of a loved one that are actually impossible to prevent. These painful moments are not about your personal ability; they are about your loved one's journey. You might not know this until you have already poured all your energy into an attempt to reverse the situation. Magic changes situations only when fate allows. Most of the time fate will allow, just not usually for the big stuff.

If you cannot afford an astrology consult, a tarot or rune reading can help you determine if you are in a magic "shut off" period. Any reading with the Hanged Man or the Tower means that the situation is beyond your power.

Maybe It Did Work ... On You

Spellcasters generally work with an eye to external results. Paradoxically, the most successful magic works on the spellcasters themselves. To see if this happened, think about a spell that failed: did the way you think about the situation change following the working? Magic transforms inner perspectives. Every spell cast, even those targeted to other people, will affect you.

An Obstacle Lies in the Energy Path

We live in a competitive world. The things you want, someone else wants too. In addition, our interconnection extends to the psychic. If you tend toward negative friendship cycles, you might have people close to you who unconsciously prefer you not to change. Most of this does not come from malice, except perhaps shame you harbor toward yourself.

Energies conflict, and despite all the words about an abundant universe, human beings see themselves in a never-ending battle for all the resources. While the Buddhist solution is to achieve a mental state that frees you from desire, the magical solution takes a little less time and therapy.

Uncrossing, a routine ritual that often accompanies protection magic, acts as a sort of road sweeper for cluttered magical paths. This ritual releases stagnant energy, banishes negative energy that has built up from daily unconscious resentments, and conciliates conflicting energies that prevent your intentions from succeeding. Several uncrossing spells exist, from burning black and gray candles to anointing the body in well-constructed oils.

You can make uncrossing oil for yourself with this recipe:

1 tablespoon olive oil
1 teaspoon dried lemongrass
1 teaspoon dried rosemary
1 broken-up stick of devil's shoestring.

Keep the ingredients in a glass vial and apply daily or rub it on candles and papers that you use as you go about your clearing work.

Maybe You Did It Wrong

While not a popular notion, you can, in fact, do magic wrong. In fact, a lot of things can make the type of magic you use wrong for the situation. The material you used

might be wrong for the spell, or the intention behind your stated intention might create an impasse. Often the block comes from a conflicted state of mind. For instance, you decide to try a Wiccan love spell and deck out your altar in lovely shades of red in hopes of a passionate fling. Yet, in the days following the spell, your love life seems DOA. When you think about your personal connection to the color red, you have problems. Upon deeper examination, you find an ancestral conflict: your ancestors saw the color red as the color of death, something you internalized while listening to your grandparents talk as a child. Your subconscious remembers everything—and put that association with death into the spell. If you go back and perform the love spell again, changing your altar colors to heavy whites or greens, you get different, livelier results because in your mind white and green express life and passion.

Ignoring the instructions can also produce an undesired result. Learning what instructions matter and what don't takes years of practice, and is helped by a solid knowledge of folklore. For example, a spell calling for basil, carnation, and spearmint might not have the desired effect when you can't produce carnation. You move forward with the spell, using just the two herbs you do have. It isn't that carnation is crucial—what is crucial is having a third herb that can produce energy in a way similar to what carnation does.

Recalibrate Your Intentions

Seriously, do you even know Ryan Gosling? While the ability to imagine any circumstance is the magician's best friend, it's also important to establish achievable intentions, since all magic requires the practitioner to do the nonmagical legwork both before and after spellcasting. Magic works by progression. If you want some

unknown person to fall madly in love with you (ethically frowned upon, but a useful example) then you need to work smaller magic that lets you meet this person, form a relationship, and then take steps toward romantic partnership. For example, if you want to meet a specific celebrity, you would need to work spells that make a trip to Los Angeles possible or enhance your own talent to make yourself a welcome addition to the entertainment industry. Even then, you face enormous amounts of crossing energy—people who want the same thing or who have intentions in conflict with your goal. The more famous the celebrity, the more obstacles you face in working that magic. The same situation applies to winning the lottery. If your end goal has no relationship to your current path in life, you need to work magic to build that metaphorical exit ramp or a side road.

~

The next time you cast a spell, consider adding some new steps to your work: Plan to repeat it over a set amount of days. Create a small uncrossing ceremony before you being your work. Weave specifics into any spoken parts: an expiration date, a request for an omen, and a means of measuring your success. Write your thoughts in a journal both before and after a casting. Assess your thought processes in the three months succeeding your work.

Magic consists of perishable skills. You can fall out of practice, and be less effective as a result. When a working fails, explore why, first, before ruling out magic altogether.

Everyday Color Magic

by Peg Aloi

The choice of color in magical work is often a combination of personal preference, folklore, research, and intuition. Why do we use red for love, green for money, and white for protection? Ceremonial and occult traditions utilize complex but accessible systems of symbolic correspondences, including color symbolism, which can be harnessed for everyday use. The vibrational power of color—the effect it has upon our physical being and psyche because of the subtle vibrations and energies it produces when we look at it—has been widely researched and its effectiveness well documented. Of course, the ancients knew all about it too! This article explores the inherent qualities of color and suggests diverse ways to use them in personal magical for improved physical, emotional, and mental well-being; magical focus; and attainment of goals.

The system of correspondences used in contemporary magical paths is both complex and accessible. Elements, planets, gems, plants, animals, and perfumes are just a few of the concepts and objects that can be employed when creating magical rituals and workings. In the Western occult tradition, which forms the basis of contemporary magical practices within Wicca and other paths, many of these correspondences are interrelated. For example, when incorporating astrology into a magical working, we usually consider the many correspondences for a specific zodiac sign. Let's take Libra: it is ruled by the planet Venus, the goddess of love and beauty; associated with the colors pink, pale green, and light blue; the opal; the element of air; and flowery scents like rose and jasmine.

Why are these colors pink, pale green, and blue considered Venusian?" Before we look at a number of colors and their value and symbolism for magic, we can look at this pleasing example for inspiration. Pink is a color associated with femininity: we dress baby girls in pale pink and little girls in pink princess dresses (I think we overdo this these days), and the color pink is the color chosen to raise awareness about breast cancer, which suggests empowerment of women and the healing power of female knowledge. The color pink is flattering to all skin tones: it imparts a rosy glow to the face, suggesting good health, which is why we say someone who is feeling and looking good is "in the pink." Pink is also associated with romance and love: think a big bouquet of pink roses delivered on Valentine's Day, or the pink prom dress worn by Molly Ringwald in the movie *Pretty in Pink*. Pink is a paler version of red, which we associate with sexuality, among other things. Pink represents the more romantic, innocent, beginning stages of love and infatuation: emotional states sacred to the goddess Venus/Aphrodite.

Pale green is likewise a more subdued version of green, one associated with nature. Pale green is the color of spring, of beginnings, and thus associated with innocence and newness. Pale blue has similar connotations of innocence: think the pale blue of a robin's egg, a pale blue morning sky, the pale blue robes worn by the Virgin Mary that radiate purity and heavenly radiance. Those powder blue morning glories we plant in spring are known as "Heavenly Blue."

Subtle Associations (Cultural and Colorful)

By now perhaps it has become obvious that much of the "magic" of different colors arises from the emotional feelings and thoughts we tend to associate with them. Blues and greens have been proven to have a calming effect, but hot pink has been shown to help reduce stress and anxiety. There is even a color known as "drunk tank pink" painted on the walls in some county jails, to help reduce violent and aggressive tendencies people display when they're inebriated.

Some of these corresponding emotions are universal, that is, they exist across cultural divides; and some are unique to certain cultures. In Japan, for example, white is worn for funerals and black and red are common at weddings. White is traditionally associated with the realm of the spiritual, but in Western culture we also associate it with purity. In magical spellworkings, many texts

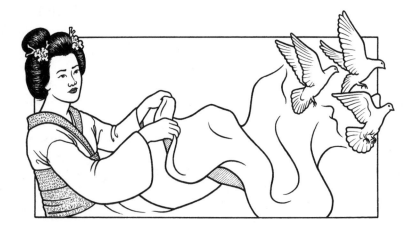

link it to protection and healing, perhaps in part because it gives us a "clean" feeling that lets us imagine our bodies and environments free of disease or negative energies.

Some magical color correspondences depend upon subtle differences in hue and shading. For the most part, using bright colors is considered most effective for magical working because the vibration is considered strongest. But paler or more subdued shades might be good choices for certain situations. Green, for example, can have a number of different connotations. Bright green, what we call "Kelly green (think Saint Patrick's Day) is a pure shade of green useful for magical purposes that call for green's most potent association: money or prosperity. But green is also the color of growth and fertility: maybe a deep, rich shade of forest green would be more appropriate for workings related to creating abundance, getting pregnant, or developing a "fertile" network of job contacts, for example. Pale green might represent the energy of spring, new beginnings, or planting "seeds" for development. Blue-green, aqua, or teal can be used for strengthening magical work connected to the water element—associated with music and creativity, healing, and the realm of the emotions and the throat chakra. Yellow-green hues (from spring green to olive) conjure up natural settings, the greens of nature. These colors might be nice to help encourage a garden project, or initiating a healthy new eating regime. (Of course, you want to add some green vegetables to that too).

Common Uses (Home Decor, Personal Flair)

So how does one use these colors in everyday magical work? Some prefer to meditate on the color, and may find that interesting variations occur the more we focus on them. But I prefer to have a very concrete and practical approach to color magic. Painting the walls of a room can have a constant effect, so be sure you want to have that general impact in your life over the long term. This is especially important in rooms where we spend a lot of time, like the bedroom. Pale blue in the bedroom is conducive to sleep; warm red tones (from salmon to pink to burgundy) are meant to help encourage sex and affection. Neutral tones (grays, beiges, etc.) can be calming too. Bright, electric colors are not recommended for the bedroom because they can disrupt sleep.

Kitchens and dining rooms should have cheery colors; orange (and shades related to it: peach, terra cotta, pumpkin) is traditional for social energy, perfect if you enjoy entertaining. Yellow is inviting for a sunny kitchen. You need not paint your walls with colors (and if you're renting, you may not be allowed to change the all-white color scheme). But using fabric to change the colors in rooms is both easy and flexible. Curtains, pillows, throws, and artwork can all provide ways to shift color in your surroundings.

On a more personal level, the color of your clothes can also help you to gain energy from color and to focus on it for your intentions. They say witches wear black more than any other color, blue and green being close seconds. Black is flattering and versatile. But accents of color can transform this neutral color and allow you to emphasize your magical purpose throughout the day.

For example, you may have green candles on your altar that you burn for prosperity magic (don't leave them lit unless you're home to keep an eye on them!), but if you wear a green scarf or jacket, you get this reminder throughout the day as you take action to help grow prosperity. When you take these actions (applying for a job, spending money wisely, being productive, etc.), you can touch or look at the green item of clothing and understand that you're connecting your actions with that synergy of color energy. Imagine green light and energy surrounding you as you visualize your intentions. Notice the colors you encounter in your daily activities and reflect on what they mean. Drape a green scarf over your window or lampshade, use green dish soap, buy the laundry detergent that comes in the green box. Buy products that are "green" (environmentally friendly). Even if using green color magic was intended for prosperity, you'll start to feel and understand the other associations of this color (health, environmental preservation) and realize these concepts are all connected.

This approach can be helpful when it's necessary to separate the most obvious associations we have with colors and use them for the best result. Red, for example, is controversial. It's under the rulership of the planet Mars (god of war); it's the color of the element of fire. We tend to associate it with passionate emotions (anger, confidence, sexuality), and with danger (think stop signs, red lights, gang colors) or violence. But we also associate red with safety and healing (fire trucks, the Red Cross, ambulances). Red

is a common color in nature that exists along a continuum that reminds us of the extremes of human existence—as with any continuum, the healthiest and best place to stay is somewhere in the middle, and this requires balance.

If we want to harness the energy of red to build our confidence and initiative, for example, we may want to downplay its associations with anger and violence. But we'll also be able, upon reflection, to understand how all of these associations work together: the courage and aggression of Mars is related to confidence and passion, after all. We may begin to understand that the same fiery essence of our being that produces anger and sexual desire is also the same "heart" that gives us drive and strengthens our will. Wearing a red scarf or shirt will draw visual attention to us: we'll want to be noticed for our physical bearing and charisma, and become a person who inspires confidence. Red lipstick may help boost a woman's sexual confidence. Confidence is a form of strength, a resiliency that allows us to understand and offer our personal best, and that also lets us balance that with humility and compassion. Think of heart and blood: the very essence of being alive. We can express our living energy with extremes, but we can also choose balance. The same heart that fuels passionate anger can also fuel tender compassion. The daily choices we make in our behavior toward others crafts our personality and social presence. Understanding the nature of the fire element and its importance to our daily energy can be a very powerful result of using red for a magical endeavor.

Complexities Abound

Other colors have seemingly conflicting or complex meanings. Purple (that witch's favorite) is associated with the occult, with death, with decadence, and with royalty. In cinema symbolism, the color purple is often a signpost for death. It is associated with the air element (and, with yellow, the primary color used to signify air). Under the rulership of Zeus, purple represents the male qualities of intellect and leadership. Its use in modern occult symbolism is very pervasive, and usually signals intense magic or ceremonial working. Pale purple (lavender) is sometimes associated with homosexuality or femininity, and this is partly because it's a cool balance between red and blue, female and male. Reddish purples can have a sexual connotation (think "Magenta" from *The Rocky Horror Picture Show*). As we have seen before, the shade or hue of a color if really important in suggesting its meaning. Witches seem to enjoy wearing purple because of its connection to the otherworld: the realms of death, faery, and the unconscious. It's also a rather glamorous color, rich and mysterious, depending on its intensity. I think using purples for altar decoration imbue magical workings with seriousness and mysticism. I also wear pale purple/lavender (a flattering color for me) when I want to have an air of neutrality, fairness, and calmness in my endeavors).

$\sim$

The use of color in everyday magical intention is both very simple and endlessly fascinating. The modes of experimentation can be as unique and varied as the individual using them. Being able to find new meaning in our surroundings and to make connections to our desire and goals through color can add a vibrant and pleasurable dimension to anyone's magical paths. After we embark upon this way of seeing, our whole world becomes more colorful, like that magical moment when Dorothy enters the Land of Oz, full of flowers and mythical creatures and wondrous occurrences.

Appalachian Bottle Tree Magic

by James Kambos

You've probably heard of a message in a bottle. And you've probably heard of a genie in a bottle, but have you ever heard of a "haint" in a bottle? If you haven't, then you've probably never heard of an Appalachian bottle tree. Bottle trees are a folk magic tradition found throughout Appalachia and the American South. It was believed, and in many places is still believed, that "haints," or evil spirits, can be trapped in empty bottles, which are slipped into place on bare tree branches with the bottle opening facing the trunk of the tree. The origin of the word *haint* is obscure. It may be an African term brought to America during slavery. Or it may be derived from the southern Appalachian pronunciation of the word "haunt." But whatever the source, the word *haint* does mean some type of mischievous spirit. Haint can also refer to restless spirits of the dead that still roam the earth, especially after dark. The word *haint* is still used today in many regions of Appalachia and the South.

Bottle Tree Magic

The magical beliefs surrounding bottle trees are based on very ancient magical traditions. For centuries, bottles were believed to have the ability to lure and trap malevolent spirits. For some reason, these spirits found empty bottles attractive; perhaps thinking of them as hiding places, the spirit would enter the bottle and then become trapped. In Appalachia you sometimes see bottles hung on the branches of trees by using twine. But the most common method of decorating a bottle tree is to simply slide an empty bottle onto a branch with the opening facing the tree trunk.

Spirits are believed to be most active at night. Once the spirit finds a bottle it likes, it enters it, and becoming confused, is trapped inside. During the night, a trapped spirit may be heard moaning in agony. The following morning, the spirit is believed to be destroyed by sunlight. Some old-timers even oil or grease the bottle opening so an evil spirit (haint) will slip inside more easily. Traditionally blue bottles were used since blue was believed to be a color of protection, but any color can be used. Modern Appalachian craftsmen skilled in metal work-

ing also make black iron "trees" with arms, which can be used as bottle trees. In this form, they appear to be garden ornaments. Occasionally you'll see old, empty jars slipped over the tops of fence posts. This is another form of bottle magic sometimes found on back-country roads.

In the old days a bottle tree in the yard served as a kind of a sign. It meant that someone who lived there was a fortune-teller, a seer, or the local wise woman.

I live in the Appalachian foothills of Ohio, and in my neck of the woods the old folk magic ways are still with us. Around here, for example, some folks still prop a broom by the door to ward off evil. And many believe a bird flying into the house is an omen of death. So you can bet bottle trees can still be found sometimes. And you can be sure they're not just for decoration. When you see a bottle tree in these parts, you know there's some serious magic going on.

In addition to being used for magical purposes in trees and on fence posts, you can sometimes find bottles used in the holes of old buildings. While researching this article, I came across an old, weathered barn about twelve miles from where I live. In a few holes of the old barn siding, someone had inserted bottles. And the bottles surrounded a cracked mirror. I believe what I found was some type of long-forgotten form of protection magic.

The History of Bottle Tree Magic

Bottle trees in the form that we know of today arrived in America as a result of the slave trade. Used at first by slaves and their descendants, the use of bottle trees as a form of folk magic gradually spread into mainstream Southern culture. My guess is that the first bottle trees appeared on American soil along the coastline of the Carolinas, especially in the region of South Carolina known as the Low Country. From there they spread throughout the South and finally into the Appalachian Mountains.

Most authorities on bottle tree history and lore agree that the concept of magical bottle trees, like those brought to the South by slaves, originated in Central Africa in about the ninth century AD. I agree with this, but bottle magic goes back much further and is a distant kin to other forms of magical practices found as far away as the British Isles involving the use of glass.

It was the ancient Egyptians who first began to make glass bottles around 1600 BCE. and they may also be the first to have used bottles for magical/religious purposes. They used many bottles to store sacred oils and spices.

Not long after, legends began to spread from North Africa through Central Africa, into Europe, and as far east as Persia and China that spirits and genies could be trapped in bottles and lamps. The tale of Aladdin and his magic lamp is a perfect example of this.

At some point, glass was thought to have the magical power to attract or repel spirits of all kinds. Glass witch balls, for example, were used in Britain to repel the evil eye by being placed inside a home near a window. About this time garden gazing balls also became popular. And, naturally, bottle trees must be closely related to the magical witch bottle.

In early times, the Irish also had their version of bottle tree magic. To repel bad spirits and attract friendly spirits, they would sometimes hang blue bottles in trees and insert a white candle in the bottle's neck. When the candles were lit, it was believed the home was protected.

As you can see, the roots of the bottle tree and its magic stretch deep into antiquity. It is linked to one of the world's most important materials used for magical purposes—glass.

Next, I will share some ideas about how you can create your own bottle tree.

How to Make and Use a Bottle Tree

The use of bottle trees is beginning to catch on around the country and the world. Bottle trees are no longer viewed as some backwoods hillbilly superstition. Bottle trees in various shapes, sizes, and forms are now being seen displayed as garden art at prestigious garden shows. Of course, many people are still unaware of their magical connections.

To make your own bottle tree is fun and easy. The only limitation should be your imagination. First decide if you want to use your tree for magic and art, or just art. It's up to you.

To begin, select your tree. Crepe myrtles were traditionally used due to their alleged mystical qualities, but any tree or shrub is fine. Your bottle tree doesn't even need to be a real tree. There are many attractive black wrought-iron trees available now at garden centers and art shows. Even a mailbox post with wooden dowels is a possibility.

Next, collect your bottles. This can be a hobby itself. Traditionally, cobalt blue bottles were used since blue is said to protect against evil. Eventually, the various shades of blue used for blue tree bottles became known as "haint blue." However, you can use any color you want. I have seen beautiful bottle trees made with only clear and pale green bottles. Collecting the bottles is a good way to recycle used bottles. Wine, beer, and vinegar bottles are a few ideas.

Once you have your bottles, rinse them out so you don't attract pests. For magical purposes, bless your bottles; a simple prayer will do. Arrange the bottles on your tree by slipping the bottles onto the branches so that the neck of the bottle is toward the tree trunk. Your bottle tree is complete.

If you'll use your tree for magic, here are some tips. To use the tree for general protection purposes, rinse out the bottles and bless them once a year. If you want to cast a specific spell, write the charm on a piece of paper and tape it on the outside of one bottle. After the spell works, remove the written charm and destroy it. This way you can reuse the bottle.

If you feel a bottle has become especially tainted by negative energy, remove the bottle and recycle it. Or, if in doubt, bury the bottle away from your home.

∼

Appalachian bottle trees can be used for magic or fun—or both. However you use yours, I hope it keeps the haints away.

Almanac Section

Calendar

Time Zones

Lunar Phases

Moon Signs

Full Moons

Sabbats

World Holidays

Incense of the Day

Color of the Day

Almanac Listings

In these listings you will find the date, day, lunar phase, Moon sign, color, and incense for the day, as well as festivals from around the world.

The Date

The date is used in numerological calculations that govern magical rites.

The Day

Each day is ruled by a planet that possesses specific magical influences:

MONDAY (MOON): Peace, sleep, healing, compassion, friends, psychic awareness, purification, and fertility.

TUESDAY (MARS): Passion, sex, courage, aggression, and protection.

WEDNESDAY (MERCURY): The conscious mind, study, travel, divination, and wisdom.

THURSDAY (JUPITER): Expansion, money, prosperity, and generosity.

FRIDAY (VENUS): Love, friendship, reconciliation, and beauty.

SATURDAY (SATURN): Longevity, exorcism, endings, homes, and houses.

SUNDAY (SUN): Healing, spirituality, success, strength, and protection.

The Lunar Phase

The lunar phase is important in determining the best times for magic.

THE WAXING MOON (from the New Moon to the Full) is the ideal time for magic to draw things toward you.

THE FULL MOON is the time of greatest power.

THE WANING MOON (from the Full Moon to the New) is a time for study, meditation, and little magical work (except magic designed to banish harmful energies).

The Moon's Sign

The Moon continuously "moves" through the zodiac, from Aries to Pisces. Each sign possesses its own significance.

ARIES: Good for starting things, but lacks staying power. Things occur rapidly, but quickly pass. People tend to be argumentative and assertive.

TAURUS: Things begun now last the longest, tend to increase in value, and become hard to alter. Brings out appreciation for beauty and sensory experience.

GEMINI: Things begun now are easily changed by outside influence. Time for shortcuts, communication, games, and fun.

CANCER: Stimulates emotional rapport between people. Pinpoints need, supports growth and nurturance. Tends to domestic concerns.

LEO: Draws emphasis to the self, central ideas, or institutions, away from connections with others and other emotional needs. People tend to be melodramatic.

VIRGO: Favors accomplishment of details and commands from higher up. Focuses on health, hygiene, and daily schedules.

LIBRA: Favors cooperation, social activities, beautification of surroundings, balance, and partnership.

SCORPIO: Increases awareness of psychic power. Precipitates psychic crises and ends connections thoroughly. People tend to brood and become secretive.

Sagittarius: Encourages flights of imagination and confidence. This is an adventurous, philosophical, and athletic Moon sign. Favors expansion and growth.

Capricorn: Develops strong structure. Focus on traditions, responsibilities, and obligations. A good time to set boundaries and rules.

Aquarius: Rebellious energy. Time to break habits and make abrupt changes. Personal freedom and individuality is the focus.

Pisces: The focus is on dreaming, nostalgia, intuition, and psychic impressions. A good time for spiritual or philanthropic activities.

Color and Incense

The color and incense for the day are based on information from *Personal Alchemy* by Amber Wolfe, and relate to the planet that rules each day. This information can be taken into consideration along with other factors when planning works of magic or when blending magic into mundane life. Please note that the incense selections listed are not hard and fast. If you cannot find or do not like the incense listed for the day, choose a similar scent that appeals to you.

Festivals and Holidays

Festivals are listed throughout the year. The exact dates of many of these ancient festivals are difficult to determine; prevailing data has been used.

Time Zones

The times and dates of all astrological phenomena in this almanac are based on **Eastern Standard Time (EST)**. If you live outside of the Eastern time zone, you will need to make the following adjustments:

PACIFIC STANDARD TIME: Subtract three hours.

MOUNTAIN STANDARD TIME: Subtract two hours.

CENTRAL STANDARD TIME: Subtract one hour.

ALASKA: Subtract four hours.

HAWAII: Subtract five hours.

DAYLIGHT SAVING TIME (ALL ZONES): Add one hour.

Daylight Saving Time begins at 2 am on March 8, 2015, and ends at 2 am on November 1, 2015.

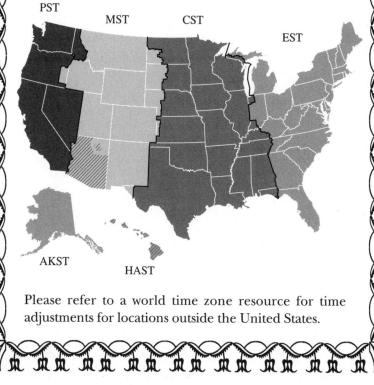

Please refer to a world time zone resource for time adjustments for locations outside the United States.

2016 Sabbats
and Full Moons

January 23	Cancer Full Moon 8:46 pm
February 2	Imbolc
February 22	Leo Full Moon 1:20 pm
March 20	Ostara (Spring Equinox)
March 23	Virgo Full Moon 8:01 am
April 22	Libra Full Moon 1:24 am
May 1	Beltane
May 21	Scorpio Full Moon 5:14 pm
June 20	Sagittarius Full Moon 7:02 am
June 20	Midsummer (Summer Solstice)
July 19	Capricorn Full Moon 6:57 pm
August 1	Lammas
August 18	Aquarius Full Moon 5:27 am
September 16	Pisces Full Moon 3:05 pm
September 22	Mabon (Fall Equinox)
October 16	Aries Full Moon 12:23 am
October 31	Samhain
November 14	Taurus Full Moon 8:52 am
December 13	Gemini Full Moon 7:06 pm
December 21	Yule (Winter Solstice)

All times are Eastern Standard Time (EST)
or Eastern Daylight Time (EDT)

2016 Sabbats in the Southern Hemisphere

Because Earth's Northern and Southern Hemispheres experience opposite seasons at any given time, the season-based Sabbats listed on the previous page and in this almanac section are not correct for those residing south of the equator. Listed here are the Southern Hemisphere sabbat dates for 2016:

February 2	Lammas
March 20	Mabon (Fall Equinox)
May 1	Samhain
June 20	Yule (Winter Solstice)
August 2	Imbolc
September 22	Ostara (Spring Equinox)
November 1	Beltane
December 21	Midsummer (Summer Solstice)

❖

Birthstone poetry reprinted from
The Occult and Curative Powers of Precious Stones
by William T. Fernie, M.D.
Harper & Row (1981)

Originally printed in 1907 as
*Precious Stones:
For Curative Wear; and Other Remedial Uses;
Likewise the Nobler Metals*

January

1 **Friday**
New Year's Day • Kwanzaa ends
Waning Moon
Moon phase: Third Quarter
Color: Rose

Moon Sign: Virgo
Moon enters Libra 1:41 am
Incense: Cypress

2 **Saturday**
First Writing Day (Japanese)
Waning Moon
Fourth Quarter 12:30 am
Color: Blue

Moon Sign: Libra
Incense: Sandalwood

3 **Sunday**
St. Genevieve's Day
Waning Moon
Moon phase: Fourth Quarter
Color: Amber

Moon Sign: Libra
Moon enters Scorpio 2:36 pm
Incense: Marigold

4 **Monday**
Frost Fairs on the Thames
Waning Moon
Moon phase: Fourth Quarter
Color: White

Moon Sign: Scorpio
Incense: Lily

5 **Tuesday**
Epiphany Eve
Waning Moon
Moon phase: Fourth Quarter
Color: Scarlet

Moon Sign: Scorpio
Incense: Geranium

6 **Wednesday**
Epiphany
Waning Moon
Moon phase: Fourth Quarter
Color: Yellow

Moon Sign: Scorpio
Moon enters Sagittarius 1:56 am
Incense: Lilac

7 **Thursday**
Rizdvo (Ukrainian)
Waning Moon
Moon phase: Fourth Quarter
Color: Purple

Moon Sign: Sagittarius
Incense: Apricot

144

8 Friday
Midwives' Day
Waning Moon
Moon phase: Fourth Quarter
Color: Pink

Moon Sign: Sagittarius
Moon enters Capricorn 10:07 am
Incense: Rose

---

9 Saturday
Feast of the Black Nazarene (Filipino)
Waning Moon
New Moon 8:31 pm
Color: Black

Moon Sign: Capricorn
Incense: Pine

---

10 Sunday
Business God's Day (Japanese)
Waxing Moon
Moon phase: First Quarter
Color: Orange

Moon Sign: Capricorn
Moon enters Aquarius 3:23 pm
Incense: Eucalyptus

---

11 Monday
Carmentalia (Roman)
Waxing Moon
Moon phase: First Quarter
Color: Ivory

Moon Sign: Aquarius
Incense: Clary sage

---

12 Tuesday
Revolution Day (Tanzanian)
Waxing Moon
Moon phase: First Quarter
Color: Red

Moon Sign: Aquarius
Moon enters Pisces 6:53 pm
Incense: Bayberry

---

13 Wednesday
Twentieth Day (Norwegian)
Waxing Moon
Moon phase: First Quarter
Color: White

Moon Sign: Pisces
Incense: Marjoram

---

14 Thursday
Feast of the Ass (French)
Waxing Moon
Moon phase: First Quarter
Color: Green

Moon Sign: Pisces
Moon enters Aries 9:48 pm
Incense: Balsam

15 Friday
Birthday of Martin Luther King, Jr. (actual)   Moon Sign: Aries
Waxing Moon   Incense: Mint
Moon phase: First Quarter
Color: Purple

◐ Saturday
Apprentices's Day   Moon Sign: Aries
Waxing Moon   Incense: Sage
Second Quarter 6:26 pm
Color: Brown

17 Sunday
St. Anthony's Day (Mexican)   Moon Sign: Aries
Waxing Moon   Moon enters Taurus 12:48 am
Moon phase: Second Quarter   Incense: Hyacinth
Color: Gold

18 Monday
Birthday of Martin Luther King, Jr. (observed)   Moon Sign: Taurus
Waxing Moon   Incense: Hyssop
Moon phase: Second Quarter
Color: Silver

19 Tuesday
Kitchen God Feast (Chinese)   Moon Sign: Taurus
Waxing Moon   Moon enters Gemini 4:13 am
Moon phase: Second Quarter   Incense: Ylang-ylang
Color: White

20 Wednesday
Inauguration Day   Moon Sign: Gemini
Waxing Moon   Sun enters Aquarius 10:27 am
Moon phase: Second Quarter   Incense: Honeysuckle
Color: Brown

21 Thursday
St. Agnes's Day   Moon Sign: Gemini
Waxing Moon   Moon enters Cancer 8:28 am
Moon phase: Second Quarter   Incense: Carnation
Color: White

146

22 Friday
St. Vincent's Day (French)
Waxing Moon
Moon phase: Second Quarter
Color: Coral

Moon Sign: Cancer
Incense: Yarrow

Saturday
St. Ildefonso's Day (French)
Waxing Moon
Full Moon 8:46 pm
Color: Indigo

Moon Sign: Cancer
Moon enters Leo 2:21 pm
Incense: Patchouli

24 Sunday
Alasitas Fair (Bolivian)
Waning Moon
Moon phase: Third Quarter
Color: Yellow

Moon Sign: Leo
Incense: Heliotrope

25 Monday
Burns' Night (Scottish)
Waning Moon
Moon phase: Third Quarter
Color: Gray

Moon Sign: Leo
Moon enters Virgo 10:46 pm
Incense: Rosemary

26 Tuesday
Republic Day (Indian)
Waning Moon
Moon phase: Third Quarter
Color: Black

Moon Sign: Virgo
Incense: Cedar

27 Wednesday
Vogelgruff (Swiss)
Waning Moon
Moon phase: Third Quarter
Color: Topaz

Moon Sign: Virgo
Incense: Lavender

28 Thursday
St. Charlemagne's Day
Waning Moon
Moon phase: Third Quarter
Color: Crimson

Moon Sign: Virgo
Moon enters Libra 9:59 am
Incense: Mulberry

29 Friday
Marty's Day (Nepalese)
Waning Moon
Moon phase: Third Quarter
Color: White

Moon Sign: Libra
Incense: Thyme

30 Saturday
Three Hierarchs Day (Eastern Orthodox)
Waning Moon
Moon phase: Third Quarter
Color: Gray

Moon Sign: Libra
Moon enters Scorpio 10:50 pm
Incense: Ivy

◐ Sunday
Independence Day (Nauru)
Waning Moon
Fourth Quarter 10:28 pm
Color: Gold

Moon Sign: Scorpio
Incense: Almond

January Birthstones

By her in January born
No gem save Garnets should be worn;
They will ensure her constancy,
True friendship, and fidelity.

Modern: Garnet   Zodiac (Capricorn): Ruby

February Birthstones

The February-born shall find
Sincerity, and peace of mind,
Freedom from passion and from care,
If they the Amethyst will wear.

Modern: Amethyst   Zodiac (Aquarius): Garnet

February

1 Monday
St. Brigid's Day (Irish)
Waning Moon
Moon phase: Fourth Quarter
Color: Lavender

Moon Sign: Scorpio
Incense: Narcissus

2 Tuesday
Imbolc • Groundhog Day
Waning Moon
Moon phase: Fourth Quarter
Color: Gray

Moon Sign: Scorpio
Moon enters Sagittarius 10:50 am
Incense: Basil

3 Wednesday
St. Blaise's Day
Waning Moon
Moon phase: Fourth Quarter
Color: White

Moon Sign: Sagittarius
Incense: Bay laurel

4 Thursday
Independence Day (Sri Lankan)
Waning Moon
Moon phase: Fourth Quarter
Color: Turquoise

Moon Sign: Sagittarius
Moon enters Capricorn 7:44 pm
Incense: Jasmine

5 Friday
Festival de la Alcaldesa (Italian)
Waning Moon
Moon phase: Fourth Quarter
Color: Purple

Moon Sign: Capricorn
Incense: Violet

6 Saturday
Bob Marley's Birthday (Jamaican)
Waning Moon
Moon phase: Fourth Quarter
Color: Brown

Moon Sign: Capricorn
Incense: Magnolia

7 Sunday
Full Moon Poya (Sri Lankan)
Waning Moon
Moon phase: Fourth Quarter
Color: Yellow

Moon Sign: Capricorn
Moon enters Aquarius 12:59 am
Incense: Frankincense

February

Monday
Chinese New Year (monkey)
Waning Moon
New Moon 9:39 am
Color: Silver

Moon Sign: Aquarius
Incense: Neroli

---

9 Tuesday
Mardi Gras (Fat Tuesday)
Waxing Moon
Moon phase: First Quarter
Color: Maroon

Moon Sign: Aquarius
Moon enters Pisces 3:31 am
Incense: Cinnamon

---

10 Wednesday
Ash Wednesday
Waxing Moon
Moon phase: First Quarter
Color: Yellow

Moon Sign: Pisces
Incense: Honeysuckle

---

11 Thursday
Foundation Day (Japanese)
Waxing Moon
Moon phase: First Quarter
Color: Green

Moon Sign: Pisces
Moon enters Aries 4:55 am
Incense: Clove

---

12 Friday
Lincoln's Birthday (actual)
Waxing Moon
Moon phase: First Quarter
Color: White

Moon Sign: Aries
Incense: Cypress

---

13 Saturday
Parentalia (Roman)
Waxing Moon
Moon phase: First Quarter
Color: Gray

Moon Sign: Aries
Moon enters Taurus 6:36 am
Incense: Rue

---

14 Sunday
Valentine's Day
Waxing Moon
Moon phase: First Quarter
Color: Orange

Moon Sign: Taurus
Incense: Juniper

February

○ Monday

Presidents' Day (observed)
Waxing Moon
Second Quarter 2:46 am
Color: Gray

Moon Sign: Taurus
Moon enters Gemini 9:35 am
Incense: Clary sage

16 Tuesday

Fumi-e (Japanese)
Waxing Moon
Moon phase: Second Quarter
Color: Red

Moon Sign: Gemini
Incense: Ginger

17 Wednesday

Quirinalia (Roman)
Waxing Moon
Moon phase: Second Quarter
Color: Topaz

Moon Sign: Gemini
Moon enters Cancer 2:24 pm
Incense: Marjoram

18 Thursday

Saint Bernadette's Second Vision
Waxing Moon
Moon phase: Second Quarter
Color: White

Moon Sign: Cancer
Incense: Nutmeg

19 Friday

Pero Palo's Trial (Spanish)
Waxing Moon
Moon phase: Second Quarter
Color: Coral

Moon Sign: Cancer
Sun enters Pisces 12:34 am
Moon enters Leo 9:17 pm
Incense: Orchid

20 Saturday

Installation of the New Lama (Tibetan)
Waxing Moon
Moon phase: Second Quarter
Color: Blue

Moon Sign: Leo
Incense: Sage

21 Sunday

Feast of Lanterns (Chinese)
Waxing Moon
Moon phase: Second Quarter
Color: Amber

Moon Sign: Leo
Incense: Eucalyptus

151

February

☺ Monday
Caristia (Roman)
Waxing Moon
Full Moon 1:20 pm
Color: Ivory

Moon Sign: Leo
Moon enters Virgo 6:24 am
Incense: Narcissus

---

23 Tuesday
Terminalia (Roman)
Waning Moon
Moon phase: Third Quarter
Color: Black

Moon Sign: Virgo
Incense: Bayberry

---

24 Wednesday
Regifugium (Roman)
Waning Moon
Moon phase: Third Quarter
Color: Brown

Moon Sign: Virgo
Moon enters Libra 5:41 pm
Incense: Bay laurel

---

25 Thursday
Saint Walburga's Day (German)
Waning Moon
Moon phase: Third Quarter
Color: Purple

Moon Sign: Libra
Incense: Myrrh

---

26 Friday
Zamboanga Festival (Filipino)
Waning Moon
Moon phase: Third Quarter
Color: Rose

Moon Sign: Libra
Incense: Alder

---

27 Saturday
Threepenny Day
Waning Moon
Moon phase: Third Quarter
Color: Black

Moon Sign: Libra
Moon enters Scorpio 6:26 am
Incense: Pine

---

28 Sunday
Kalevala Day (Finnish)
Waning Moon
Moon phase: Third Quarter
Color: Orange

Moon Sign: Scorpio
Incense: Heliotrope

March

29 **Monday**
Leap Day
Waning Moon
Moon phase: Third Quarter
Color: White

Moon Sign: Scorpio
Moon enters Sagittarius 6:56 pm
Incense: Hyssop

○ **Tuesday**
Matronalia (Roman)
Waning Moon
Fourth Quarter 6:11 pm
Color: Maroon

Moon Sign: Sagittarius
Incense: Cinnamon

2 **Wednesday**
St. Chad's Day (English)
Waning Moon
Moon phase: Fourth Quarter
Color: Topaz

Moon Sign: Sagittarius
Incense: Lavender

3 **Thursday**
Doll Festival (Japanese)
Waning Moon
Moon phase: Fourth Quarter
Color: Crimson

Moon Sign: Sagittarius
Moon enters Capricorn 5:01 am
Incense: Carnation

4 **Friday**
Purim
Waning Moon
Moon phase: Fourth Quarter
Color: Coral

Moon Sign: Capricorn
Incense: Vanilla

5 **Saturday**
Isis Festival (Roman)
Waning Moon
Moon phase: Fourth Quarter
Color: Indigo

Moon Sign: Capricorn
Moon enters Aquarius 11:22 am
Incense: Rue

6 **Sunday**
Alamo Day
Waning Moon
Moon phase: Fourth Quarter
Color: Gold

Moon Sign: Aquarius
Incense: Frankincense

March

7 Monday
Bird and Arbor Day
Waning Moon
Moon phase: Fourth Quarter
Color: Gray

Moon Sign: Aquarius
Moon enters Pisces 2:08 pm
Incense: Lily

Tuesday
International Women's Day
Waning Moon
New Moon 8:54 pm
Color: White

Moon Sign: Pisces
Incense: Geranium

9 Wednesday
Forty Saints' Day
Waxing Moon
Moon phase: First Quarter
Color: Brown

Moon Sign: Pisces
Moon enters Aries 2:40 pm
Incense: Lilac

10 Thursday
Tibet Day
Waxing Moon
Moon phase: First Quarter
Color: Purple

Moon Sign: Aries
Incense: Jasmine

11 Friday
Feast of the Gauri (Hindu)
Waxing Moon
Moon phase: First Quarter
Color: Pink

Moon Sign: Aries
Moon enters Taurus 2:44 pm
Incense: Mint

12 Saturday
Receiving the Water (Buddhist)
Waxing Moon
Moon phase: First Quarter
Color: Black

Moon Sign: Taurus
Incense: Ivy

13 Sunday
Purification Feast (Balinese)
Waxing Moon
Moon phase: First Quarter
Color: Amber

Moon Sign: Taurus
Moon enters Gemini 5:03 pm
Incense: Marigold
Daylight Saving Time begins

March ♈

14 Monday
Mamuralia (Roman)
Waxing Moon
Moon phase: First Quarter
Color: Lavender

Moon Sign: Gemini
Incense: Neroli

☽ Tuesday
Phallus Festival (Japanese)
Waxing Moon
Second Quarter 1:03 pm
Color: Gray

Moon Sign: Gemini
Moon enters Cancer 8:57 pm
Incense: Ylang-ylang

16 Wednesday
St. Urho's Day (Finnish)
Waxing Moon
Moon phase: Second Quarter
Color: White

Moon Sign: Cancer
Incense: Lavender

17 Thursday
St. Patrick's Day
Waxing Moon
Moon phase: Second Quarter
Color: Turquoise

Moon Sign: Cancer
Incense: Nutmeg

18 Friday
Sheelah's Day (Irish)
Waxing Moon
Moon phase: Second Quarter
Color: Rose

Moon Sign: Cancer
Moon enters Leo 3:54 am
Incense: Thyme

19 Saturday
St. Joseph's Day (Sicilian)
Waxing Moon
Moon phase: Second Quarter
Color: Brown

Moon Sign: Leo
Incense: Rue

20 Sunday
Palm Sunday • Ostara • Spring Equinox
Waxing Moon
Moon phase: Second Quarter
Color: Orange

Moon Sign: Leo
Sun enters Aries 12:30 am
Moon enters Virgo 1:39 pm
Incense: Hyacinth

March ♈

21 Monday
Juarez Day (Mexican)
Waxing Moon
Moon phase: Second Quarter
Color: Silver

Moon Sign: Virgo
Incense: Rosemary

---

22 Tuesday
Hilaria (Roman)
Waxing Moon
Moon phase: Second Quarter
Color: Scarlet

Moon Sign: Virgo
Incense: Basil

☺ Wednesday
Pakistan Day
Waxing Moon
Full Moon 8:01 am
Color: Yellow

Moon Sign: Virgo
Moon enters Libra 1:23 am
Incense: Marjoram

---

24 Thursday
Purim
Waning Moon
Moon phase: Third Quarter
Color: Green

Moon Sign: Libra
Incense: Apricot

---

25 Friday
Good Friday
Waning Moon
Moon phase: Third Quarter
Color: White

Moon Sign: Libra
Moon enters Scorpio 2:09 pm
Incense: Cypress

---

26 Saturday
Prince Kuhio Day (Hawaiian)
Waning Moon
Moon phase: Third Quarter
Color: Blue

Moon Sign: Scorpio
Incense: Sandalwood

---

27 Sunday
Easter
Waning Moon
Moon phase: Third Quarter
Color: Yellow

Moon Sign: Scorpio
Incense: Almond

March

28 Monday
Oranges and Lemons Service (English)
Waning Moon
Moon phase: Third Quarter
Color: White

Moon Sign: Scorpio
Moon enters Sagittarius 2:46 am
Incense: Hyssop

29 Tuesday
Feast of Eastace's of Luxeuil
Waning Moon
Moon phase: Third Quarter
Color: Black

Moon Sign: Sagittarius
Incense: Ginger

30 Wednesday
Seward's Day (Alaskan)
Waning Moon
Moon phase: Third Quarter
Color: White

Moon Sign: Sagittarius
Moon enters Capricorn 1:45 pm
Incense: Honeysuckle

○ Thursday
The Borrowed Days (Ethiopian)
Waning Moon
Fourth Quarter 11:17 am
Color: Crimson

Moon Sign: Capricorn
Incense Myrrh

March Birthstones

Who in this world of ours, her eyes
In March first opens, shall be wise.
In days of peril, firm and brave,
And wear a Bloodstone to her grave.

Modern: Aquamarine
Zodiac (Pisces): Amethyst

April

1 Friday
April Fools' Day
Waning Moon
Moon phase: Fourth Quarter
Color: Pink

Moon Sign: Capricorn
Moon enters Aquarius 9:37 pm
Incense: Mint

2 Saturday
The Battle of Flowers (French)
Waning Moon
Moon phase: Fourth Quarter
Color: Gray

Moon Sign: Aquarius
Incense: Pine

3 Sunday
Thirteenth Day (Iranian)
Waning Moon
Moon phase: Fourth Quarter
Color: Orange

Moon Sign: Aquarius
Incense: Juniper

4 Monday
Megalesia (Roman)
Waning Moon
Moon phase: Fourth Quarter
Color: Lavender

Moon Sign: Aquarius
Moon enters Pisces 1:45 am
Incense: Clary sage

5 Tuesday
Tomb-Sweeping Day (Chinese)
Waning Moon
Moon phase: Fourth Quarter
Color: White

Moon Sign: Pisces
Incense: Ylang-ylang

6 Wednesday
Chakri Day (Thai)
Waning Moon
Moon phase: Fourth Quarter
Color: Yellow

Moon Sign: Pisces
Moon enters Aries 2:46 am
Incense: Lilac

🌑 Thursday
Festival of Pure Brightness (Chinese)
Waning Moon
New Moon 7:24 am
Color: Turquoise

Moon Sign: Aries
Incense: Clove

April ♈

8 Friday
Buddha's Birthday
Waxing Moon
Moon phase: First Quarter
Color: Rose

Moon Sign: Aries
Moon enters Taurus 2:10 am
Incense: Alder

9 Saturday
Valour Day (Filipino)
Waxing Moon
Moon phase: First Quarter
Color: Blue

Moon Sign: Taurus
Incense: Patchouli

10 Sunday
The Tenth of April (English)
Waxing Moon
Moon phase: First Quarter
Color: Gold

Moon Sign: Taurus
Moon enters Gemini 1:59 am
Incense: Hyacinth

11 Monday
Heroes Day (Costa Rican)
Waxing Moon
Moon phase: First Quarter
Color: Ivory

Moon Sign: Gemini
Incense: Lily

12 Tuesday
Cerealia (Roman)
Waxing Moon
Moon phase: First Quarter
Color: Gray

Moon Sign: Gemini
Moon enters Cancer 4:07 am
Incense: Cinnamon

☽ Wednesday
Thai New Year
Waxing Moon
Second Quarter 11:59 pm
Color: Brown

Moon Sign: Cancer
Incense: Bay laurel

14 Thursday
Sanno Festival (Japanese)
Waxing Moon
Moon phase: Second Quarter
Color: White

Moon Sign: Cancer
Moon enters Leo 9:53 am
Incense: Mulberry

15 Friday
Plowing Festival (Chinese)   Moon Sign: Leo
Waxing Moon   Incense: Rose
Moon phase: Second Quarter
Color: Purple

16 Saturday
Zurich Spring Festival (Swiss)   Moon Sign: Leo
Waxing Moon   Moon enters Virgo 7:23 pm
Moon phase: Second Quarter   Incense: Pine
Color: Black

17 Sunday
Yayoi Matsuri (Japanese)   Moon Sign: Virgo
Waxing Moon   Incense: Frankincense
Moon phase: Second Quarter
Color: Yellow

18 Monday
Flower Festival (Japanese)   Moon Sign: Virgo
Waxing Moon   Incense: Narcissus
Moon phase: Second Quarter
Color: Lavender

19 Tuesday
Cerealia last day (Roman)   Moon Sign: Virgo
Waxing Moon   Moon enters Libra 7:24 am
Moon phase: Second Quarter   Sun enters Taurus 11:29 am
Color: Red   Incense: Bayberry

20 Wednesday
Drum Festival (Japanese)   Moon Sign: Libra
Waxing Moon   Incense: Honeysuckle
Moon phase: Second Quarter
Color: White

21 Thursday
Tiradentes Day (Brazilian)   Moon Sign: Libra
Waxing Moon   Moon enters Scorpio 8:17 pm
Moon phase: Second Quarter   Incense: Balsam
Color: Purple

April

☺ Friday
Earth Day
Waxing Moon
Full Moon 1:24 am
Color: Coral

Moon Sign: Scorpio
Incense: Yarrow

---

23 Saturday
Passover begins
Waning Moon
Moon phase: Third Quarter
Color: Indigo

Moon Sign: Scorpio
Incense: Magnolia

---

24 Sunday
St. Mark's Eve
Waning Moon
Moon phase: Third Quarter
Color: Amber

Moon Sign: Scorpio
Moon enters Sagittarius 8:46 am
Incense: Eucalyptus

---

25 Monday
Robigalia (Roman)
Waning Moon
Moon phase: Third Quarter
Color: Gray

Moon Sign: Sagittarius
Incense: Neroli

---

26 Tuesday
Arbor Day
Waning Moon
Moon phase: Third Quarter
Color: Scarlet

Moon Sign: Sagittarius
Moon enters Capricorn 7:54 pm
Incense: Basil

---

27 Wednesday
Humabon's Conversion (Filipino)
Waning Moon
Moon phase: Third Quarter
Color: Topaz

Moon Sign: Capricorn
Incense: Lavender

---

28 Thursday
Floralia (Roman)
Waning Moon
Moon phase: Third Quarter
Color: Green

Moon Sign: Capricorn
Incense: Clove

April

Friday
Orthodox Good Friday
Waning Moon
Fourth Quarter 11:29 pm
Color: White

Moon Sign: Capricorn
Moon enters Aquarius 4:47 am
Incense: Violet

---

30 Saturday
Passover ends • Walpurgis Night • May Eve
Waning Moon
Moon phase: Fourth Quarter
Color: Brown

Moon Sign: Aquarius
Incense: Patchouli

April Birthstones

She who from April dates her years,
Diamonds shall wear, lest bitter tears
For vain repentance flow; this stone
Emblem for innocence is known.

Modern: Diamond
Zodiac (Aries): Bloodstone

May

1 Sunday
Orthodox Easter • Beltane • May Day
Waning Moon
Moon phase: Fourth Quarter
Color: Gold

Moon Sign: Aquarius
Moon enters Pisces 10:33 am
Incense: Almond

2 Monday
Big Kite Flying (Japanese)
Waning Moon
Moon phase: Fourth Quarter
Color: Gray

Moon Sign: Pisces
Incense: Rosemary

3 Tuesday
Holy Cross Day
Waning Moon
Moon phase: Fourth Quarter
Color: Maroon

Moon Sign: Pisces
Moon enters Aries 1:04 pm
Incense: Geranium

4 Wednesday
Bona Dea (Roman)
Waning Moon
Moon phase: Fourth Quarter
Color: White

Moon Sign: Aries
Incense: Marjoram

5 Thursday
Cinco de Mayo (Mexican)
Waning Moon
Moon phase: Fourth Quarter
Color: Crimson

Moon Sign: Aries
Moon enters Taurus 1:10 pm
Incense: Carnation

6 Friday
Martyrs' Day (Lebanese)
Waning Moon
New Moon 3:30 pm
Color: White

Moon Sign: Taurus
Incense: Yarrow

7 Saturday
Pilgrimage of St. Nicholas (Italian)
Waxing Moon
Moon phase: First Quarter
Color: Black

Moon Sign: Taurus
Moon enters Gemini 12:35 pm
Incense: Sage

May

8 Sunday
Mother's Day
Waxing Moon
Moon phase: First Quarter
Color: Yellow

Moon Sign: Gemini
Incense: Marigold

9 Monday
Lemuria (Roman)
Waxing Moon
Moon phase: First Quarter
Color: Ivory

Moon Sign: Gemini
Moon enters Cancer 1:24 pm
Incense: Narcissus

10 Tuesday
Census Day (Canada)
Waxing Moon
Moon phase: First Quarter
Color: White

Moon Sign: Cancer
Incense: Cedar

11 Wednesday
Ukai Season Opens (Japanese)
Waxing Moon
Moon phase: First Quarter
Color: Topaz

Moon Sign: Cancer
Moon enters Leo 5:32 pm
Incense: Bay laurel

12 Thursday
Florence Nightingale's Birthday
Waxing Moon
Moon phase: First Quarter
Color: Purple

Moon Sign: Leo
Incense: Jasmine

☽ Friday
Pilgrimage to Fatima (Portuguese)
Waxing Moon
Second Quarter 1:02 pm
Color: Coral

Moon Sign: Leo
Incense: Orchid

14 Saturday
Carabao Festival (Spanish)
Waxing Moon
Moon phase: Second Quarter
Color: Indigo

Moon Sign: Leo
Moon enters Virgo 1:52 am
Incense: Rue

May

♊

15 Sunday
Festival of St. Dympna (Belgian)
Waxing Moon
Moon phase: Second Quarter
Color: Amber

Moon Sign: Virgo
Incense: Heliotrope

---

16 Monday
St. Honoratus' Day
Waxing Moon
Moon phase: Second Quarter
Color: Silver

Moon Sign: Virgo
Moon enters Libra 1:33 pm
Incense: Lily

---

17 Tuesday
Norwegian Independence Day
Waxing Moon
Moon phase: Second Quarter
Color: Red

Moon Sign: Libra
Incense: Ginger

---

18 Wednesday
Las Piedras Day (Uruguayan)
Waxing Moon
Moon phase: Second Quarter
Color: Yellow

Moon Sign: Libra
Incense: Lilac

---

19 Thursday
Pilgrimage to Treguier (French)
Waxing Moon
Moon phase: Second Quarter
Color: White

Moon Sign: Libra
Moon enters Scorpio 2:29 am
Incense: Nutmeg

---

20 Friday
Pardon of the Singers (British)
Waxing Moon
Moon phase: Second Quarter
Color: Pink

Moon Sign: Scorpio
Sun enters Gemini 10:36 am
Incense: Vanilla

☺ Saturday
Victoria Day (Canadian)
Waxing Moon
Full Moon 5:14 pm
Color: Brown

Moon Sign: Scorpio
Moon enters Sagittarius 2:48 pm
Incense: Patchouli

May

22 Sunday

Heroes' Day (Sri Lankan)
Waning Moon
Moon phase: Third Quarter
Color: Gold

Moon Sign: Sagittarius
Incense: Juniper

23 Monday

Tubilustrium (Roman)
Waning Moon
Moon phase: Third Quarter
Color: Lavender

Moon Sign: Sagittarius
Incense: Clary sage

24 Tuesday

Culture Day (Bulgarian)
Waning Moon
Moon phase: Third Quarter
Color: Black

Moon Sign: Sagittarius
Moon enters Capricorn 1:34 am
Incense: Cedar

25 Wednesday

Urbanas Diena (Latvian)
Waning Moon
Moon phase: Third Quarter
Color: Brown

Moon Sign: Capricorn
Incense: Marjoram

26 Thursday

Pepys' Commemoration (English)
Waning Moon
Moon phase: Third Quarter
Color: Green

Moon Sign: Capricorn
Moon enters Aquarius 10:27 am
Incense: Apricot

27 Friday

St. Augustine of Canterbury's Day
Waning Moon
Moon phase: Third Quarter
Color: Purple

Moon Sign: Aquarius
Incense: Violet

28 Saturday

St. Germain's Day
Waning Moon
Moon phase: Third Quarter
Color: Blue

Moon Sign: Aquarius
Moon enters Pisces 5:06 pm
Incense: Magnolia

May

○ **Sunday**
Royal Oak Day (English)
Waning Moon
Fourth Quarter 8:12 am
Color: Orange

Moon Sign: Pisces
Incense: Heliotrope

---

30 Monday
Memorial Day (actual)
Waning Moon
Moon phase: Fourth Quarter
Color: White

Moon Sign: Pisces
Moon enters Aries 9:09 pm
Incense: Neroli

---

31 Tuesday
Flowers of May
Waning Moon
Moon phase: Fourth Quarter
Color: Gray

Moon Sign: Aries
Incense: Geranium

May Birthstones

Who first beholds the light of day,
In spring's sweet flowery month of May,
And wears an Emerald all her life,
Shall be a loved, and happy wife.

Modern: Emerald
Zodiac (Taurus): Sapphire

June

♊

1   Wednesday
National Day (Tunisian)   Moon Sign: Aries
Waning Moon   Moon enters Taurus 10:46 pm
Moon phase: Fourth Quarter   Incense: Lilac
Color: Topaz

2   Thursday
Rice Harvest Festival (Malaysian)   Moon Sign: Taurus
Waning Moon   Incense: Balsam
Moon phase: Fourth Quarter
Color: Green

3   Friday
Memorial to Broken Dolls (Japanese)   Moon Sign: Taurus
Waning Moon   Moon enters Gemini 11:01 pm
Moon phase: Fourth Quarter   Incense: Thyme
Color: Pink

☽ Saturday
Full Moon Day (Burmese)   Moon Sign: Gemini
Waning Moon   Incense: Patchouli
New Moon 11:00 pm
Color: Indigo

5   Sunday
Constitution Day (Danish)   Moon Sign: Gemini
Waxing Moon   Moon enters Cancer 11:41 pm
Moon phase: First Quarter   Incense: Marigold
Color: Amber

6   Monday
Ramadan begins   Moon Sign: Cancer
Waxing Moon   Incense: Hyssop
Moon phase: First Quarter
Color: White

7   Tuesday
St. Robert of Newminster's Day   Moon Sign: Cancer
Waxing Moon   Incense: Basil
Moon phase: First Quarter
Color: Maroon

June ♊

8 Wednesday
St. Medard's Day (Belgian)
Waxing Moon
Moon phase: First Quarter
Color: Brown

Moon Sign: Cancer
Moon enters Leo 2:47 am
Incense: Lavender

9 Thursday
Vestalia (Roman)
Waxing Moon
Moon phase: First Quarter
Color: White

Moon Sign: Leo
Incense: Mulberry

10 Friday
Time-Observance Day (Chinese)
Waxing Moon
Moon phase: First Quarter
Color: Purple

Moon Sign: Leo
Moon enters Virgo 9:46 am
Incense: Mint

11 Saturday
Kamehameha Day (Hawaiian)
Waxing Moon
Moon phase: First Quarter
Color: Gray

Moon Sign: Virgo
Incense: Sandalwood

☽ Sunday
Shavuot
Waxing Moon
Second Quarter 4:10 am
Color: Orange

Moon Sign: Virgo
Moon enters Libra 8:33 pm
Incense: Almond

13 Monday
St. Anthony of Padua's Day
Waxing Moon
Moon phase: Second Quarter
Color: Gray

Moon Sign: Libra
Incense: Rosemary

14 Tuesday
Flag Day
Waxing Moon
Moon phase: Second Quarter
Color: Scarlet

Moon Sign: Libra
Incense: Bayberry

June

15 Wednesday
Father's Day
Waxing Moon
Moon phase: Second Quarter
Color: White

Moon Sign: Libra
Moon enters Scorpio 9:18 am
Incense: Honeysuckle

---

16 Thursday
Bloomsday (Irish)
Waxing Moon
Moon phase: Second Quarter
Color: Purple

Moon Sign: Scorpio
Incense: Myrrh

---

17 Friday
Bunker Hill Day
Waxing Moon
Moon phase: Second Quarter
Color: Coral

Moon Sign: Scorpio
Moon enters Sagittarius 9:34 pm
Incense: Vanilla

---

18 Saturday
Independence Day (Egyptian)
Waxing Moon
Moon phase: Second Quarter
Color: Black

Moon Sign: Sagittarius
Incense: Ivy

---

19 Sunday
Father's Day
Waxing Moon
Moon phase: Second Quarter
Color: Yellow

Moon Sign: Sagittarius
Incense: Eucalyptus

☺ Monday
Midsummer • Summer Solstice
Waxing Moon
Full Moon 7:02 am
Color: Ivory

Moon Sign: Sagittarius
Moon enters Capricorn 7:55 am
Sun enters Cancer 6:34 pm
Incense: Lily

---

21 Tuesday
U.S. Constitution ratified
Waning Moon
Moon phase: Third Quarter
Color: Black

Moon Sign: Capricorn
Incense: Cinnamon

June

22 Wednesday
Rose Festival (English)
Waning Moon
Moon phase: Third Quarter
Color: Topaz

Moon Sign: Capricorn
Moon enters Aquarius 4:08 pm
Incense: Bay laurel

23 Thursday
St. John's Eve
Waning Moon
Moon phase: Third Quarter
Color: Turquoise

Moon Sign: Aquarius
Incense: Jasmine

24 Friday
St. John's Day
Waning Moon
Moon phase: Third Quarter
Color: Rose

Moon Sign: Aquarius
Moon enters Pisces 10:30 pm
Incense: Orchid

25 Saturday
Fiesta of Santa Orosia (Spanish)
Waning Moon
Moon phase: Third Quarter
Color: Blue

Moon Sign: Pisces
Incense: Rue

26 Sunday
Pied Piper Day (German)
Waning Moon
Moon phase: Third Quarter
Color: Gold

Moon Sign: Pisces
Incense: Frankincense

☽ Monday
Day of the Seven Sleepers (Islamic)
Waning Moon
Fourth Quarter 2:19 pm
Color: Silver

Moon Sign: Pisces
Moon enters Aries 3:08 am
Incense: Hyssop

28 Tuesday
Paul Bunyan Day
Waning Moon
Moon phase: Fourth Quarter
Color: Red

Moon Sign: Aries
Incense: Ylang-ylang

June

29 Wednesday
Feast of Saints Peter and Paul
Waning Moon
Moon phase: Fourth Quarter
Color: Yellow

Moon Sign: Aries
Moon enters Taurus 6:03 am
Incense: Lilac

30 Thursday
The Burning of the Three Firs (French)
Waning Moon
Moon phase: Fourth Quarter
Color: Crimson

Moon Sign: Taurus
Incense: Apricot

June Birthstones

Who comes with summer to this earth,
And owes to June her hour of birth,
With ring of Agate on her hand,
Can health, wealth, and long life command.

Modern: Moonstone or Pearl
Zodiac (Gemini): Agate

July

1 Friday
Climbing Mount Fuji (Japanese)
Waning Moon
Moon phase: Fourth Quarter
Color: Coral

Moon Sign: Taurus
Moon enters Gemini 7:44 am
Incense: Violet

2 Saturday
Heroes' Day (Zambian)
Waning Moon
Moon phase: Fourth Quarter
Color: Black

Moon Sign: Gemini
Incense: Ivy

3 Sunday
Indian Sun Dance (Native American)
Waning Moon
Moon phase: Fourth Quarter
Color: Yellow

Moon Sign: Gemini
Moon enters Cancer 9:20 am
Incense: Almond

☽ Monday
Independence Day
Waning Moon
New Moon 7:01 am
Color: Lavender

Moon Sign: Cancer
Incense: Neroli

5 Tuesday
Ramadan ends
Waxing Moon
Moon phase: First Quarter
Color: Red

Moon Sign: Cancer
Moon enters Leo 12:28 pm
Incense: Ginger

6 Wednesday
Khao Phansa Day (Thai)
Waxing Moon
Moon phase: First Quarter
Color: Topaz

Moon Sign: Leo
Incense: Honeysuckle

7 Thursday
Weaver's Festival (Japanese)
Waxing Moon
Moon phase: First Quarter
Color: White

Moon Sign: Leo
Moon enters Virgo 6:41 pm
Incense: Balsam

July

8 Friday
St. Elizabeth's Day (Portuguese)
Waxing Moon
Moon phase: First Quarter
Color: Pink

Moon Sign: Virgo
Incense: Rose

9 Saturday
Battle of Sempach Day (Swiss)
Waxing Moon
Moon phase: First Quarter
Color: Gray

Moon Sign: Virgo
Incense: Pine

10 Sunday
Lady Godiva Day (English)
Waxing Moon
Moon phase: First Quarter
Color: Amber

Moon Sign: Virgo
Moon enters Libra 4:32 am
Incense: Hyacinth

◐ Monday
Revolution Day (Mongolian)
Waxing Moon
Second Quarter 8:52 pm
Color: Silver

Moon Sign: Libra
Incense: Clary sage

12 Tuesday
Lobster Carnival (Nova Scotian)
Waxing Moon
Moon phase: Second Quarter
Color: White

Moon Sign: Libra
Moon enters Scorpio 4:52 pm
Incense: Basil

13 Wednesday
Festival of the Three Cows (Spanish)
Waxing Moon
Moon phase: Second Quarter
Color: Brown

Moon Sign: Scorpio
Incense: Bay laurel

14 Thursday
Bastille Day (French)
Waxing Moon
Moon phase: Second Quarter
Color: Purple

Moon Sign: Scorpio
Incense: Clove

July

15 Friday
St. Swithin's Day
Waxing Moon
Moon phase: Second Quarter
Color: Rose

Moon Sign: Scorpio
Moon enters Sagittarius 5:14 am
Incense: Yarrow

16 Saturday
Our Lady of Carmel
Waxing Moon
Moon phase: Second Quarter
Color: Blue

Moon Sign: Sagittarius
Incense: Magnolia

17 Sunday
Rivera Day (Puerto Rican)
Waxing Moon
Moon phase: Second Quarter
Color: Gold

Moon Sign: Sagittarius
Moon enters Capricorn 3:33 pm
Incense: Marigold

18 Monday
Gion Matsuri Festival (Japanese)
Waxing Moon
Moon phase: Second Quarter
Color: Ivory

Moon Sign: Capricorn
Incense: Narcissus

☺ Tuesday
Flitch Day (English)
Waxing Moon
Full Moon 6:57 pm
Color: Black

Moon Sign: Capricorn
Moon enters Aquarius 11:10 pm
Incense: Ylang-ylang

20 Wednesday
Binding of Wreaths (Lithuanian)
Waning Moon
Moon phase: Third Quarter
Color: Yellow

Moon Sign: Aquarius
Incense: Lavender

21 Thursday
National Day (Belgian)
Waning Moon
Moon phase: Third Quarter
Color: Crimson

Moon Sign: Aquarius
Incense: Carnation

22 Friday

St. Mary Magdalene's Day
Waning Moon
Moon phase: Third Quarter
Color: White

Moon Sign: Aquarius
Moon enters Pisces 4:35 am
Sun enters Leo 5:30 am
Incense: Cypress

23 Saturday

Mysteries of Santa Cristina (Italian)
Waning Moon
Moon phase: Third Quarter
Color: Brown

Moon Sign: Pisces
Incense: Ivy

24 Sunday

Pioneer Day (Mormon)
Waning Moon
Moon phase: Third Quarter
Color: Orange

Moon Sign: Pisces
Moon enters Aries 8:33 am
Incense: Frankincense

25 Monday

St. James' Day
Waning Moon
Moon phase: Third Quarter
Color: Lavender

Moon Sign: Aries
Incense: Rosemary

○ Tuesday

St. Anne's Day
Waning Moon
Fourth Quarter 7:00 pm
Color: Scarlet

Moon Sign: Aries
Moon enters Taurus 11:37 am
Incense: Geranium

27 Wednesday

Sleepyhead Day (Finnish)
Waning Moon
Moon phase: Fourth Quarter
Color: White

Moon Sign: Taurus
Incense: Marjoram

28 Thursday

Independence Day (Peruvian)
Waning Moon
Moon phase: Fourth Quarter
Color: Green

Moon Sign: Taurus
Moon enters Gemini 2:17 pm
Incense: Myrrh

29 Friday
Pardon of the Birds (French)
Waning Moon
Moon phase: Fourth Quarter
Color: Pink

Moon Sign: Gemini
Incense: Vanilla

---

30 Saturday
Micman Festival of St. Ann
Waning Moon
Moon phase: Fourth Quarter
Color: Indigo

Moon Sign: Gemini
Moon enters Cancer 5:09 pm
Incense: Sage

---

31 Sunday
Weighing of the Aga Kahn
Waning Moon
Moon phase: Fourth Quarter
Color: Amber

Moon Sign: Cancer
Incense: Juniper

July Birthstones

The glowing Ruby shall adorn
Those who in warm July are born;
Then will they be exempt and free
From love's doubt, and anxiety.

Modern: Ruby
Zodiac (Cancer): Emerald

August

1 Monday
Lammas
Waning Moon
Moon phase: Fourth Quarter
Color: Silver

Moon Sign: Cancer
Moon enters Leo 9:12 pm
Incense: Lily

Tuesday
Porcingula (Native American)
Waning Moon
New Moon 4:45 pm
Color: White

Moon Sign: Leo
Incense: Cinnamon

3 Wednesday
Drimes (Greek)
Waxing Moon
Moon phase: First Quarter
Color: Brown

Moon Sign: Leo
Incense: Lavender

4 Thursday
Cook Islands Constitution Celebration
Waning Moon Waxing
Moon phase: First Quarter
Color: Crimson

Moon Sign: Leo
Moon enters Virgo 3:34 am
Incense: Nutmeg

5 Friday
Benediction of the Sea (French)
Waxing Moon
Moon phase: First Quarter
Color: Purple

Moon Sign: Virgo
Incense: Cypress

6 Saturday
Hiroshima Peace Ceremony
Waxing Moon
Moon phase: First Quarter
Color: Blue

Moon Sign: Virgo
Moon enters Libra 12:57 pm
Incense: Rue

7 Sunday
Republic Day (Ivory Coast)
Waxing Moon
Moon phase: First Quarter
Color: Orange

Moon Sign: Libra
Incense: Heliotrope

August

8   Monday
Dog Days (Japanese)
Waxing Moon
Moon phase: First Quarter
Color: Gray

Moon Sign: Libra
Incense: Hyssop

9   Tuesday
Nagasaki Peace Ceremony
Waxing Moon
Moon phase: First Quarter
Color: Maroon

Moon Sign: Libra
Moon enters Scorpio 12:51 am
Incense: Ginger

☽   Wednesday
St. Lawrence's Day
Waxing Moon
Second Quarter 2:21 pm
Color: Yellow

Moon Sign: Scorpio
Incense: Bay laurel

11   Thursday
Puck Fair (Irish)
Waxing Moon
Moon phase: Second Quarter
Color: Turquoise

Moon Sign: Scorpio
Moon enters Sagittarius 1:24 pm
Incense: Carnation

12   Friday
Fiesta of Santa Clara
Waxing Moon
Moon phase: Second Quarter
Color: Rose

Moon Sign: Sagittarius
Incense: Yarrow

13   Saturday
Women's Day (Tunisian)
Waxing Moon
Moon phase: Second Quarter
Color: Gray

Moon Sign: Sagittarius
Incense: Magnolia

14   Sunday
Festival at Sassari
Waxing Moon
Moon phase: Second Quarter
Color: Gold

Moon Sign: Sagittarius
Moon enters Capricorn 12:11 am
Incense: Eucalyptus

August

15 Monday
Assumption Day
Waxing Moon
Moon phase: Second Quarter
Color: White

Moon Sign: Capricorn
Incense: Neroli

16 Tuesday
Festival of Minstrels (European)
Waxing Moon
Moon phase: Second Quarter
Color: Gray

Moon Sign: Capricorn
Moon enters Aquarius 7:52 am
Incense: Cedar

17 Wednesday
Feast of the Hungry Ghosts (Chinese)
Waxing Moon
Moon phase: Second Quarter
Color: White

Moon Sign: Aquarius
Incense: Marjoram

☺ Thursday
St. Helen's Day
Waxing Moon
Full Moon 5:27 am
Color: Green

Moon Sign: Aquarius
Moon enters Pisces 12:34 pm
Incense: Apricot

19 Friday
Rustic Vinalia (Roman)
Waning Moon
Moon phase: Third Quarter
Color: Pink

Moon Sign: Pisces
Incense: Orchid

20 Saturday
Constitution Day (Hungarian)
Waning Moon
Moon phase: Third Quarter
Color: Black

Moon Sign: Pisces
Moon enters Aries 3:18 pm
Incense: Ivy

21 Sunday
Consualia (Roman)
Waning Moon
Moon phase: Third Quarter
Color: Yellow

Moon Sign: Aries
Incense: Juniper

August

22 Monday
Feast of the Queenship of Mary (English)
Waning Moon
Moon phase: Third Quarter
Color: Ivory

Moon Sign: Aries
Sun enters Virgo 12:38 pm
Moon enters Taurus 5:19 pm
Incense: Clary sage

23 Tuesday
National Day (Romanian)
Waning Moon
Moon phase: Third Quarter
Color: Red

Moon Sign: Taurus
Incense: Bayberry

☾ Wednesday
St. Bartholomew's Day
Waning Moon
Fourth Quarter 11:41 pm
Color: Topaz

Moon Sign: Taurus
Moon enters Gemini 7:40 pm
Incense: Lilac

25 Thursday
Feast of the Green Corn (Native American)
Waning Moon
Moon phase: Fourth Quarter
Color: White

Moon Sign: Gemini
Incense: Clove

26 Friday
Pardon of the Sea (French)
Waning Moon
Moon phase: Fourth Quarter
Color: Coral

Moon Sign: Gemini
Moon enters Cancer 11:06 pm
Incense: Rose

27 Saturday
Summer Break (English)
Waning Moon
Moon phase: Fourth Quarter
Color: Indigo

Moon Sign: Cancer
Incense: Sandalwood

28 Sunday
St. Augustine's Day
Waning Moon
Moon phase: Fourth Quarter
Color: Gold

Moon Sign: Cancer
Incense: Frankincense

29 **Monday**
St. John's Beheading
Waning Moon
Moon phase: Fourth Quarter
Color: Lavender

Moon Sign: Cancer
Moon enters Leo 4:11 am
Incense: Lily

30 **Tuesday**
St. Rose of Lima Day (Peruvian)
Waning Moon
Moon phase: Fourth Quarter
Color: Scarlet

Moon Sign: Leo
Incense: Geranium

31 **Wednesday**
Unto These Hills Pageant (Cherokee)
Waning Moon
Moon phase: Fourth Quarter
Color: White

Moon Sign: Leo
Moon enters Virgo 11:22 am
Incense: Honeysuckle

August Birthstones

Wear Sardonyx, or for thee
No conjugal felicity;
The August-born without this stone,
'Tis said, must live unloved, and lone.

Modern: Peridot
Zodiac (Leo): Onyx

September ♍

☽ Thursday
Greek New Year
Waning Moon
New Moon 5:03 am
Color: Purple

Moon Sign: Virgo
Incense: Myrrh

---

2 Friday
St. Mama's Day
Waxing Moon
Moon phase: First Quarter
Color: Rose

Moon Sign: Virgo
Moon enters Libra 8:55 pm
Incense: Rose

---

3 Saturday
Founder's Day (San Marino)
Waxing Moon
Moon phase: First Quarter
Color: Brown

Moon Sign: Libra
Incense: Patchouli

---

4 Sunday
Los Angeles' Birthday
Waxing Moon
Moon phase: First Quarter
Color: Amber

Moon Sign: Libra
Incense: Almond

---

5 Monday
Labor Day • First Labor Day (1882)
Waxing Moon
Moon phase: First Quarter
Color: Silver

Moon Sign: Libra
Moon enters Scorpio 8:38 am
Incense: Narcissus

---

6 Tuesday
The Virgin of Remedies (Spanish)
Waxing Moon
Moon phase: First Quarter
Color: Red

Moon Sign: Scorpio
Incense: Basil

---

7 Wednesday
Festival of the Durga (Hindu)
Waxing Moon
Moon phase: First Quarter
Color: Yellow

Moon Sign: Scorpio
Moon enters Sagittarius 9:20 pm
Incense: Marjoram

September ♍

8   Thursday
Birthday of the Virgin Mary   Moon Sign: Sagittarius
Waxing Moon   Incense: Jasmine
Moon phase: First Quarter
Color: Turquoise

☾   Friday
Chrysanthemum Festival (Japanese)   Moon Sign: Sagittarius
Waxing Moon   Incense: Cypress
Second Quarter 7:49 am
Color: White

10   Saturday
Festival of the Poets (Japanese)   Moon Sign: Sagittarius
Waning Moon   Moon enters Capricorn 8:55 am
Waxing phase: Second Quarter   Incense: Sage
Color: Blue

11   Sunday
Coptic New Year   Moon Sign: Capricorn
Waxing Moon   Incense: Heliotrope
Moon phase: Second Quarter
Color: Yellow

12   Monday
National Day (Ethiopian)   Moon Sign: Capricorn
Waxing Moon   Moon enters Aquarius 5:28 pm
Moon phase: Second Quarter   Incense: Rosemary
Color: White

13   Tuesday
The Gods' Banquet (Roman)   Moon Sign: Aquarius
Waxing Moon   Incense: Ylang-ylang
Moon phase: Second Quarter
Color: Black

14   Wednesday
Holy Cross Day   Moon Sign: Aquarius
Waxing Moon   Moon enters Pisces 10:23 pm
Moon phase: Second Quarter   Incense: Lavender
Color: Topaz

15 Thursday

Birthday of the Moon (Chinese)
Waxing Moon
Moon phase: Second Quarter
Color: Crimson

Moon Sign: Pisces
Incense: Carnation

☺ Friday

Mexican Independence Day
Waxing Moon
Full Moon 3:05 pm
Color: Coral

Moon Sign: Pisces
Incense: Violet

---

17 Saturday

Von Steuben's Day
Waning Moon
Moon phase: Third Quarter
Color: Gray

Moon Sign: Pisces
Moon enters Aries 12:22 am
Incense: Pine

---

18 Sunday

Dr. Johnson's Birthday
Waning Moon
Moon phase: Third Quarter
Color: Gold

Moon Sign: Aries
Incense: Hyacinth

---

19 Monday

St. Januarius' Day (Italian)
Waning Moon
Moon phase: Third Quarter
Color: Gray

Moon Sign: Aries
Moon enters Taurus 12:58 am
Incense: Neroli

---

20 Tuesday

St. Eustace's Day
Waning Moon
Moon phase: Third Quarter
Color: Maroon

Moon Sign: Taurus
Incense: Ginger

---

21 Wednesday

UN International Day of Peace
Waning Moon
Moon phase: Third Quarter
Color: White

Moon Sign: Taurus
Moon enters Gemini 1:53 am
Incense: Bay laurel

22 Thursday
Mabon • Fall Equinox
Waning Moon
Moon phase: Third Quarter
Color: Green

Moon Sign: Gemini
Sun enters Libra 10:21 am
Incense: Balsam

◖ **Friday**
Shubun no Hi (Chinese)
Waning Moon
Fourth Quarter 5:56 am
Color: Rose

Moon Sign: Gemini
Moon enters Cancer 4:33 am
Incense: Thyme

24 Saturday
Schwenkenfelder Thanksgiving (German-American)
Waning Moon
Moon phase: Fourth Quarter
Color: Black

Moon Sign: Cancer
Incense: Ivy

25 Sunday
Dolls' Memorial Service (Japanese)
Waning Moon
Moon phase: Fourth Quarter
Color: Orange

Moon Sign: Cancer
Moon enters Leo 9:48 am
Incense: Eucalyptus

26 Monday
Feast of Santa Justina (Mexican)
Waning Moon
Moon phase: Fourth Quarter
Color: Silver

Moon Sign: Leo
Incense: Narcissus

27 Tuesday
Saints Cosmas and Damian's Day
Waning Moon
Moon phase: Fourth Quarter
Color: White

Moon Sign: Leo
Moon enters Virgo 5:43 pm
Incense: Cedar

28 Wednesday
Confucius's Birthday
Waning Moon
Moon phase: Fourth Quarter
Color: Brown

Moon Sign: Virgo
Incense: Lilac

29 **Thursday**
Michaelmas   Moon Sign: Virgo
Waning Moon   Incense: Mulberry
Moon phase: Fourth Quarter
Color: White

 Friday
St. Jerome's Day   Moon Sign: Virgo
Waning Moon   Moon enters Libra 3:52 am
New Moon 8:11 pm   Incense: Cypress
Color: Purple

September Birthstones

A maiden born when autumn leaves
Are rustling in September's breeze,
A Sapphire on her brow should bind;
'Twill cure diseases of the mind.

Modern: Sapphire
Zodiac (Virgo): Carnelian

October

1 **Saturday**
Armed Forces Day (South Korean)
Waxing Moon
Moon phase: First Quarter
Color: Gray

Moon Sign: Libra
Incense: Sage

---

2 **Sunday**
Islamic New Year
Waxing Moon
Moon phase: First Quarter
Color: Gold

Moon Sign: Libra
Moon enters Scorpio 3:43 pm
Incense: Marigold

---

3 **Monday**
Rosh Hashanah
Waxing Moon
Moon phase: First Quarter
Color: Lavender

Moon Sign: Scorpio
Incense: Rosemary

---

4 **Tuesday**
St. Francis's Day
Waxing Moon
Moon phase: First Quarter
Color: Black

Moon Sign: Scorpio
Incense: Bayberry

---

5 **Wednesday**
Republic Day (Portuguese)
Waxing Moon
Moon phase: First Quarter
Color: White

Moon Sign: Scorpio
Moon enters Sagittarius 4:26 am
Incense: Lilac

---

6 **Thursday**
Dedication of the Virgin's Crowns (English)
Waxing Moon
Moon phase: First Quarter
Color: Green

Moon Sign: Sagittarius
Incense: Nutmeg

---

7 **Friday**
Kermesse (German)
Waxing Moon
Moon phase: First Quarter
Color: White

Moon Sign: Sagittarius
Moon enters Capricorn 4:40 pm
Incense: Orchid

October ♎

8 Saturday
Okunchi (Japanese)
Waxing Moon
Moon phase: First Quarter
Color: Black

Moon Sign: Capricorn
Incense: Sandalwood

☾ Sunday
Alphabet Day (South Korean)
Waxing Moon
Second Quarter 12:33 am
Color: Amber

Moon Sign: Capricorn
Incense: Juniper

10 Monday
Columbus Day (observed)
Waxing Moon
Moon phase: Second Quarter
Color: Ivory

Moon Sign: Capricorn
Moon enters Aquarius 2:33 am
Incense: Hyssop

11 Tuesday
Medetrinalia (Roman)
Waxing Moon
Moon phase: Second Quarter
Color: Gray

Moon Sign: Aquarius
Incense: Cinnamon

12 Wednesday
Yom Kippur
Waxing Moon
Moon phase: Second Quarter
Color: Yellow

Moon Sign: Aquarius
Moon enters Pisces 8:43 am
Incense: Honeysuckle

13 Thursday
Fontinalia (Roman)
Waxing Moon
Moon phase: Second Quarter
Color: Purple

Moon Sign: Pisces
Incense: Clove

14 Friday
Battlefield Festival (Japanese)
Waxing Moon
Moon phase: Second Quarter
Color: Pink

Moon Sign: Pisces
Moon enters Aries 11:08 am
Incense: Alder

15 Saturday

The October Horse (Roman)
Waxing Moon
Moon phase: Second Quarter
Color: Blue

Moon Sign: Aries
Incense: Magnolia

☺ Sunday

The Lion Sermon (British)
Waxing Moon
Full Moon 12:23 am
Color: Orange

Moon Sign: Aries
Moon enters Taurus 11:04 am
Incense: Almond

---

17 Monday

Sukkot begins
Waning Moon
Moon phase: Third Quarter
Color: Silver

Moon Sign: Taurus
Incense: Clary sage

---

18 Tuesday

Brooklyn Barbecue
Waning Moon
Moon phase: Third Quarter
Color: Maroon

Moon Sign: Taurus
Moon enters Gemini 10:30 am
Incense: Cedar

---

19 Wednesday

Our Lord of Miracles Procession (Peruvian)
Waning Moon
Moon phase: Third Quarter
Color: Brown

Moon Sign: Gemini
Incense: Lavender

---

20 Thursday

Colchester Oyster Feast
Waning Moon
Moon phase: Third Quarter
Color: Turquoise

Moon Sign: Gemini
Moon enters Cancer 11:28 am
Incense: Balsam

---

21 Friday

Feast of the Black Christ
Waning Moon
Moon phase: Third Quarter
Color: Rose

Moon Sign: Cancer
Incense: Yarrow

October ♏

○ **Saturday**
Goddess of Mercy Day (Chinese)
Waning Moon
Fourth Quarter 3:14 pm
Color: Indigo

Moon Sign: Cancer
Moon enters Leo 3:34 pm
Sun enters Scorpio 7:46 pm
Incense: Patchouli

23 Sunday
Sukkot ends
Waning Moon
Moon phase: Fourth Quarter
Color: Yellow

Moon Sign: Leo
Incense: Marigold

24 Monday
United Nations Day
Waxing Moon
Moon phase: Fourth Quarter
Color: White

Moon Sign: Leo
Moon enters Virgo 11:16 pm
Incense: Lily

25 Tuesday
St. Crispin's Day
Waning Moon
Moon phase: Fourth Quarter
Color: Red

Moon Sign: Virgo
Incense: Ylang-ylang

26 Wednesday
Quit Rent Ceremony (English)
Waning Moon
Moon phase: Fourth Quarter
Color: Topaz

Moon Sign: Virgo
Incense: Bay laurel

27 Thursday
Feast of the Holy Souls
Waning Moon
Moon phase: Fourth Quarter
Color: Crimson

Moon Sign: Virgo
Moon enters Libra 9:51 am
Incense: Jasmine

28 Friday
Ochi Day (Greek)
Waning Moon
Moon phase: Fourth Quarter
Color: Coral

Moon Sign: Libra
Incense: Vanilla

October ♏

29 Saturday
Iroquois Feast of the Dead
Waning Moon
Moon phase: Fourth Quarter
Color: Brown

Moon Sign: Libra
Moon enters Scorpio 10:01 pm
Incense: Rue

☽ Sunday
Meiji Festival (Japanese)
Waning Moon
New Moon 1:38 pm
Color: Amber

Moon Sign: Scorpio
Incense: Hyacinth

---

31 Monday
Halloween • Samhain
Waxing Moon
Moon phase: First Quarter
Color: Lavender

Moon Sign: Scorpio
Incense: Neroli

October Birthstones

October's child is born for woe,
And life's vicissitudes must know;
But lay an Opal on her breast,
And hope will lull those foes to rest.

Modern: Opal or Tourmaline
Zodiac (Libra): Peridot

November ♏

1 Tuesday
All Saints' Day
Waxing Moon
Moon phase: First Quarter
Color: Scarlet

Moon Sign: Scorpio
Moon enters Sagittarius 10:43 am
Incense: Geranium

2 Wednesday
All Souls' Day
Waxing Moon
Moon phase: First Quarter
Color: Yellow

Moon Sign: Sagittarius
Incense: Marjoram

3 Thursday
St. Hubert's Day (Belgian)
Waxing Moon
Moon phase: First Quarter
Color: Turquoise

Moon Sign: Sagittarius
Moon enters Capricorn 11:05 pm
Incense: Apricot

4 Friday
Mischief Night (British)
Waxing Moon
Moon phase: First Quarter
Color: White

Moon Sign: Capricorn
Incense: Alder

5 Saturday
Guy Fawkes Night (British)
Waxing Moon
Moon phase: First Quarter
Color: Blue

Moon Sign: Capricorn
Incense: Pine

6 Sunday
Daylight Saving Time ends
Waxing Moon
Moon phase: First Quarter
Color: Orange

Moon Sign: Capricorn
Moon enters Aquarius 8:55 am
Incense: Hyacinth

☽ Monday
Mayan Day of the Dead
Waxing Moon
Second Quarter 2:51 pm
Color: Gray

Moon Sign: Aquarius
Incense: Clary sage

November ♏

8 Tuesday
Election Day (general)
Waxing Moon
Moon phase: Second Quarter
Color: Black

Moon Sign: Aquarius
Moon enters Pisces 4:45 pm
Incense: Basil

---

9 Wednesday
Lord Mayor's Day (British)
Waxing Moon
Moon phase: Second Quarter
Color: White

Moon Sign: Pisces
Incense: Honeysuckle

---

10 Thursday
Martin Luther's Birthday
Waxing Moon
Moon phase: Second Quarter
Color: Crimson

Moon Sign: Pisces
Moon enters Aries 8:45 pm
Incense: Nutmeg

---

11 Friday
Veterans Day
Waxing Moon
Moon phase: Second Quarter
Color: Pink

Moon Sign: Aries
Incense: Violet

---

12 Saturday
Tesuque Feast Day (Native American)
Waxing Moon
Moon phase: Second Quarter
Color: Black

Moon Sign: Aries
Moon enters Taurus 9:24 pm
Incense: Rue

---

13 Sunday
Festival of Jupiter (Roman)
Waxing Moon
Moon phase: Second Quarter
Color: Yellow

Moon Sign: Taurus
Incense: Marigold

☺ Monday
The Little Carnival (Greek)
Waxing Moon
Full Moon 8:52 am
Color: Ivory

Moon Sign: Taurus
Moon enters Gemini 8:23 pm
Incense: Narcissus

15 Tuesday

St. Leopold's Day
Waning Moon
Moon phase: Third Quarter
Color: Maroon

Moon Sign: Gemini
Incense: Bayberry

16 Wednesday

St. Margaret of Scotland's Day
Waning Moon
Moon phase: Third Quarter
Color: Topaz

Moon Sign: Gemini
Moon enters Cancer 7:57 pm
Incense: Lilac

17 Thursday

Queen Elizabeth's Day
Waning Moon
Moon phase: Third Quarter
Color: White

Moon Sign: Cancer
Incense: Carnation

18 Friday

St. Plato's Day
Waning Moon
Moon phase: Third Quarter
Color: Purple

Moon Sign: Cancer
Moon enters Leo 10:14 pm
Incense: Cypress

19 Saturday

Garifuna Day (Belizean)
Waning Moon
Moon phase: Third Quarter
Color: Brown

Moon Sign: Leo
Incense: Patchouli

20 Sunday

Revolution Day (Mexican)
Waning Moon
Moon phase: Third Quarter
Color: Amber

Moon Sign: Leo
Incense: Frankincense

◑ Monday

Repentance Day (German)
Waning Moon
Fourth Quarter 3:33 am
Color: White

Moon Sign: Leo
Moon enters Virgo 4:34 am
Sun enters Sagittarius 4:22 pm
Incense: Lily

November

22 Tuesday

St. Cecilia's Day
Waning Moon
Moon phase: Fourth Quarter
Color: Red

Moon Sign: Virgo
Incense: Ginger

23 Wednesday

St. Clement's Day
Waning Moon
Moon phase: Fourth Quarter
Color: White

Moon Sign: Virgo
Moon enters Libra 2:42 pm
Incense: Lavender

24 Thursday

Thanksgiving Day
Waning
Moon phase: Fourth Quarter
Color: Purple

Moon Sign: Libra
Incense: Myrrh

25 Friday

St. Catherine of Alexandria's Day
Waning
Moon phase: Fourth Quarter
Color: Rose

Moon Sign: Libra
Incense: Mint

26 Saturday

Festival of Lights (Tibetan)
Waning Moon
Moon phase: Fourth Quarter
Color: Gray

Moon Sign: Libra
Moon enters Scorpio 3:01 am
Incense: Sandalwood

27 Sunday

St. Maximus' Day
Waning Moon
Moon phase: Fourth Quarter
Color: Gold

Moon Sign: Scorpio
Incense: Heliotrope

28 Monday

Day of the New Dance (Tibetan)
Waning Moon
Moon phase: Fourth Quarter
Color: Gray

Moon Sign: Scorpio
Moon enters Sagittarius 3:46 pm
Incense: Rosemary

November

🌙 **Tuesday**
Tubman's Birthday (Liberian)
Waning Moon
New Moon 7:18 pm
Color: White

Moon Sign: Sagittarius
Incense: Cinnamon

---

30 Wednesday
St. Andrew's Day
Waxing Moon
Moon phase: First Quarter
Color: Brown

Moon Sign: Sagittarius
Incense: Honeysuckle

November Birthstones

Who first come to this world below,
With drear November's fog, and snow,
Should prize the Topaz's amber hue,
Emblem of friends, and lovers true.

Modern: Topaz or Citrine
Zodiac (Scorpio): Beryl

December

1 Thursday
Big Tea Party (Japanese)
Waxing Moon
Moon phase: First Quarter
Color: White

Moon Sign: Sagittarius
Moon enters Capricorn 3:52 pm
Incense: Mulberry

2 Friday
Republic Day (Laotian)
Waxing Moon
Moon phase: First Quarter
Color: Pink

Moon Sign: Capricorn
Incense: Vanilla

3 Saturday
St. Francis Xavier's Day
Waxing Moon
Moon phase: First Quarter
Color: Black

Moon Sign: Capricorn
Moon enters Aquarius 2:44 pm
Incense: Magnolia

4 Sunday
St. Barbara's Day
Waxing Moon
Moon phase: First Quarter
Color: Yellow

Moon Sign: Aquarius
Incense: Eucalyptus

5 Monday
Eve of St. Nicholas' Day
Waxing Moon
Moon phase: First Quarter
Color: Silver

Moon Sign: Aquarius
Moon enters Pisces 11:31 pm
Incense: Hyssop

6 Tuesday
St. Nicholas' Day
Waxing Moon
Moon phase: First Quarter
Color: Red

Moon Sign: Pisces
Incense: Geranium

☽ Wednesday
Burning the Devil (Guatemalan)
Waxing Moon
Second Quarter 4:03 am
Color: Topaz

Moon Sign: Pisces
Incense: Lilac

December

8   Thursday
Feast of the Immaculate Conception
Waxing Moon
Moon phase: Second Quarter
Color: Purple

Moon Sign: Pisces
Moon enters Aries 5:15 am
Incense: Clove

9   Friday
St. Leocadia's Day
Waxing Moon
Moon phase: Second Quarter
Color: Coral

Moon Sign: Aries
Incense: Orchid

10   Saturday
Nobel Day
Waxing Moon
Moon phase: Second Quarter
Color: Gray

Moon Sign: Aries
Moon enters Taurus 7:41 am
Incense: Ivy

11   Sunday
Pilgrimage at Tortugas
Waxing Moon
Moon phase: Second Quarter
Color: Orange

Moon Sign: Taurus
Incense: Juniper

12   Monday
Fiesta of Our Lady of Guadalupe (Mexican)
Waxing Moon
Moon phase: Second Quarter
Color: Lavender

Moon Sign: Taurus
Moon enters Gemini 7:41 am
Incense: Lily

☻   Tuesday
St. Lucy's Day (Swedish)
Waxing Moon
Full Moon 7:06 pm
Color: White

Moon Sign: Gemini
Incense: Basil

14   Wednesday
Warriors' Memorial (Japanese)
Waning Moon
Moon phase: Third Quarter
Color: Brown

Moon Sign: Gemini
Moon enters Cancer 7:09 am
Incense: Marjoram

15 Thursday

Consualia (Roman)
Waning Moon
Moon phase: Third Quarter
Color: Crimson

Moon Sign: Cancer
Incense: Jasmine

16 Friday

Posadas (Mexican)
Waning Moon
Moon phase: Third Quarter
Color: White

Moon Sign: Cancer
Moon enters Leo 8:15 am
Incense: Mint

17 Saturday

Saturnalia (Roman)
Waning Waning Moon
Moon phase: Third Quarter
Color: Indigo

Moon Sign: Leo
Incense: Pine

18 Sunday

Feast of the Virgin of Solitude
Waning Moon
Moon phase: Third Quarter
Color: Gold

Moon Sign: Leo
Moon enters Virgo 12:52 pm
Incense: Almond

19 Monday

Opalia (Roman)
Waning Moon
Moon phase: Third Quarter
Color: Ivory

Moon Sign: Virgo
Incense: Rosemary

◑ Tuesday

Commerce God Festival (Japanese)
Waning Moon
Fourth Quarter 8:56 pm
Color: Gray

Moon Sign: Virgo
Moon enters Libra: 9:40 pm
Incense: Cinnamon

21 Wednesday

Yule • Winter Solstice
Waning Moon
Moon phase: Fourth Quarter
Color: White

Moon Sign: Libra
Sun enters Capricorn 5:44 am
Incense: Honeysuckle

December

22 Thursday
Saints Chaeremon and Ischyrion's Day Moon Sign: Libra
Waning Moon Incense: Myrrh
Moon phase: Fourth Quarter
Color: Green

23 Friday
Larentalia (Roman) Moon Sign: Libra
Waning Moon Moon enters Scorpio 9:32 am
Moon phase: Fourth Quarter Incense: Thyme
Color: Purple

24 Saturday
Christmas Eve Moon Sign: Scorpio
Waning Moon Incense: Sage
Moon phase: Fourth Quarter
Color: Brown

25 Sunday
Christmas Day • Hanukkah begins Moon Sign: Scorpio
Waning Moon Moon enters Sagittarius 10:19 pm
Moon phase: Fourth Quarter Incense: Marigold
Color: Amber

26 Monday
Kwanzaa begins Moon Sign: Sagittarius
Waning Moon Incense: Clary sage
Moon phase: Fourth Quarter
Color: White

27 Tuesday
Boar's Head Supper (English) Moon Sign: Sagittarius
Waning Moon Incense: Cedar
Moon phase: Fourth Quarter
Color: Black

28 Wednesday
Holy Innocents' Day Moon Sign: Sagittarius
Waning Moon Moon enters Capricorn 10:12 am
Moon phase: Fourth Quarter Incense: Bay laurel
Color: Yellow

December

Thursday
Feast of St. Thomas à Becket
Waning Moon
New Moon 1:53 am
Color: Turquoise

Moon Sign: Capricorn
Incense: Carnation

---

30 **Friday**
Republic Day (Madagascan)
Waning Moon
Moon phase: First Quarter
Color: Rose

Moon Sign: Capricorn
Moon enters Aquarius 8:29 pm
Incense: Yarrow

---

31 **Saturday**
New Year's Eve
Waning Moon
Moon phase: First Quarter
Color: Blue

Moon Sign: Aquarius
Incense: Rue

Kwanzaa and Hanukkah end January 1, 2017

December Birthstones

If cold December gives you birth,
The month of snow, and ice, and mirth,
Place in your hand a Turquoise blue;
Success will bless whate'er you do.

Modern: Turquoise or Blue Topaz
Zodiac (Sagittarius): Topaz

Fire Magic

The Wild Hunt

by Charlynn Walls

There is a great deal of mystery surrounding the Wild Hunt, especially as it deals with the Fae, or the Fair Folk. The Hunt is said to ride across the fields and moors, silently unless they choose for the Hunt to be heard. What would be more chilling to witness: a procession of riders on horseback and hounds moving at a ground-eating gallop, the crunch of the earth pulsing beneath them as they move forward—or that same group of charging participants that move without a hoof betraying a footfall?

The Hunt itself is relentless. It seeks out the prey with the single-mindedness of a lone individual, which is then extended to the hunting party and its hounds. They tear across the landscape in pursuit, seemingly tireless, and do not stop until the prey is caught. The prey can sometimes be an animal or a person.

Those who have glimpsed the Wild Hunt on a moonlit night are either fortunate to witness as it passes by, or they themselves fall victim and become a part of the Hunt. Either way they leave the encounter profoundly changed.

In Welsh lore, the Hunt is usually led by the King of the Fairies and his hounds. The sound of those riding by gives life to the sounds of the night. The Hunt itself is neither good nor evil; like nature itself, it is neutral. It is the embodiment of nature itself and how we relentlessly pursue life.

The Hunt does not usually leave the realm of the Fae, but at times it can. If the Hunt is summoned elsewhere, it can appear, or if the prey slips into the mortal realm, the hounds will sense that and pursue it through that realm.

Harnessing the Power of the Hunt

The Hunt is a powerful force. It should not be called upon lightly and should be used with the utmost care. One way you can harness the power of the Hunt is as a means of protection. Should you fear for your own safety or that of your family, you can call on the Hunt to pursue the person/entity attempting to cause you harm.

Being responsible, and staying as neutral as possible, you will want to include the directions to pursue, but not to catch. The pursuit will cause sufficient anxiety and fear that the person attempting to harm you will stop.

The following is a scenario for someone who is being stalked. If the typical and mundane means of persuasion including legal channels have failed to yield results, then you might want to utilize this ritual.

Ritual to Summon the Hunt

You will want to gather the following items to be used during your ritual:

A black candle
A white candle
Sage or sandalwood incense or spray
Herbs related to the Fae: moonflower, thyme, elecampane, elderberry, clover
Honey cakes, milk and honey, mead
Offering of a coin or other shiny item

The ritual should take place near dusk, as the Hunt typically rides at night. As with any dealing with the Fair Folk, you should be careful to show your respect.

Make sure that you are alone or will not be interrupted. Set up your ritual space and cleanse the area. Cleansing the area with sage or sandalwood is a good choice and often has spray alternatives if you are unable to use smoke because of an allergy. You will want to have a black and a white candle at the center of your workspace. The black will be for your prey and the white for the pursuers. Set out your quarter candles in the correct alignment for your area. Spread about bits of greenery such as moonflowers, thyme, elecampane, elderberry, or clover. These are all plants and herbs that share a connection to the realm of the Fae.

Set out cakes and ale onto the altar along with a seperate plate and cup. Typical offerings consist of honey cakes and mead or milk and honey. You will also want to have a shiny trinket or coin that you are willing to part with.

Cast your circle with a formal calling to the elementals associated with each quarter.

Calling the Quarters

North: *Hail to the Guardians of the Watchtowers of the North. I call to the Gnomes, the guardians of earth. Grant me stability within my current situation. Hail and welcome!*

East: *Hail to the Guardians of the Watchtowers of the East. I call to the Sylphs, the guardians of air. Grant me your wisdom on this delicate situation on this night. Hail and welcome!*

South: *Hail to the Guardians of the Watchtowers of the South. I call to the Salamanders, the guardians of fire. Grant me the flame of protection to keep those I love safe from harm. Hail and welcome!*

West: *Hail to the Guardians of the Watchtowers of the West. I call to the Undines, the guardians of water. Grant me control of my emotions and hear my plea. Hail and welcome!*

Invocation

This is the time to acknowledge the Fae associated with the Wild Hunt. You will want to be specific in your request. Make certain they understand that while you want them to give chase, you do not wish the individual in question true harm. Provide a length of time that the Hunt will last. A week to two should be sufficient time to refocus the individual. A suggested invocation would be:

Lords and Ladies of the Wild Hunt, I ask tonight for your assistance. A person of questionable intention has made themselves known to me. I fear for my safety. For the next fortnight, set the hounds and hunters on his/her scent. Keep only to the chase and once the time has passed release them from the Hunt. I seek only to refocus their sights upon themselves. Please take this coin as a token of my appreciation.

Do not make the Fae any promises you cannot keep. If you promise to set out offerings each week for the next month, make sure you do so or you may end up losing items that will reappear a month or more after they have gone missing.

Honoring Your Guests/Cakes and Ale

Take a moment to acknowledge your honored guests. Make no mistake, they are there, and you will be best served in acknowledging them and offering them refreshments. You can set out your honey cakes and offering on a small plate along with a cup of milk and honey or mead reserved just for them. You can say the following to make the offering complete:

Honored guests, Lords and Ladies of the Fae, Guardians of the Watchtowers, you honor me by your presence and by listening to my plea. Please accept my tokens of appreciation and restore yourselves this night.

Once you have presented the cakes and ale to your guests you can take some for yourself and begin to restore your own strength before closing out the circle.

Releasing the Quarters

West: *Guardians of the Watchtowers of the West, the Undines, I thank you for your time and tempering of my own emotional waters. Hail and farewell!*

South: *Guardians of the Watchtowers of the South, the Salamanders, I thank you for your time and your flames of protection. Hail and farewell!*

East: *Guardians of the Watchtowers of the East, the Sylphs, I thank you for your time and your wisdom regarding these issues. Hail and farewell!*

North: *Guardians of the Watchtowers of the North, the Gnomes, I thank you for your time and your strength in order to give me stability. Hail and farewell!*

Closing the Circle

Take a moment to contemplate the strength of the Fae, the elementals, and all those who have gathered to participate in your rite. Thank them all again and make certain you realease them back to their realms.

I thank all who have gathered to lend their energies to this task. You have your own responsibilities to which you must now attend. This circle is open. Hail and farewell to you all!"

This should hopefully keep any unwanted visitors from lingering.

Urban Crossroads:
Magick in the City

by Cassius Sparrow

Crossroads magick is one of the oldest forms of magick, dating back to ancient Greco-Roman times. Crossroads have been widely regarded as an area between worlds, neither here nor there, where anything could—and would—happen. They are a place where deals are struck, bargains are made, and a witch can shake hands with a god.

Crossroads magick commonly conjures the image of a lone, dark, usually dirt road, so practitioners understandably want some measure of security. The full moon hangs low and heavy in the sky. As the witch approaches the crossroads, they know they are alone out there.

However, for many witches this scenario simply isn't possible. Whether by circumstance or by choice, the nearest deserted road could be hours away. So what's a city witch to do? With some planning and resourcefulness, crossroads magick can even be accessible to a witch living and practicing in a big city.

Finding the Crossroads

Sometimes not just any crossroads will work for your spell or deal. A crossroads—especially in a city—is brimming with energy that is waiting to be accessed. Before you begin, ask yourself what kind of crossroads you might need for your work. Would your spell benefit more from a crossroads that is busy, filled with the constant rush of traffic, or do you need to find somewhere quieter? Are you working a spell or are you trying to contact a crossroads spirit? Hermes, god of the crossroads, is more partial to the number four, and a witch wishing to contact him would have the most luck at a four-way crossroads. Similarly, Hekate is best summoned at a three-way crossroads.

When making your handy list of crossroads, it's best to have a map—or maps—of the area. Pick several crossroads options and begin staking your claim. Observe the traffic schedule and make note of the best times for safety and discretion. Mark your crossroads on your map and keep your schedule close by. You should also make a note of how to get to the crossroads. Can you walk, or do you have to drive? Is there safe parking available nearby? Can you access the crossroads by public transportation?

At this point, crossroads magick in the city may seem daunting, but don't let the effort overwhelm you! The reward will be well worth the extra work.

The Spell

So you've found the perfect crossroads, drawn up your map, and are ready to work some magick. Now what?

Now, you take a look at your spell itself.

Does your spellwork require you to leave an element of your work or offerings at the crossroads?

Environmental impact should be your first concern. Keep local wildlife in mind when leaving out food offerings, and try not to leave the container, even if it is biodegradable.

Be aware of your surroundings when leaving spellwork elements. In residential areas and business areas, leaving burnt candle stubs, pictures, or poppets could be taken the wrong way. There are also littering laws to consider. If you are able, try burying the spell "ingredients" at the crossroads to prevent problems, and to ensure that they will not be disturbed by curious passerby or local wildlife.

Perhaps part of your spell requires actions on your part at the crossroads. Your crossroads schedule plays an important role in this. Hopefully, you were able to find a crossroads where you could be afforded some privacy for discreet spellwork at some point in the day—or night. In some cases, though, discretion is simply not an option. At this point, you'll need to bring the crossroads to you by making your own.

The earliest roads were little more than dirt and stone, well-worn by pedestrian traffic. You'll use both to build your symbolic crossroads. Clear your altar or workspace, giving yourself plenty of room to work. Collect stones from the crossroads that you would have liked to work at and arrange them in an "X." Sprinkle them with dirt, also collected from your preferred crossroads. To further enhance this, craft a small road sign, as crude or elaborate as you wish. When you are finished working your spell, carefully gather the remnants of your work and leave them at the real crossroads. You can deconstruct the symbolic crossroads you created and respectfully return what you borrowed, or you leave it up at your altar or workspace for future use. If you do decide to leave it up, remember to periodically return to the original crossroads to collect small amounts of dirt to keep the energy flowing and to feed the magickal properties of your miniature crossroads.

The Traveler on the Road

Nearly every culture has a cautionary tale regarding finding a stranger at a crossroads, usually after midnight. The details vary from tale to tale, but in many, there is a lot of syncretism between this "stranger" and the most famous god of the crossroads—Hermes.

Hermes is most well-known as the divine messenger from the Greek Pantheon, as well as being a notorious trickster god. But Hermes is well-acquainted with those secret places where realms meet—and intersect. As a psychopomp as well, it is also his job to guide souls to the underworld. This busy god *can* be petitioned to aid the adventurous witch, provided the reasons and cause are interesting enough to get his attention.

To call on Hermes, you must travel to his domain. This means your symbolic crossroads will not be enough to get his favor. Go to a four-way crossroads either at sunrise or sunset. Appeal to him as god of merchants by bringing something physical to exchange. Gifts of honey, wine (or honeyed wine), cinnamon, goat's milk, and gold or copper coins are all suitable. If you want to petition him for help with accomplishing a goal, bring symbols of his own conquests and accomplishments: caduceus charms, peacock feathers, and representations of the lyre or winged sandals are perfect for this. You can also appeal to him as a parent who loves his children fiercely. So if you are requesting his aid concerning your own, bring pictures of your children, and his—the most famous of these being the god Pan and the daimon Hermaphroditos.

Big-city crossroads are truly the prime place to invoke Hermes. They are nearly as busy as he is! If you are approaching him for help in monetary matters, be prepared for anything. This trickster god wears many masks, and the god of merchants and small-business owners also happens to be a patron of thieves. Always be aware of what is going on in the environment around you; never sacrifice safety for discretion. Bring a cellphone with you—you won't offend him, as he is a god of communication—though be sure to set it to *silent*, as not to be disrespectful. He will want your full attention. Let a friend know where you are going, though if you're not comfortable explaining why, you can keep that to yourself.

Approach the crossroads with your offering and the details of your petition. You can call on him for nearly anything. From money to luck, writers, gamblers, parents, and thieves can all approach Hermes to make a deal. It's the details that are important. You'll want to get his attention—and keep it—leaving little room for tricks.

Hermes is a wild god, so offer your gift first. Whistle, hum, or sing a tune to stir the energy in the area. Then talk: tell him your request, be as detailed as possible and be specific about what you intend to do in return for his aid—remember, you are making a deal with a crossroads god for help, and he will expect payment. Don't worry—Hermes has very few uses for souls. Payment can be in the form of actual money offered to the god, a promise to maintain a shrine for him, food and wine as an offering, or volunteer work in his honor. Be sure that it is an equal exchange. When you are finished, thank him for his time.

≈

So, you left your offering, called upon Hermes, and offered your deal. How do you know it's been heard?

Hermes has ways of making himself known. The sudden appearance of a hawk or a rabbit is the most obvious sign that the god has heard and agreed to your terms, especially in very urban areas. Look for signs around you as well, especially in traffic. Wing motifs on a car that passed you? Vanity plates with interesting messages? Those are also good signs that you've been heard. But perhaps you've been waiting for a while, with no sign of wildlife or traffic—or maybe the signs you've received seem inconclusive.

Set a signal for yourself, such as when you see a neon sign or when a red car passes. Plug your ears, open your eyes, and walk—keeping safe or walk on the sidewalk—toward a crowd or busy area. When you see your signal, unplug your ears and listen carefully. Music is a powerful message from Hermes, so pay careful attention to any song lyrics you may hear. The first words you heard will be your answer.

Don't allow an obvious *No* of silence to discourage you. Take some time, ask yourself if this is something you truly wanted or needed. Think about your petition and be sure that it wasn't impossible or demanding—did you ask for a lot all at once? Was your payment acceptable and equal? Answer these questions, rework your petition, and try again. After a reasonable amount of silence, however, it's safe to say that you were unable to pique his curiosity regarding the deal. Always thank Hermes for his time—you never know when you may need his help.

If you have struck a bargain with this crossroads god, make certain to fulfill your end of the deal in a timely and respectful manner.

It's never a good idea to try and cheat a trickster!

The Magic of Twin Souls

by Shawna Galvin

When the connection between two people is so powerful it's like magic—it's as if it is of an otherworldly source or supernatural. Romantic love can feel this way, and so can a friendship. Sometimes bonds are so potent that two people feel as one, or twin souls. For example, the characters of Catherine (Cathy) and Heathcliff, from Emily Brontë's *Wuthering Heights*, have a connection that oftentimes leaves the readers with an over-whelming haunting sensation about these fictional characters' lives. Throughout the years, so many have been influenced by the magic of Emily Brontë's telling of this soul connection between Cathy and Heathcliff.

As I began to examine how this piece of the story relates to the overwhelming haunting feeling of love Cathy and Heathcliff have for one another, I dug deeper into other elements that relate to the idea of love as a twin soul.

Musician Kate Bush was so mesmerized by *Wuthering Heights* that she wrote a song with the same title, which was also her debut in the late 1970s. As a girl, Bush watched a film version and said, "I just caught the end where Cathy's ghost was coming through the window to Heathcliff. I had always been interested in spooks and sci-fi and that grabbed me." Through her lyrics, live performances, and videos of her song, she "becomes" Cathy's ghost looking for Heathcliff. She believes she has the ghost of Brontë to thank for the massive success of her debut song, "Wuthering Heights." Bush said she felt "a closeness" to the dead writer that went beyond just sharing a birthday with her—July 30. Kate Bush gives Emily Brontë credit for inspiring her—and helping the song's success from beyond. In a sense, Bush was promoting her book in a commercial way. The song was so popular that was referenced in a well-known *Wuthering Heights* textbook.

I had never read *Wuthering Heights* or seen any of the films until my husband brought home a free copy from our local book shack, where people drop off their unwanted books. My husband just thought it looked like something I'd like to read. Emily Brontë's story led me to research the idea of twin souls and so much more. Brontë was a mystic in her own right. She created fictional characters who demonstrate the supernatural and spiritual connection of their soul love (which is also tormented) and soul connection. She created literary magic that transcends time, and can link into deeper reflections and meditations on topics such as love, mysteries, and secrets, and how these can translate into our present lives. Before getting more in-depth about twin souls, I will start to examine how the ideas came about by analyzing the narrator of *Wuthering Heights*.

The Narrator's Perspective

While reading *Wuthering Heights*, it's easy to forget that Lockwood is the narrator who "writes" the actual story of Wuthering Heights in his diary in the year 1801. The intellect of Emily Brontë's storytelling is genius; we see the story relayed from

Lockwood's perspective as the history of Cathy and Heathcliff was told to him by their lifelong housekeeper, Ellen (Nelly) Dean. Not much is known about Lockwood's character, unless one analyzes him a bit closer. He reflects on his stay, and how he came to Wuthering Heights in the first place after a summer of failed *amour* (romance). Lockwood inquires about renting Thrushcross Grange as a way to escape, or get away from society. He talks about his first meeting with Heathcliff in his diary, and what he has seen and heard in Yorkshire, 1801.

When Lockwood goes to Wuthering Heights to inquire about renting out Heathcliff's vacant residency, Thrushcross Grange, he meets Heathcliff and experiences his odd lifestyle that leads to further unpleasant experiences while there. He ends up spending the night at Wuthering Heights due to bad weather and other incidents. Before his overnight stay, Lockwood reveals glimpses of his own lost love. As he examines Heathcliff's character and his home, Lockwood flashes back to his own amour that he let go of. He reveals this by talking about enjoying a month of "fine weather at the sea-coast" and how he was "thrown into the company of a most fascinating creature: a real goddess in my eyes, as long as she took no notice of me. I 'never told my love' vocally; still if looks have language, the merest idiot might have guessed I was over head and ears: she understood me at last, and looked a return— the sweetest of all imaginable looks. And what did I do? I confess it with shame—shrunk icily into myself, like a snail; at every glance retired colder, and farther; till finally the poor innocent was left to doubt her own senses, and overwhelmed with confusion at her supposed mistake ... " This sets up the premise for the entire story, and Lockwood's curiosity about the love between Heathcliff and Cathy becomes a great lesson to both him and the reader. As he discovers more about them, their story unfolds. Lockwood talks about being cold (maybe afraid to love this "goddess") and that he knew he made a mistake, which grieved his heart, and that is most likely why he was in seclusion at Thrushcross Grange. When Lockwood meets Heathcliff, he seems to understand that there is more to Heathcliff than a monster, and that a broken heart is the cause of this. In this way, Lockwood identifies with Heathcliff and wants to know more about him and his relationship with Cathy.

Their love story comes into play right away in the first chapters of *Wuthering Heights*.

Lockwood talks about how Heathcliff is handsome but morose. He knows by instinct that Heathcliff will not show his feelings or kindness in any way, due to his loss, and will never be loved or hated again. And after making his observations of Heathcliff, Lockwood says, "No, I'm running on too fast: I bestow my own attributes over liberally on him." And after this meeting with Heathcliff, we see Lockwood's experiences when he spends the night at Wuthering Heights. From here, Lockwood's curiosity unleashes a story of twin souls: Heathcliff and Cathy.

Heathcliff's servant of two years, Zillah, has motives of her own. She gives Lockwood brandy and takes him to a room to sleep, then warns him that her master, Heathcliff, would never let anyone lodge in that particular room willingly. Zillah tells Lockwood to hide his candle and to make no noise.

Lockwood's experience in this room opens the mystery of Heathcliff and Cathy. He places his candle on the window ledge and sees writing scratched in paint: "*Catherine Earnshaw, Catherine Heathcliff, and Catherine Linton.*" He then finds an antique calfskin book containing the writings of a

young Catherine Earnshaw dating back a quarter of a century. There is a sketch of one of the longtime caretakers, the terrifying religious tyrant, Joseph. The passage Lockwood reads from her diary talks about how it was an awful Sunday. Cathy misses her father (who passed away), and talks about how her brother, Hindley, and the caretaker, Joseph, are mean to both her and Heathcliff (who was adopted into the family by her father, and he adored Heathcliff). They live in a sheltered and isolated place where Joseph and Hindley seemingly abuse Catherine and Heathcliff. Her document is a disturbing account of their lives, but it demonstrated their bond, even at a young age. Catherine talks about how she and Heathcliff are going to rebel. And then Lockwood falls into a dream while reading Catherine's diary. It is Lockwood's dream that further unleashes the mystery and love between Catherine and Heathcliff.

The most haunting and revealing part of Lockwood's dream is when he has a dream within a dream. It starts with a fir branch hitting his window and stirring his sleep, and then he hears the voice of Cathy. Lockwood punches through the glass to stop the noise, but when he does, her voice comes through and she grabs his wrist. Lockwood screams in terror at Cathy's ghost trying to get in through the window and wakes up Heathcliff.

Heathcliff finds Lockwood in the room, which angers him, but at the same time, Heathcliff dashes tears from his eyes. Then Heathcliff sends Lockwood away to his own room. Lockwood is angry and terrified, and before going to Heathcliff's room, he witnesses Heathcliff open the lattice in an uncontrollable passion of tears as he calls out: "Come in! Come in!" "Cathy, do come. Oh do—*once more*! Oh! My heart's darling; hear me this time Catherine, at last!" Lockwood observes that no spectre or ghost shows itself, but snow and wind whirl wildly through the window—and blow out the light. Lockwood feels this presence from across the room. Heathcliff goes into deeper agony after this night.

Lockwood's night in Catherine's old room was instigated by Zillah's own curiosities about the supernatural in that household, but also it is as if Catherine's ghost wanted Lockwood to see her and the things that led him to investigate the story of love and Heathcliff and Cathy. His dream is a supernatural experience that spooked him, as it felt like more than a dream. This experience causes the story of Catherine and Heathcliff to further unfold.

Lockwood's breaking of the window in his dream is a constant movement in this story to break through the constant constraint of civilization and personal consciousness, and also a movement toward "passionate fulfillment of consciousness." A powerful force develops, where life unifies dark and light, and this is seen through the beauty and the pain of Catherine and Heathcliff's love, which is of a higher level and takes us into the twin soul realm.

The Intenstity of Twin Souls

It's easy to become so lost in the dream that the reader forgets that Lockwood is telling it through his diary. He's writing this story in his diary from Thrushcross Grange as he recovers from his journey to Wuthering Heights. Through the telling of *Wuthering Heights*, we see the importance and bond of a love that cannot be broken because it is so powerful, even from beyond. This story of Heathcliff and Catherine changes Lockwood, since he is the "writer" of it—telling it through his point of view, as Nelly Dean had told it to him.

Twin soul love even haunts the fictional characters in the story, those who knew Catherine and those who did not. The story lives on in fiction and in reality, and causes greater thoughts about the aspect of soul twins, and greater insight and understanding of twin souls and soul mates. Twin soul love is eternal and even lives on in fictional characters as a great lesson to us.

When thinking about the magic and higher power of love, there are many ways to view it, and it is commonly described as a soul mate (or romantic partner). A general outline of soul mates includes but is not limited to:

Temporary Soul Mate (Karmic): Two people enter each other's lives for a reason—to teach a lesson. This can be romantic love, but doesn't last long. Or this can be a friendship, to teach you about yourself—we have many of these types of relationships in a lifetime. This is a connection of human nature, and not believed to be that of a connection on a higher spiritual plane— although the lessons learned from these relationships might help us move to a higher plane individually. These relationships can include coworkers, family members, or even close friends.

Companion Soul Mate: This partnership can be intimate and romantic; this person can be a spouse (though not destined to be with us forever) for a purpose, short-lived relationship, maybe to help progress in life, or give birth to a child, or for other reasons.

Twin Flame, also called Twin Soul: This is believed to be the highest form of soul mate connection. This is like your other half, like finding yourself. This kind of connection might always be around us, but not apparent. One soul at human level involves awareness, balance, and integration of masculine and feminine components—raising individual and joint consciousness. Soul consciousness.

~

It's believed by some that twin souls choose to journey apart throughout lifetimes to gain a full spectrum of the human experience—and then move closer together through the final lifetime together on the planet to ascend together.

This love is a gift, blessing life at a planetary level and beyond—even these fictional twin flames. Thus, the magic of love, soul twins, and stories.

There are so many beliefs and teachings on how soul mates should be understood and even categorized, and even how they recognize each other or not in certain lifetimes. Also, there is the belief that once together, their soul will automatically bring to the surface past experiences that need to be released. This can be hard at times in the healing process, where soul twins might lash out at one another.

Emily Brontë put up so many obstacles in *Wuthering Heights* to demonstrate how overpowering Catherine and Heathcliff's soul connection was, but in their lifetime together, they were unable to really experience and let go to truly love and trust each other in the environment they were raised in and lived in. This also shows that sometimes life situations might keep you and your twin soul apart, but you never let go and eventually might come back to each other if it is a true soul connection, as Cathy and Heathcliff's was. Later, when Cathy says she is Heathcliff, the idea of soul twins/love is where one cannot live in peace without the other in life. Heathcliff and Catherine were restless without each other.

The continued importance of dreams and soul twins unfolds when, later in *Wuthering Heights*, Nelly tells Lockwood of her con-

versation with Catherine, who said to Nelly: "I've dreamt in my life dreams that have stayed with me ever after, and changed my ideas; they've gone through me, like wine through water, and altered the color of my mind." Then Catherine reveals her great love for Heathcliff in an ironic conversation that he will overhear; Heathcliff only catches the part of it that makes it clear that Catherine will not marry him. Heathcliff leaves before hearing Catherine reveal her love for him to Nelly when she famously says: "He's more myself than I am. Whatever souls are made of, his and mine are the same . . .Nelly, I am Heathcliff!" A line referenced in pop culture to this day.

Although there are only hints of Lockwood's lost love, in a sense, this is his love—or twin soul story too. Perhaps he might have learned a lesson about his own lost love, and we can only speculate on this at the end of the book. It could be that Lockwood might meet up with his lost love another time? Perhaps this is a lesson for all who encounter this, as a deeper and higher plane level of understanding of twin souls.

Some believe that the characters of Cathy and Heathcliff were based on local legends of the two giants or gods of the Moors, Belenus, one of the most ancient and widespread deities worshiped in

Celtic Britain, Austria, Italy, and Spain, and his consort, Belisama, the goddess of lakes, rivers, fire, crafts, metalworking, and light—later known as Rombald and Saint Catherine by the Christians in their quest to pacify all Pagan deities, in Keighley, United Kingdom.

Belenus ("bright one") likely gave his name to the fire festival of Beltane, which was originally linked with his cult. Celts associated him with pastoralism, healing, and fountains; the Romans connected Belenus as the god of light with their god Apollo.

Christian Celts prayed to their most powerful goddess, Belisama ("summer bright" or "most brilliant one"), who shared common traits with the goddess Brigid, as well as the Roman goddess Minerva. Many inscriptions bearing the name "Belisama Minerva" reflect the blending of deities and traditions that often occurred in Roman-occupied lands. There is also the River of Belisama—The River Ribble, in Lancashire, England.

No myths of Belenus or Belisama have survived to modern times. Their names have only been found in classical texts and stone inscriptions, suggesting the presence of sanctuaries; the names of geographic features also hint at the existence of their cults.

~

As humans, sometimes we are "trapped" in certain circumstances throughout our physical lifetimes—the soul is much more than this, and the soul in the afterlife as Brontë demonstrates with Catherine and Heathcliff, who are wandering the moors in eternal bliss. One can only wonder if Emily Brontë thought her story was being channeled to her from a higher power, like Marguerite Porete, Kate Bush, and now, even me. Such is the literary magic of Emily Brontë. Through her writing, she shares the love of twin souls on a higher plane, and we continue to learn from it and wonder about the mysteries of the twin soul love, despite Catherine and Heathcliff's situation at Wuthering Heights.

Through the immortality and the afterlife of literature and the magic of literature, Cathy and Heathcliff remain restless without each other. Only in death are they truly happy together forever. Their love story haunted Lockwood so much that he understood love on a higher level, as a divine love, and this made him wonder about his own love that he'd let go of—a goddess, as he said from the start—and led to one of the greatest stories of all time, in the brilliant mastery of Emily Brontë's *Wuthering Heights*.

For Futher Study

Campbell, Marie. *Strange World of the Brontës*. Wilmslow, Cheshire: Sigma Leisure, 2001.

Melani, Lilia. "Emily Bronte. Religion, Metaphysics, and Mysticism." Brooklyn College. October 16, 2003. http:// academic.brooklyn.cuny.edu/english/melani/novel_19c /wuthering/mystic.html

Nicholson, Monique. "From Pre-Christian Goddess of Light to Saints of Light." *Canadian Woman Studies* 17/1 (1997): 14. ProQuest Central. October 20, 2013. http:// pi.library.yorku.ca/ojs/index.php/cws/article/view/8893.

Porete, Marguerite. Trans. Ellen L. Babinsky.*The Mirror of Simple Souls*. New York: Paulist Press, 1993.

Thompson, Dorothy. "Demystifying the Soul Mate Relationship." *Goddess Flight*. http://www.goddessflight.com /articles/Demystifying-the-Soul-Mate-Relationship.html #.U8bLp41dVQY

Williamson, Mitch. "Belenus and Belisama." *Old Maps, Expeditions and Explorations*. September 5, 2012. mitchtestone .blogspot.com/2012/09/belanus-and-belisama.html

Concentrated Candle Magic: A Surprising Method

by Mickie Mueller

The witch had cast her spell and sent her energy, and as she gathered her magical tools and packed them lovingly away in the old trunk, her spell candle flickered brightly upon the altar. She knew it worked its magic even as she got ready for bed and the moon sunk deep in the night sky. By the next morning the candle would be low in the jar, but still burning while she got ready for work. Later on, she would dispose of the leftover wax. Over the next month or so, she would see the magical working manifest.

We all have performed candle magic in this way. Gather our tools, work our spell, and leave the candle to burn out. What if you could continue to send your intention into that candle flame for the entire time that it burns, from the moment that it's lit until the flame is extinguished and only a small tendril of smoke dances forth? That would be great, but we have dishes to wash, jobs to go to, e-mails to answer. In this modern world, no one has time for that. We all love those little spell candles; they burn for about two hours, so if we do our work early enough, the candle is burned up before bedtime. Tealights are very convenient; they're gone in about four hours or so. But even with those small candles, few people even have time for a two- or four-hour ritual. Plus, how would you possibly keep your concentration going for that long? I have come up with a new method of candle magic that takes about twenty minutes from start to finish and is a superconcentrated blast of energy that from my experiments seems to manifest both quickly and concisely.

I have two words for you: birthday candles. No, I'm not kidding. Many of you reading this have grabbed one out of the kitchen drawer to use in a pinch, but you didn't consider

it serious magic, more like a dirty little secret. If you're one of those people (admit it, you know you are), you probably found that it worked fine. Of course it worked, because as we all know it's your powerful intention that creates the magic and that's what's important: your focus. Enter the humble birthday candle. The concept here is that this is a tiny candle. A standard birthday candle burns for about twenty minutes. If you're capable of taking the time to sit down and watch a TV show while fast-forwarding through commercials on your DVR, then you have time to make some groundbreaking, life-altering magic! So let's think outside the box, shall we?

Concentrated Candle Magic Method

Here's my method of concentrated candle magic, from start to finish. First set your intention, and draft a short couplet or sentence. It should be something you can easily memorize after repeating it a couple of times because you'll be focusing on the candle flame, not reading a big long magical charm from a book. There is also no room for ultraflowery language; simplicity is the key. Write down your finalized sentence or couplet on a small slip of paper. Now you may inscribe and anoint your candle if you wish, then surround it with or roll it in herbs. You may also place other symbols around your candle like stones, coins, or flowers to add their energy to the magic. As you light the candle, you'll begin repeating your intention over and over. Continue chanting the intention over and over as you stare at the base of the flame. Don't take your eyes off of it. As you chant, the words will become more and more intense. At times, the words will become more like sounds than words; this means you're entering a trance state. The words develop a slight tune on their own as you weave your magic. This is the point when your creative mind is in control; this is where manifestation is created. Continue, unwavering, and watch the flame; this flame lives only to serve your purpose. Finally as it shrinks and disappears into a tiny finger of smoke, you utter the words:

By my will, with harm to none, so mote it be.

Zam, pow, bam! Didn't know you had that in you did you? I've seen signs of manifesting within ten minutes to twenty-four hours of using this concentrated candle magic method.

Using a birthday candle to create magic as described above has many benefits. Birthday candles come in every color you can imagine, even black, gold, and silver. You can easily find them at your local grocery store or party supply store, and you can store a large selection of candles in a small box or drawer. On top of that, the fact that you can use them for some quick and powerful spells means you have a great new magical tool in your magical arsenal. If you want to get really fancy, you can easily find sources online for hand-dipped birthday candles created by artisans and craftspeople.

Candle Colors, Stripes, and Dots
Birthday candles come in a variety of colors and color combinations, so let's explore how to use these color correspondences in some concentrated candle magic of your own. If you usually use color correspondences that differ from these listed, feel free to use colors as you are accustomed.

White: A balance of all colors; cleansing, healing, spiritual enlightenment, truth-seeking, lunar energy, may be substituted for any color candle

Yellow: Activity, creativity, joy, brings power of concentration and imagination to a ritual, confidence, solar energy

Orange: Communication, creativity, ability to speak one's mind, ambition, career matters, legal matters, self-confidence

Pink: Friendship, romance, feminine energy, honor, healing the heart, inviting love

Red: Passion, love, fertility, strength, courage, willpower; increases magnetism, health

Purple: Psychic power, success, ambition, independence, financial rewards, healing

Blue: Spiritual energy, obtain wisdom, harmony, peace, truth, guidance, tranquility

Green: Prosperity, fertility, success, good luck, money, harmony, and rejuvenation, wealth, abundance

Black: Banish evil or negativity, uncrossing, banishing bad habits, protection

Silver: Remove negativity, protection, stability, psychic abilities, lunar and goddess energy

Gold: Luck, prosperity, abundance, success, harnessing the powers of the universe, solar and god energy

Peppermint striped candles: When using these candles with spirals of both color and white, apply the appropriate color correspondence from above and add an extra boost of energy from your higher power for the greatest good. These candles also represent the connections to our spiraling universe and all life.

White candles with polka dots: Use these candles to lift joyful energy surrounding the situation and infuse your magic with laughter.

Now that you have your collection of candles in concentrated candle magic form, you'll need little candleholders. We're familiar with using birthday candles for a different kind of candle magic—making a wish and blowing them out. This time, our candle will burn all the way down until nothing is

left, so those plastic candleholders are probably not the best idea, but don't worry, I have options. The simplest one is a small dish of sand or salt. You can just pop that candle right into the sand or salt and you're ready to go. You'll need a minimum of ¼ inch of sand or salt and then be very careful to have it on a very stable surface before you light it or it will just tip over. When you use this method, you'll have a little blob of wax left at the end to dispose of as you see fit.

You can also make a nice little candleholder from a used tealight holder. You'll need the kind with the little round, metal wick tabs on the bottom of the candle. After burning a tealight, save the round metal wick tab. Pull out any little bit of wick that remains and then use a small nail to round out the pinched neck part. Then all you have to do is press the bottom of the birthday candle onto the wick tab. (The neck will dig into the candle, holding it upright). Now you can place the candle into most candleholders, tealight holders, votive holders, even most taper holders will work. If you put it back into the tealight holder when you burn it, be sure to remove any wax left over from the tealight out of it first. If you don't, the wax will melt down and pool up at the end of your candle burning and add a lot of extra time to the burning of your candle.

I also found some really sweet, silver-plated birthday candleholders online by searching for "metal birthday candleholders." Some are shaped like different animals, so you could choose a totem animal or an animal that corresponds with your magical purpose—dove for love, frog for transformation, fish for abundance, etc.

Concentrated Candle Magic Spells

Here are a few examples of concentrated candle magic using birthday candles. You should feel free to change theses spells to fit your needs. I also hope you use them as inspiration to create some concentrated candle magic spells of your own.

Fast-Cash Spell

Use a green or gold birthday candle, anoint with your favorite money oil, mint, or olive oil. Place coins, acorns, malachite, or any prosperity symbols you like around the candle.

Light your candle and using the method described above as you visualize all the cash you need already in your hands or the dollar amount in your bank account, repeat the following chant to raise energy, repeating until the candle burns out:

I need money, make it fast, owed or earned, check or cash.

Once your spell is done, money that you are owed or an opportunity to earn some extra money should be forthcoming.

Quick Negative Influence Destruction

This spell breaks up negative influences coming from other people whether sent purposefully or accidentally. Jealousy, anger, or belittling thoughts projected toward you can build up and become a very real negative force, so burn it off. Use a black candle; anoint it with protection oil like lavender or olive oil. Either set the candle in sea salt or surround it with a circle of sea salt. Include black onyx, agate, or any protective talismans or amulets around the candle that you wish.

Light your candle and using the concentrate candle magic method described above visualize any powers against you being drawn to the black candle and becoming trapped there by the sea salt; see it coming from every nook and cranny of your life. Repeat the following chant to raise energy, repeating until the candle burns out:

Negative force to candle black, I draw you in, you can't go back.

When the candle burns out, all the negative influences expire with it, unable to escape. If there's any wax left behind, wrap it in brown paper and drop it in a public trash can or Dumpster far from your home. The salt can become a barrier across your front door.

Clear the Air Spell

Life can be stressful, and sometimes the little annoyances of daily life can bog down the flow of happy energy. If there was a big blowout that put everyone is on edge, those energies can linger in your home, feeding the flame. It's time to give the environment a boost, clear the air, and raise the energy that will promote healing—and you need to do it on the double.

Use a white, blue, or a white and blue striped candle anointed with lavender or peppermint oil. Include sandalwood or frankincense incense, clear quartz, rose quartz, amethyst, a Quan Yin statue, a dove, or any symbols you like for peace or spiritual positive energy.

Light your candle and using the concentrate candle magic method described above visualize ripples of positive energy emanating from the candle and filling the house. Repeat the following chant to raise energy, repeating until the candle burns out:

Raise the vibes, clear the air, lighten up, with great care.

When your spell is done, shake off the gloom and watch as things start to run more smoothly.

Successful Day Spell

If you've got a big day ahead, job interview, house hunting, or big meeting, you can do this one either the night before,

or wake up a half hour early and get a jump on a successful outcome to your plans.

Use a purple or gold candle, depending on the situation; you might use a green striped candle anointed with success oil of your choice, cinnamon, or bergamot oil. Include tiger eye, citrine, and oak. You may place your business cards, resume, or symbols of the success you plan to achieve around the candle if you wish.

Light your candle and using the method described above as you visualize yourself already achieving a favorable outcome and feeling successful, repeat the following chant to raise energy repeating until the candle burns out:

Success is mine, as I command;
I have it all in the palm of my hand.

As soon as the candle burns out, go out there into the world with confidence and make it happen!

Pre-Party House Blessing

If you have a houseful of guests arriving and you want to add some extra mojo to help make the gathering full of fun and enjoyable for everyone involved, this is your spell. Take a little time in the morning before you finish your preparations and make some magic.

Use a white candle with yellow or orange polkadots, and anoint with oil squeezed from the outside of an orange peel. Include an invitation if you used one, a CD of music you plan to play, flowers that will be on your table, turquoise, clear quartz, green chrysoprase, or any items that bring you joy and remind you of fun.

Light your candle and using the concentrated candle magic method described above visualize smiles on the faces of your guests, hear the sound of laughter, glasses clinking, and lively conversation. Repeat the following chant to raise energy, repeating until the candle burns out:

We gather today in laughter and fun, from the first arrival till the day is done!

Finish your last-minute preparations for your party. It will be a magnificent success!

~

These are just a few examples of what you can do with the concentrated candle method of candle magic using birthday candles. Most candle spells can be converted to this method as long as you remember the simple rules: keep your chant short and simple, raise energy during the entire life of the flame, and plan on about twenty minutes of time to focus on your goal. Use your imagination and have fun working with the surprising power of the simple birthday candle.

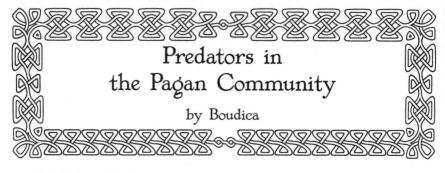

Predators in the Pagan Community

by Boudica

With a title like that, I am sure many of you have chills just thinking that this could actually happen in your community. There are others who should be warned that this article might contain triggers, and it might be a good idea to read this in small doses and avoid the parts that may hurt. Or get someone to give you the "digest" version.

Discussing predators is not a gentle topic. So, warnings have been given. Let's discuss what issues we have faced and the solutions available to handle this in our communities today.

This article is not meant to excuse predatory behavior. People do this for all sorts of reasons, and sometimes for no reason at all. Whatever the reasons, the fact remains that predators exist, they are attracted to our community for many reasons, and we have to deal with them.

What do we mean by a predator? When the topic comes up, many people immediately think of sexual predators, but there are many types—and all of them try to obtain something illicitly from someone else. In this article, we are discussing predators in all forms—those who prey on our community, taking what is not theirs from those who trust, who don't know any better, or who had a moment when they weren't thinking clearly.

The Pagan community is comprised of many lifestyle groups, among which we can count poly-pagans, sexually expressive Pagans, gay, lesbian, bisexual, and transgender Pagans, and those who just like taking off their clothes and running around as nature intended. We are a trusting community, offering help and assistance where and when we can—even when we have very little to offer. We love being who we are and should not repress our choices because of the behavior of others. Rather, we are looking at what to do when we find predatory behavior in our community.

For some, our sexual expressiveness sets off many triggers, especially for those who have suffered sexual suppression or have been at the mercy of deviant behavior. Some predators see it as a free-for-all, a feast of sexual promiscuity. Others see this as open season and find us a niche in which to prey upon the innocent.

And because we are often so giving of ourselves, our time, and our funds, we also open a door to those who feel free to take what is offered. They feel that taking it all is their right or their privilege. We also offer potential financial resources to those who are inclined to take a free ride on such assets.

We have a culture that attracts two extreme types: the naive and those who exploit the same. Our community is full of triggers, and we have events that can set these triggers off in susceptible individuals without our realizing it.

Good Intentions

When I first started on the festival circuit, many of us had gone through the sexual revolution of the late 1960s. Free love and an end to sexual repression was a good thing. Workshops discussing sexuality and inviting individuals to push the old boundaries and live sexually unrepressed lives were offered at festivals. However,

many of those teaching the workshops did not have the necessary credentials. Some individuals attending these events and workshops jumped into these lifestyles without a second thought, and some embraced them fully without thinking about any kind of repercussions. There were no consequences—just embrace the freedom and the love. The workshops led us along, and we were pretty much convinced this was the way to go. And, for all intents and purposes, free love is a wonderful thing.

We should never encourage a lifestyle to anyone who is unsure. But yet, I remember teachers saying if you do not embrace this lifestyle fully then there is something wrong with you. Yes, I heard it several times, and it scared me half to death. Because, in a way, they were correct—some people may have issues that they need to deal with, and we were not providing the correct support or environment to deal with these issues. "Yeah, yeah," they said. "If you need help, get it." Where? How? The support resources just weren't there. Looking back on some of those classes, someone just wasn't thinking. It was simply assumed that everyone at those classes knew what they were doing and knew if they belonged there. They were wrong.

Looking back, it's easy to see how ill-prepared we were. We didn't have properly trained medical personnel available who could handle the situations that these kinds of workshops could create. And let's face it; most were there for the free love and the openness of relationships. No one was thinking about being responsible.

As a result, we had instances of rape. And while not all instances were actual rape, charges were filed. And charges were dropped. In the end, formal charges notwithstanding, the incidents at these events definitely and directly caused broken relationships, unintended pregnancies, and mental breakdowns.

These things did not happen often, and many folks never heard about these "side effects" of our events. But it did happen. And in some cases, workshops like this were never offered again. Some were offered privately. And the love-ins still happen at certain events. In many cases, there is no harm, no foul. But there are always the exceptions.

We have learned. We have grown.

Getting Responsible

It is up to the community hosting these events to try their best to make sure we are protected. No, it is not our place to try to prevent people from indulging in the freedoms we take for granted, but we do have the responsibility to offer a safe place for our community members should any issues arise. People are free to choose what courses they take and to also accept responsibility for their actions. But sometimes people are not aware of their own condition. While we cannot always prevent bad things from happening, the community should offer some kind of support system for those who fall into this category, because that is what community does. When we gather into a community, we choose to be responsible for all our members. And to be a true community, we need to realize this and take up all the associated responsibilities.

I know there will be a lot of shaking of heads and denying responsibility for these possibilities. What does it take to have a phone number handy to tap a mental health professional to be a resource, or ask a family planning organization if they would be willing to donate condoms or provide education at our events? You would be surprised by how much some organizations are willing to assist. We have competent doctors and nurses within our community who already volunteer to provide some basic help. I am sure they would know who to tap to provide an extra layer of protection and security to our community. All we have to do is ask. Open the dialogue, see what resources we have, and make that information available to our community members. This is really simple and costs us nothing.

Some communities already do this, and they deserve recognition for their initiative. But there are always beginners. Sharing this kind of information is another line of communication we need to cultivate.

～

Up to this point, I've focused on sexual predators, who deservedly garner a lot of attention. Yes, they are out there, we have seen them, and we have reported them. Sometimes they are removed; sometimes they run. We have their names and many communities will exchange information about well-known predators with each other. There are resources now in place that we need to tap on a regular basis in order to protect our communities and ourselves. Communicate with other communities. Communicate with authorities. Communication is our best weapon against most types of predators. And there are other types of predators.

Swindlers and Scammers

We also have instances where individuals in our community prey on our people financially. They may be from our own groups, or they may be attracted to our community because we are so open.

These people pick our pocketbooks and steal our assets. From the house guest who never leaves to those who rob our community savings, these predators come from within as well as from outside our communities. We have the scammers, the con artists, and the suit-wearing financial executives who will take your money and then disappear. Some of them come in and hit fast; others will stick around and take from us slowly so we don't realize our pockets are being picked. Then there are the ones who

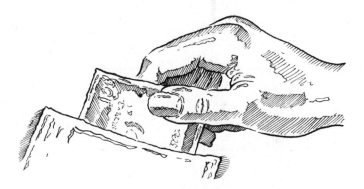

will repeatedly steal from individuals again and again until they are recognized, at which point they move on to another community to steal again.

We are such a trusting community of people. When we see someone in need, we tend to be very generous—even to the point of opening our doors and inviting them into our homes. This can get real messy, to the point of lawsuits.

I've also seen this played in reverse, where the predator invites someone in need into their home, takes everything they have, and then kicks them out, leaving them truly destitute.

We also have the Internet swindles. Although this type of predatory bottom-feeding has been around for a while, it seems to be taking off lately. Be careful of the "crowdfunding" option. We have some very worthwhile individuals we can support within the community, but there are "opportunities" out there to lose your hard-earned money. Not too long ago, starting a store or running an event was a major undertaking, in part because of the financial commitment. On the plus side, that monetary investment demonstrated how serious people were about the project.

These days, someone calling themselves a pagan and needing startup cash to run an "Internet storefront" or start a new "Pagan event" can post on a crowdfunding site, and we tend to jump in with both feet, only to find there is no floor.

How can we manage these problems? How do we deal with this?

There are two answers. First, always vet your resources. Get references; do not trust until you have a reason to trust. This is especially true when dealing with money. Banking institutions are always your best bet for holding your funds and putting a legal instrument in place to assure that your money is protected. Retain a lawyer when contracts are placed on the table. If you are going to spend money, make sure it will be well spent and that you have a legal way to address a failed contract. Do your homework! Be aware! If you don't know the individual personally and you don't have the cash, then leave it alone and let those with investment resources and a good background checker handle the heavy lifting.

Second, we should do the same with new members. Ask where they have been before they came to you, and get references. Make sure you know who you are dealing with when you invite someone into your home. Call those references—don't just look at them and say, "Ooohh, a big name! Impressive!" People drop names all the time. That does not mean they have ever met.

For festivals and events—I cannot say this enough—vet your presenters and vendors and make sure you are dealing with honest and reputable individuals. Even then, you should have professional resources and insurance in place to handle potential legal

240

and financial issues. Going the extra mile not only makes the community safer at your festival, it also protects you. If you don't know how to deal with every scam and perpetrator, ask those who hold successful events and learn how to deal with potential issues before they happen to you.

Policing Your Event

When dealing with predators, I want to make sure each community understands this clearly. If you encounter a predator and someone in your community is harmed, or the community itself is a victim, please press charges. Take it directly to the police and a lawyer! It's tempting to deal with the "small" issues yourself to avoid giving your event a black eye, but even a minor incident could spiral out beyond your capabilities.

We seem to want to protect the community when it comes to someone being seriously injured. But if you witnessed a car crash, wouldn't you report it to the police? The same goes with predators. The reason they can get away with things is because we let them. If we are not willing to take the responsibility to report and press charges, then this individual is free to do it again and again. By our inaction, we are essentially responsible if this person injures another time.

We are talking about rape, physical harm, unintended pregnancy, abuse, illegal drug use, forced drug use, theft, embezzlement, and whatever else these people see fit to impose on an individual before they are done and move on. Yes, this has happened in the Pagan community, as well as all other communities where people would rather remain silent than speak up.

To bring this home even further, websites run by the U.S. Department of Justice have statistics on abuse and sexual offenders available for everyone to read—Google NSOPW, the National Sex Offender Public Website, and read it. The FBI also has a website chock-full of crime statistics that will give you some idea of the scope of what is going on out there.

Addressing Incidents and Proactive Measures

And for those who are victims, please get professional help coping with the issues that arise—even if the repercussions do not surface until well after the initial incident. Whether it is losing

cash or being raped, there are social services out there, many of which are free of charge. Seek the help you need so you do not end up being a lifelong victim—or worse. We love our community members and it is tragic when we lose them. Always ask for help; there is nothing wrong with that. If we teach nothing else to our community members, we should be teaching that there is no shame in asking for help and support.

We also need to establish clear channels of communication between our organizations and our communities. We need to get the word out that we are connected, that we are not victims, and that we will react as a community when we are attacked by any kind of predator. And by making it known that we will not tolerate predators within our communities, we will lessen the chance of being infiltrated by predators and con artists. By taking this discussion to our membership, we put in place a support mechanism to combat predatory behavior and enable our membership to handle these kinds of issues when they arise. There is no "if," there is only "when."

Open dialogues in your communities and openly discuss this topic. Discuss what your community will and will not tolerate, discuss resources that are available in your communities, and make plans "just in case." Be prepared and hope you never have to implement these options.

Establish communication with other groups and organizations and make them aware that you are willing to get involved. Get to know who your law enforcement people are and find out who would be "Pagan friendly." You would be surprised how far we have come and how, in many communities, law enforcement is very Pagan friendly. If you don't know who to contact, we do have an organization of first responders, Officers of Avalon, and you can contact them.

～

We are but small communities, which makes us ideal for anyone who is looking for quick pickings, so we need to learn to protect ourselves. And while our communities are close-knit, there are times we need to make use of institutional support to handle issues that are beyond our scope. This means alerting the authorities. The only way we can prevent predators from repeating their crimes is to report them and press charges. What I have been discussing here are all crimes. Sexual violence, sex without permission, rape, theft, and embezzlement—these are all crimes! Treat them as such! Identify and report!

Take this discussion to the next level, your level, and let's see if we can bring safety to the Pagan community as a whole.

Polyamory and Paganism

by Autumn Damiana

O f all our deeply rooted societal norms, I would say that monogamy is extremely high on the list, if not at the very top. For some reason, people find it difficult to imagine a life outside of most traditional relationship patterns, even those who are extremely liberal in every other sense. And yet, because Pagans are a group that pushes cultural and societal limits further than most, nonmonogamy is pretty widely accepted in Pagan circles and even embraced in some cases, especially in the form of polyamory. I myself have been both polyamorous and Pagan for most of my adulthood. And let me tell you, it's not easy. If someone believes you are perverted because you are polyamorous or sinful because you are Pagan, watch how they react when they find out you are both! That being the case, why would Pagans want to add one more controversy to their lives? Are Pagans all just a bunch of attention-seeking libertines, or what?

The truth of the matter is that, unfortunately, many Pagans dabble in polyamory for all the wrong reasons, but there are some real diehards out there who make it work and would not want to live any other way. For starters, polyamory has a lot in common with Paganism. Much more so than most other religions, Paganism puts a strong emphasis on gender equality and respecting gender differences. The same is true of polyamory, which unlike many forms of nonmonogamy considers the needs and desires of women equal to men. Throughout the world, nonmonogamy is almost always structured around one man having many wives, mistresses, courtesans, or even prostitutes. In some societies, men might "lend" their women to other men like property. Polyamory not only rejects this idea of completely male-dominated relationships, it also values and encourages the feminine experience, which often has more to do with feelings than matters of the flesh. In addition, both Paganism and polyamory hold sexuality as sacred and believe that every human being is inherently sexual and has a right to sexual expression and gratification. In polyamory, the idea that sexually active men are "studs" and sexually active women are "sluts" is nonexistent. Polyamorists, like most Pagans, are also extremely accepting of LGBTQ lifestyles and will typically display a greater sensitivity toward same-sex involvement and gender identity. But in order to understand the deeper reasons that Pagans are attracted to polyamory, it is important to take a closer look and define what polyamory is and what it is not.

A Quick Exploration of Polyamory

Nonmonogamy has existed throughout history in many different forms, but polyamory is a fairly recent invention. The word itself was coined in the 1990s, purportedly by Morning Glory and Oberon Zell-Ravenheart, who are both well-known Pagans. The word "polyamory" loosely means "many loves," and differs in a few significant ways from other systems of nonmonogamy. Here is a basic breakdown:

Love

This is central to the concept of polyamory and is intrinsic in its definition. Polyamory is all about forming deep, loving, and sometimes lasting commitments with people other than your partner. This can take many forms: a long-distance love relationship, occasional sex with a lifelong friend, plural marriages, and many other possibilities. It may even be about loving or appreciating someone just because they make your partner happy, known in polyamorous circles as "compersion."

Sex

Obviously nonmonogamy may include intimacy with others. However, because polyamory is primarily about love, some polyamorous relationships do not include sex or even any physical contact at all. Polyamory is *not* about orgies, sex clubs, "swinging," "key parties," or "wife-swapping." These are all sexually based, nonmonogamous activities, and while polyamory can include any of these, sex is not the primary focus. Love, loving relationships, and emotional connections to others are what polyamory is all about, with or without sex.

Honesty

Transparency in all relationships is also a major tenet, and a truly successful polyamorous arrangement is one in which all participants, including spouse(s)/partner(s), lovers, and potential love interests are open and honest with each other. More importantly, you must be honest with yourself in determining what you want out of life, what you want out of your relationships, and what you are willing and not willing to do in practicing polyamory.

Respect

The only real "cheating" that goes on in polyamory is dishonesty. Because polyamory is about openness and transparency, each person must negotiate his or her terms, desires, goals, and boundaries, much in the same way that people do with BDSM. It is considered morally and ethically wrong to lie or withhold information about romantic involvements because consent is required among all partners. Common problems like hurt feelings, jealousy, possessiveness, fear, and other conflicts will arise sometimes, because even polyamorists are only human. However, being a respectful polyamorist means dealing with these issues calmly by communicating, negotiating, compromising, and honoring whatever agreements are made.

Responsibility

This is both the "no-brainer" and conversely the most important thing to consider in polyamory: *act responsibly*. Use protection. Practice safe sex. Avoid the drama/victim routine. Follow the rules you and your partner(s) have decided on. Do not neglect your personal obligations (family, partner/ spouse, kids, work, finances, etc.). That being said, polyamory is usually not just a "fling" or sexual recreation, so part of your responsibility is to help meet your partner(s) needs. Not all polyamorous relationships are "out"; many are kept secret because of societal pressures, family disapproval, or even legal issues. Responsibility includes having an understanding among individuals how public or private their polyamorous relationships and lifestyles should be.

Happiness

Ultimately, polyamory is about achieving a greater happiness than a monogamous relationship can provide. When sustained correctly, a polyamorous relationship can extend the love, affection, intimacy, and/or emotional fulfillment between two people to three, four, five, or even more, because love begets love, and people soon realize that the more love they give, the more they have. Common polyamorous patterns involve primary and secondary relationships (for example, having a primary spouse and a secondary lover); a V (or Vee), in which two partners are involved with another partner, but not each other; a Triad, in which three partners are all involved (which can have primary/secondary relationships or be equal); a Quad, in which a couple is involved with another couple (of any gender combination); or various group structures, which can include plural marriage, "polyfidelity" (polyamory restricted to a specific group of people), and general open relationships.

How Is This Related to Paganism?

Polyamory really doesn't have to do with any religion or culture per se. It is decidedly different from polygamy, in which one marries multiple spouses—usually one man with multiple wives (found in both the Mormon religion and Islam, among others). And yet, Pagans overall seem to be a culture that is particularly attracted to the idea of polyamory, even though there is no spiritual "duty" to have multiple partners, and partners are not required to be spouses or to bear children as is the case with most religiously sanctioned nonmonogamy. However, there are a number of reasons Pagans can benefit from polyamory.

The Charge of the Goddess

In this well-loved and often-cited piece, the Goddess states that "all acts of love and pleasure are my rituals." Polyamorists assume that this really means *all* acts of love and pleasure, not just those experienced with one's spouse or primary partner. Granted, the "harm none" rule of the Wiccan Rede should also be observed in these acts, which is where the ethics of polyamory come into play.

The Great Rite

Some covens still enact the true Great Rite, and I can't imagine how difficult it would be if the pair who did this were expected not to feel any attachment to each other afterward.

If the two performing the Rite are not already involved but have other existing partners, a polyamorous relationship may be the answer to exploring this newfound connection. In this case, the two people in question may decide to put restrictions on the relationship, such as being intimate only in a sacred or ritual context.

Beltane Fires (or similar celebrations)

A traditional Beltane fire ritual supposedly suspends ordinary relationship attachments, and anyone and everyone is invited to dance, drink, make merry, and perhaps indulge in a little promiscuity for the night. While a "one-night stand" of this sort can be sacred to the God and Goddess, it does not qualify as polyamory by itself. However, it can be the catalyst for a future polyamorous relationship or a short-term way to test the compatibility between potential love interests. It might also provide an outlet or experimental opportunity for people to test the polyamorous lifestyle.

Ritual Energy Exchange

Polyamory most certainly exists among Pagans in a coven or circle setting, even if they don't know it. Sometimes the ritual exchange of energy, coupled with the long-standing friendship, trust, and familiarity of another member is enough to fuel romantic feelings for that person. In some cases, a powerful ritual can trigger lasting emotions between participants in a group even if they have never met before. If any of these people are in an existing relationship, polyamory can be a way to explore these new emotions with each other, since there is no implicit expectation of sex or intimacy. Things can progress slowly while each person processes their feelings and decides if they want to pursue a deeper relationship.

Multiplicity

Some polyamorists claim that the ability to love more than one partner is a natural ability that we all possess and is akin to loving more than one friend or more than just one of your children. Pagans are famous for this "more than one" philosophy: we may worship many deities, work with different pantheons,

uphold more than one tradition, have multiple religious practices, or travel many different spiritual paths. It is no wonder,
then, that Pagans might also gravitate toward this idea of "many
loves." For some, the freedom of a polyamorous relationship
pairs nicely with the freedom they find in a Pagan religious
practice, and the two become complementary lifestyles.

Further Investigation

So, have I piqued your interest in polyamory? I certainly don't
expect every Pagan who reads this article to adopt the lifestyle, but because polyamory has become so prevalent among
Pagans, I felt that an introduction was necessary. There are
currently quite a few books on polyamory that I have not read
because they were not around when I first became polyamorous. However, here are some excellent resources I found
immensely helpful and can personally recommend.

Pagan Polyamory: Becoming a Tribe of Hearts, by Raven Kaldera
(Llewellyn Publications, 2005.) This book is *the* authority
on polyamory relating specifically to Pagans.

The Ethical Slut, by Dossie Easton and Janet W. Hardy (Celestial Arts, 2009.) A fascinating read that I practically devoured, packed with useful information.

The Myth of Monogamy: Fidelity and Infidelity in Animals and People, by David P. Barash and Judith Eve Lipton (Henry Holt and Company, 2001.) This book provides scientific evidence that monogamy is not as natural as everyone assumes it is.

"A Bouquet of Lovers," by Morning Glory Zell (*Green Egg Magazine*, 1990.) Here is the article that started it all.

www.polyamory.org. Home of the alt.polyamory page, the original online polyamory resource. There are a lot of great links and must-read articles here.

www.lovemore.com. Originally a magazine about polyamory, Loving More has developed into an entire organization dedicated to polyamory education and support.

www.polymatchmaker.com. A tasteful polyamory dating site—people come here to find real relationships, *not* casual sex!

Envisioning Magic

by Dallas Jennifer Cobb

Vision boards are used in so many places and so many ways that they can sometimes seem like a tool of Corporate America. They are commonly used to brainstorm and develop ideas, to track a project's progress, or to visually keep track of the big picture. I have used vision boards to inspire weight loss, get fit, manifest a healthy relationship, and call in the house of my dreams. Recently, practitioners of "the law of attraction" have popularized vision boards as a tool for manifesting money, success, and financial gain.

Magic is "the power to transform energy at will" according to Pagan author Starhawk in *Dreaming the Dark: Magic, Sex, and Politics*, and envisioning magic is about using a vision board as a tool to work powerful magic by developing imagery, focusing intention, raising energy, affirming success, and generating transformation using images, words, color, and shape.

What Is a Vision Board?

A vision board is a tool that is both a process and product, enabling us to "envision" our dreams and invest multiple sources of energy into that vision in order to make it real. Making a vision board is the action that brings transformative energy to ideas.

In the mundane world, a vision board is a collage of words, pictures, colors, and images that represents our desires. It's a collection of symbols representing emotional yearning and determination while simultaneously evoking belief and commitment.

In the magical world, a vision board is a "place between the worlds," a magical place that anchors emotion and energy that duly engage the Law of Attraction, magnetically attracting good things to us. A vision board is a tool for working envisioning magic, and we all know that what happens between the worlds affects all worlds.

Steps to Envisioning Magic

The first step to envisioning magic is to be precise about your vision. Focus and be specific about what you want to manifest. Don't cast the net too wide or your energy will be diffused and ineffective. Focus on the positive versus the negative, and state what you want rather than what you don't want.

When I was selling my house and preparing to move into a new space, I learned the power of precision. I started a vision board that at first was highly chaotic and unfocused. Sure, I knew what I didn't want—a big house with

lots of yard and home-maintenance chores. I started my vision board with lists of what I didn't want, and then realized that I needed to focus on the solution, so I made lists of what I did want. Lots of ideas emerged about the sort of house I wanted, and this propelled me to find images reflecting those desires.

I kept looking at it, and then one day it dawned on me what was wrong. I had focused the board on the concept of "a house" and what I "wanted," when in actuality what I "needed" was to cultivate "a home." I took down the images, printed out the word HOME in block letters, and placed it in the center of the board. With precision, the vision quickly unfolded. HOME was joined by the words SAFETY, SECURITY, NURTURE, and COMFORT, and then the images began to amass. Letting the concept of "home" guide me, I was able to identify what features I needed to satisfy my deepest needs. Images reflecting the emotions associated with "home" replaced the vague wants of "a house." Precision brought the vision board to life and filled it with power.

Affirm the Goal

Once you have a precise vision, the next step is to put yourself in the picture. I added photos of me and my daughter: our faces turned toward the Sun; eating together at our harvest table, in circle with friends and community, and even a picture of us snuggled together on the couch. I wanted the home I was trying to manifest for the two of us to be filled with spirit, joy, nourishment, community, and connection. Images are not just about "picturing" what you are trying to manifest, but reminders to create and experience these emotional states. Choose pictures that evoke joy, feelings of love, contentment, and belonging, and these will draw more of those to you.

Be sure that your vision is something realistic and possible, grounded in your current economic reality and lifestyle. I live in Ontario, Canada, so I discarded pictures of Caribbean oceanside pavilions. I knew I wanted my new home to be in my current community, so I added a lot of little pictures of the village and the beach that we currently call home to the vision board. And I avoided pictures of million-dollar houses because they were not monetarily possible. We don't have to limit ourselves, and I encourage you to dream, but let those dreams be seeded in reality to have a chance to grow and flourish.

Believing in your vision and believing that you deserve it is fundamental to the success of manifesting it. For the most part, belief is the transformational energy behind envisioning magic, so make sure that you truly believe in what you seek to create. My most powerful vision boards are grounded in spiritual and emotional values versus purely material gain or resources.

Always inject your own health and well-being into the vision board. Include images that represent your mental, physical, spiritual, and emotional health, vitality, and safety. Pictures of good food, exercise, meditation and prayer, and loving community will help draw more of these to you. Remember, without our essential health and well-being, we will be powerless to enjoy the visions that we manifest.

Once you have a precise vision—one with you in it that is realistic and possible—that you fervently believe in and provides for your well-being and health, add some verbal affirmations that will help you harness the envisioning magic. My favorite all-time affirmation is:

I now have enough time, energy, wisdom, and money to accomplish all my desires.

I use it daily, and generally. More specific affirmations are good too. As I was working on my "home" vision board I added the phrases "*Home is where the heart is,*" and "*There's no place like home.*"

Be Grateful

The perfect companion to affirmation is gratitude. I love the Meister Eckhart quote: "If the only prayer I ever say in my entire life is "thank you," it will be enough." Gratitude is a powerful transformational tool, and the Law of Attraction people agree it works wonders.

In addition to harnessing the power of gratitude, employ other positive emotions: joy, happiness, feeling worthy and deserving, and abundance. See if you can root these emotions on your vision board by adding words or pictures that evoke these feelings in you. As neuroscientist Rick Hanson says, with practice we can learn to "hardwire happiness" into our daily lives.[1] Research shows that reminding ourselves to cultivate happiness, desire, belief, and satisfaction can actually increase the incidence of their

1 Rick Hanson, *Hardwiring Happiness: The New Brain Science of Contentment, Calm and Confidence*. New York: Harmony Books, 2013.

presence in our experience. And this is the magic that envisioning magic is founded on.

When you have amassed all this positive energy in one place, find a space for your vision board where you will see it daily, many times a day if possible. Create a ritual of spending a few minutes with the vision board each day, using breath work, meditation, prayer, intention, and affirmation to consciously cultivate the positive emotions within you. Let the visions on your board stimulate your imagination. Use creative visualization to see yourself in the picture—see yourself happy, successful in your dream job, or living joyously in your new home.

The Law of Attraction

We hear a lot about the Law of Attraction these days, but what is it really? The Law of Attraction is one of the Seven Natural Laws of the Universe, and is considered a subset of the Law of Vibration. [2]

The Law of Vibration holds that everything in the universe is vibrating because everything is made up of energy, and energy particles vibrate. All matter contains atoms, which are always vibrating. All sound, electricity, heat, and even thought are forms of energy, and are vibrations.

The Law of Attraction states that "like attracts like." So when two oxygen particles meet up, they join together. But when two different particles meet up, they generally repel. Using this simple natural law, we can understand that the cultivation of gratitude and feelings of abundance will naturally bring more gratitude and more abundance to us, as the vibrational energy of these feelings attracts more of the same.

But remember, when using the Law of Attraction, you can't just wish for what you want and expect it to come to

2 http://www.creative-wealthbuilding.com/the-law-of-vibration.html, accessed August 26, 2014.

you. You actually have to experience joy, abundance, and success in order to attract more joy, abundance, and success. Doing the physical work of creating a vision board is the finite action that will help you to cultivate the energy of that desire, and draw more of the things, experiences, and circumstances that you desire to you. Never neglect the action work, because wishing alone will not manifest magic.

What to Use Vision Boards For

Envisioning magic is a process that can be undertaken at home in private to shape a personal intention and manifest it. The process of daily focus and raising energy is powerful work, best done solo.

But envisioning magic can also be done in more public places and still have a powerful magical effect. It not only harnesses the energy of the person constructing the board, but a vision board also affects the energy of those who come into contact with it, so it can also be a powerful tool for transformation of energy in a workplace, or shared community space.

Relationship Building

I am a visual thinker, and I use images, color, texture, and shape to convey thoughts. When I am puzzling over a project or needing to bring more detail to a nebulous or murky idea, I have used a vision board to help bring things into focus.

When I first left my life partner and was in massive transition socially, economically, relationally, and practically, I used a vision board to help envision my new life. Because I had lived for so long as a partner in a family, I had few images to draw on. I needed to develop imagery, focus intention, raise my own energy, and generate transformation in order to create a new way of life, so I employed a vision board. I gathered images of sports and social activities I wanted to try, added photos of my daughter and myself enjoying life, and interspersed these with currency, paid bills, and my projected household budget, which showed us saving and enjoying money. The vision board helped me contemplate new ways of being and new ideas. And it helped me believe that a happy and prosperous future was possible.

Last year I created a vision board specifically devoted to cultivating a healthy, loving, and growing relationship. I put quotes from self-help literature I was reading on the board, added flowers (the language of emotions), made lists of qualities I sought in a partner, added blessings and notes of love and support from friends, and put in photographs of happy, connected people. As my vision clarified, the vision board changed, and I realized that instead of manifesting a partner with the qualities I had identified, I wanted to become a person who possessed those qualities.

I am still single and am joyously learning and becoming more intimate with myself.

Various Goals

Vision boards can be used for specific singular goals, and enable you to bring your dreams to life. They can also be used to clarify nebulous ideas, which brings them closer to existence.

Vision boards can also be used to provide inspiration. Maybe you don't specifically seek something, but instead have a desire to "be happier." A board devoted to happiness can help inspire and cultivate happiness in your daily life, making you more aware of all that makes you happy: friends, family, pets, and companions; favorite foods, drinks, desserts, and treats; beautiful flowers, stones, and scents; and uplifting lyrics, poems, quotes, and excerpts from favorite books. There is so much that evokes happiness.

Constructing the Board

Vision boards can be made with easily available items. The first thing to think about is a base, or setting. I have used corkboards, cardboard, Bristol board, wood, old frames, and even cloth. I like using a corkboard best because I can pull out thumbtacks and pins and remove items used to create the vision and then start on the same surface with a new vision later on.

I've made permanent vision boards by gluing stuff onto cardboard and Bristol board. The advantage to these is that paint, marker, pastels, and crayons can be used to color the project. It's easy to find old frames with their backing still attached to use as a base. A frame gives definition and formality to the project. Look for old frames at yard sales or thrift shops.

Once you have a base, decide how to attach materials to it. If you use a corkboard, get pins and thumbtacks. If you are using paper or cardboard, get out the glue stick and gesso. For old frames, it may be useful to paint over the old surface to seal and prepare it for use.

When I am searching for "vision" materials, I look through recycled magazines and newspapers; personal photographs and mementos; old theater tickets, souvenirs, and postcards; quotes from books I'm reading; and lines from notes from my friends. Just about anything that inspires joy, raises energy, and stimulates good feelings is useful on a vision board.

Where to Get Ideas

Vision boards come from our visions, so the best vision board is something that brings your internal vision of a thing, a place, a relationship, or an experience to life in great detail, color, and evocative imagery.

Think of the word "envision"—to be "in" the "vision." So a vision board helps to put you in the picture with what you are trying to manifest. The clearer you can "see it," the easier it is to "feel it," and the easier it is to attract more. The more detailed the vision board, the easier the manifestation becomes.

~

Use envisioning magic to propel your dreams, goals, and desires into reality. The action of making a vision board is the "footwork" necessary to flesh out your desires, making them visible, tactile, tangible, and defined.

As Meister Echhart says: "What we plant in the soil of contemplation, we shall reap in the harvest of action."

Photos for Magical Manifestation

by Suzanne Ress

The first step in all magic is specifying your intention. The more well-defined your intention, the more likely your magic will work. In order to specify your intent, you must have a clear idea of what you want. Writing down your desired outcome is one way to clarify intent. However, in order to write down or put into words what you want, you must also be able to visualize it.

In Shakti Gawain's classic groundbreaking book *Creative Visualization* (MJF Books, New York, 1978), the author sets down the basics of creative visualization as:

1. Set your goal
2. Create a clear idea or picture
3. Focus on it often
4. Give it positive energy

Visually oriented people may find it easy to create a clear mental picture of their intended goal, but for others this may be difficult. I have found it helpful to place a photographic representation of my intended outcome where I can focus on it often, and this increases my chance for a positive outcome.

A Photo Mandala

A mandala is a magic circle used in Eastern meditation and in some Native Peoples' sacred rites. Mandalas are also some-times used by psychologists as a powerful aid to integrating one's inner and outer selves.

When you have an hour or so of free time, sit down at a comfortable table (or on the floor) with a pile of old maga-zines. Relax, let go of any tensions or worrisome thoughts, and brew yourself a cup of herbal tea, if desired.

With your magical goal firmly in mind—let's say your goal is to find a job—flip quickly through the magazines, page by page. Give your eyes time to register what they are seeing, but do not analyze. Whenever you see a picture you like and that somehow represents your goal of finding a job (or whatever your goal is), tear it out and set it aside. Remember, do not analyze or try to understand why, just see and tear. Keep on with this activity until you have about twenty pictures.

Next, you will need a poster-sized sheet of paper (or four regular-sized sheets taped together), a glue stick, and a pair of scissors. You can do this in the same session, or a day or even a week later, depending on your time and urgency.

Lay the large sheet of paper in front of you and use the scissors to trim around all of the magazine pictures. Arrange the pictures in a round formation on the paper. Keep rearranging them until you are completely satisfied with the way it looks. Then leave it, undisturbed, until the following day. Look at it again, and make any necessary changes before gluing the pictures to the backing paper.

Charge your photographic mandala during the same magical ceremony at which you make your request. Afterwards, tack or tape the mandala somewhere you will see it daily, such as behind your desktop computer screen, on your refrigerator door, inside a locker door, or on the wall beside your bed. In less time than you would expect, you are likely to notice changes in your life that move you closer to the intention pictured on your mandala.

A Photographic Labyrinth

Labyrinths symbolize transformation. They are used all over the world for spiritual contemplation in the form of visual, or walking, pathways. The pathways form a maze, and at the center of the maze is your goal, or intent. You must keep your focus constantly upon it or you risk getting lost.

Creating a maze on paper or poster board, with a photograph representing the final outcome of your spell at its heart, is a powerful help in spell manifestation.

Let's say you have performed a spell to find true and lasting love. Even if you do have a particular person in mind, to avoid manipulating another's free will and to increase your possibility for success, you should look for magazine photographs of anonymous couples that appear (to you, anyway) to be truly in love. Do not choose photos of celebrities or anyone else you can identify. Choose photos that best illustrate the feeling of being truly in love. Maybe the couple is kissing, or holding hands, or simply gazing at each other lovingly. Maybe they are sitting together on a park bench talking, or on a sofa, cuddling in front of a television. Try to put yourself into the photograph and imagine how you feel.

When you have three or four pictures, arrange and glue them on to the center of a sheet of blue construction paper or poster board. Leave plenty of space around them for the maze.

Before drawing the maze, look at a few examples on the Internet to understand the basic set-up of a labyrinth.

Using a pencil, lightly draw a circle or oval around your photo grouping, leaving a small opening, or passageway, in front of the photos. Then draw an even number of concentric, ever larger circles or ovals around the first one, leaving space to "walk through" between each. Leave an opening in the outermost circle, in front of the photos.

Starting from the outermost circle, visually walk through the opening and follow the pathway about a quarter of the

way around, going clockwise, and draw a small "wall" line perpendicular between two circles. Use an eraser to open up a passageway into the next circle, walk on in either direction, and continue on in the same way until you reach the opening at the center. This is your true path.

Go back to the outermost circle, enter, and turn counterclockwise. Go through the maze again, creating false paths that end in blockages. When you have the maze the way you like it, carefully draw over the pencil lines with a fine-tipped black marker. If you wish, add other magazine photos or stickers around the outside of the maze to represent things that delay you from reaching your goal. These could be pictures of any number of obstacles including food snacks, alcohol, television, and people.

Charge your labyrinth during a regular magical ceremony, then tack or tape it somewhere you will see it daily. Whenever your eyes settle on it, visually walk through the maze, to your goal at the center. The more often you do this, the sooner your magical intention will manifest.

Image-Enhanced Spells

In general, you should not use photos of specific people you can identify by name unless you are doing a banishing spell or a helping/healing spell for that individual. In spells for individual gain, whether for love, money, work, or luck, you should use magazine photos that illustrate the feeling or situation you desire.

A Fertility Spell

Collect magazine photos of babies. When you have about twenty of these, on a clear night of the full moon, go outside to a place you will not be seen or disturbed.

Open your magic circle as you normally do.

Sit on the ground underneath the moonlight and arrange the photos of babies all around you in a circle. If there is a breeze, you will have to weigh them down with small rocks, but do not cover the babies' faces.

266

Gazing all around you at the baby photos, slowly say these words:

> *Let me multiply,*
> *By conceiving a child,*
> *Healthy and beautiful,*
> *Longed for and desired,*
> *In Love's name,*
> *I multiply.*

Turn your face up toward the moon and observe her motherliness. Close your eyes and feel your skin bathed in the moon's light. Imagine your baby in your arms. Continue this meditation for as long as you see fit.

Then collect the baby photos, kissing each one before putting it away, and close your circle.

~

In some spells you should use photos of specific people. If you are asking for help or healing for someone, using a photograph of that person looking happy and healthy adds strength to your spell.

If you need to cast a blocking or banishing spell regarding someone who is causing problems for you or someone close to you, a small photograph of that person can substitute for hair or fingernail clippings, which are sometimes difficult to acquire.

In certain love spells you can use photos of people you know, but only if the spell is to strengthen or otherwise alter an existing love relationship that involves that person.

Spell to Deepen an Existing Love Relationship

You will need a separate photograph of each of the people involved in the relationship, a red candle with two joined hearts carved into it that has been anointed with rose oil, and a small red bag containing the petals of a red rose. The two photos should be about the same size, and clearly show their faces.

Set up your magic circle in the usual way, and when you are ready, light the red candle. Place the two photos side by side in front of the candle, facing you.

Recite these lines:

Two hearts together are knit,
So that but one heart can be made of it.

Stare hard at the two photographs, and do not blink. Let your eyes lose focus, until the images of the two photos merge into one. Keep this single, blurred image for as long as you are able.

Refocus your eyes, and put the two photos together, face to face, and slide them underneath the candle.

Now repeat:

Two hearts together are knit,
So that but one heart can be made of it.

Imagine the souls of the two persons in the photographs merging together. See them melding into a single entity.

Watch the candle flame and concentrate on this vision for several minutes. Then say:

It is done!

And blow out the candle.

Without separating the photos, slip them into the small red bag. Close the bag and put it away in a safe place where it will not be disturbed.

Banishing Spell

You can use a photograph of a specific person to get rid of his or her unwanted attentions, whether these are amorous or predatory.

Go to your magic circle or altar on a Tuesday night when the moon is waning. Bring with you a small photograph of the offending person inside a small black bag, a four-square of black paper (approximately), a small jar containing a tea-spoonful of mixed garlic and hot chili powder, a black candle, a fireproof burning surface, and a lighter.

Open your circle as usual.

When you feel centered and relaxed, light the black candle before you. Take the photograph from the black bag and place it onto the black paper. Sprinkle some of the garlic and chili powders over it as you say:

Pest be gone,
Burn away,
Go away,
Stay away.
Banished from my life,
Turned to ash.
Pest be gone!

Fold the black paper away from you to tightly enclose the photo and the powder. Place this small black packet on the fireproof incense burner, stone, or brick, and use the flame of the black candle to set it on fire.

Watch it burn down to ash.

Close your circle.

When the ash is cool, take it away, and flush it down a toilet.

Direct Photo Manifestation

The previous spells will all work with existing photos, either personal pictures, stock images, or professionally shot images clipped out of a magazine. However, today we have the technology to manifest photos more directly.

If you are skilled in digital-image editing, you can use graphics-editing computer software such as Photoshop to manipulate and transform digital photographic images of real scenes or situations to make them more closely match your magical intention. For example, you might remove excess body fat from a photo of yourself, or remove clutter from a photo of your garage.

You could create a composite image illustrating yourself in a faraway place you long to visit, or at a desk in the office you wish to work in, or walking along a lovely beach, holding hands with a dear friend you would like to be closer to.

Be careful with digital manipulation of photographs for magical use, though. Photography comes across very literally to our unconscious minds, so make certain that your finished composition does not stray too far into fantasy, or you may regret it!

Water Magic

Simple Shell Magic

by Ember Grant

Natural items such as stones, feathers, and shells seem to be part of nearly every magical tradition. They serve as symbols, talismans, and charms and are used in a variety of spells and spiritual practices. Shells are found in myriad shapes, sizes, and colors, and have been used in jewelry and other decorative objects throughout history. They have been used as tools, forms of currency, and to make buttons.

I'd like to spend time focusing on shell magic as a way to expand and diversify their use. Many people use shells to represent water, which makes sense because many of them are derived from creatures that lived in oceans or in freshwater lakes and rivers. But I want to include the shells of land snails as well, and distinguish the different types of shells for particular uses.

First of all, I don't want to encourage any collecting of threatened or endangered species. I prefer to use shells that have already been abandoned by the animals. Shells are relatively easy to find in some regions, and you can also purchase them from stores that sell them for aquariums or home décor. (Unfortunately, many of these shells have been collected from living organisms.) If you do practice collecting shells, dead or alive, in the wild, please abide by all conservation regulations.

You can use a detailed shell identification guide if you wish, but you can still use shells in magic based solely on their appearance without knowing specifically from what type of animal the shell originated. For the purpose

of this article, I'm grouping them by shape because that's how I will approach their magical functions.

Now, let's consider exactly what shells are. Shells, like feathers, are part of an animal's body. We find them after the animal has died and its remains have decayed or been scavenged by another animal. I think it's important to respect the life that created the shell and always consider that in your magical practice. If it helps, do some research on the shell and find pictures of the animals so you can think of the shell as more than just an inanimate object.

Seashells are made mainly of calcium carbonate, but they're not technically minerals. Minerals are naturally occurring; shells are made by the animal. They grow in layers as the animal grows and secretes the minerals, along with a small amount of protein. (They're not made of living cells, like a turtle's shell, which are more like human bones.) What's interesting is that in seashells, the mineral formation does include minerals that form crystals, such as aragonite and calcite. Aragonite is present in the nacre (mother of pearl) of shells, that pearly iridescent layer that gives some of them such a lovely appearance.

Bivalves are one of the most common types of shell you can find. These are a type of mollusk whose shells usually consist of two pieces hinged together. They can be found in both marine and freshwater environments. These creatures include mussels, clams, oysters, and scallops. The shell shape is receptive, like a cup or bowl, or sometimes flat or curved. Some can be oblong in shape while others are more rounded. Bowl-shaped shells can be used to hold small stones, herbs, water, sand, salt, or earth. If you have both pieces, you can also place things inside and possibly even close the pieces (depending on the type of shell). These are excellent for use in healing and abundance spells. If you have one that is large enough, you can even place a small candle inside.

Snail shells (gastropods) are mainly noted for their spiral shapes. There are many varieties, including those of the land snail. The abalone, murex, whelk, periwinkle, and conch are also part of this class, among many others. Sea snail shells can range from a flattened coil shape to a very long spiral. Because of their spiral shape, shells like this can be used to represent the life force. Due to their phallic appearance, the long, turret-shaped shells can be used for fertility and passion spells. Murex shells are ornate, spiny, and often colorful; these are excellent for protection due to their appearance. "Top" shells (calliostoma) have a pyramid shape and look as though you could spin them like a top. They are also spiral shaped, and can be used for strength, courage, and focus.

Conch is often used to refer to the shape of a shell that comes to a point on each end, one end having a long spire, and having a flared outer "lip" that extends from the side. True conch shells are a specific genus of marine mollusk but, for magical use, we'll just consider the shape. You may be familiar with the use of these shells as a horn. In some Asian cultures, conch shells have a long history of religious associations. They are one of the Eight Auspicious Symbols in Buddhism, and the god Vishnu is said to hold a special conch shell that represents life-giving waters. For these reasons, we can consider it a symbol of life. Be careful in purchasing a conch—export of these shells is banned in some countries.

Abalone shells, the slightly convex, oval-shaped shells with patterns resembling an ear, are excellent for use in prosperity spells. But use caution—some species are endangered or threatened. If you have one of these shells, treasure it. They are very strong, so protection spells using this shell would be also be appropriate. They are among the loveliest of shells and are commonly sold as incense burners in some metaphysical shops.

Cowrie shells (or cowry) have long been associated with the appearance of female genitalia. They are egg-shaped, flat on the bottom with a slit-like opening, and usually quite smooth and shiny in appearance. Some are speckled brown and white. Use these shells for nurturing, love, and fertility as well as abundance and wealth.

Sand dollars are a type of sea urchin; their skeleton is called a *test*. These can be found in many different shapes. In some of these, there are five loose pieces inside that look like flying birds. These are the animal's jaws. Some have referred to this as "Aristotle's lantern." If you have these pieces, they can be glued together to create a five-pointed star.

Starfish are a related species; contrary to popular belief, some do have more than five arms. Like sand dollars, starfish skeletons can be used to represent life—the number five is associated with the five senses, the human form, regeneration, and humanity. These make lovely additions to an altar; they can be used to symbolize the water element or used in spells based on the numerology of five.

Shell Spells

Small shells can be easily carried with you or worn as jewelry. Large shells are best suited to being displayed on an altar or placed in a significant location. Remember you can also buy shells and pearls with holes drilled to create your own jewelry, or perhaps you have a piece of shell jewelry that's ready to wear. In either case, charge them for your specific purpose. You can also combine shells with crystals, herbs, and candles. For each of these spells, prepare your space and visualize your goal as needed.

Cowrie for Keeps

On a tiny strip of paper, write down what you wish to receive or attract. Fold the paper and slip it into the shell, visualizing these qualities being drawn to you. Carry the shell with you or keep it on your altar.

Longevity Amulet

Create a bundle that contains one land snail shell, a small clear quartz point, and some dried sage. The crystal is to enhance the energy, the shell is for life force, and the herb represents wisdom and longevity. Wrap all ingredients in a white cloth or bag and carry it with you. If the shell breaks, replace it.

Prosperity

Use a bivalve half-shell for this spell, and keep it on your altar. Sprinkle dried basil into the shell. Next, add a small coin or piece of tiger's-eye (or both). Alternately, to create a charm to carry, rub basil or ginger essential oil on a small half-shell that you can keep in your purse or pocket.

Passion

Place a snail shell in a shallow, clear glass dish and add water. Use a long, spiral-shaped shell if you have one. If not, any snail shell will do. Sprinkle five drops of rose oil on the water and add a floating candle, if desired. Place this on a dresser or nightstand in the bedroom to set the

mood. You can create a more elaborate design by adding crystals and other appropriate stones to the bowl, using more than one shell, and adding multiple candles.

Protection Spell

If possible, use a murex shell or other snail shell that has a spiny appearance for this spell. A type of conch shell would also be appropriate. The shell should be placed near an entryway or window, or even on a porch. Place eight grains of sea salt inside the shell—you may need to tilt it a few times so the salt crystals go all the way down inside the shell and won't fall out. Turn it over, and leave it in place.

~

Even if you're landlocked, like me, you can still find shells. I have found dozens of snail shells while hiking, and also found bivalve shells near rivers and streams. I believe shells we find are special because they come to us by chance. But whether you buy them or find them, enjoy your discovery of shells and have fun experimenting with them in magic.

Enchant Your Beauty Routine with DIY Products

by Mickie Mueller

In this busy world, it's great to find ways to work tried-and-true magical formulas into your everyday routines. A great way to do that is to add a touch of magic to your usual health and beauty products. These techniques are not just for the ladies but are great for the guys too; after all, you're all beautiful! Enchant your crowning glory for success every time you shampoo, add a time-honored beauty charm to your face moisturizer; magical protection every day is as close as the body wash you're using anyway. Adding magic to your favorite standard daily products is easy, and you can even add a couple homemade magical products to your routine.

It should be noted that even though the herbs used here are in very small quantities, if you have an allergy, can't find an herb, or prefer another herb to what's listed here, you may substitute as you see fit. There are many herbs with similar magical correspondences, so have fun, get creative, and make some beauty magic that's as unique as your own beauty!

Magical Protection Body Wash

Pick out your favorite body wash—there are many that are made with herbs included in their ingredients—or just choose one that makes you feel great and smells wonderful. Pour out a couple teaspoons worth into a small jar to save for later and make room for your magical addition.

To a small pan of about ½ cup of water, combine a pinch of each of the following:

Earl Grey tea (made of tea leaves and bergamot for strength and success)
Powdered dragon's blood resin (protection)
Powdered frankincense resin (protection, raises vibrations)
Powdered myrrh resin (protection, raises vibrations)
Sea salt (blessing, banishing negativity)

Use the following charm to enchant your brew as it boils:

Magic resins and powers combine,
Protection magic shall be mine,
Every time I use this brew,
Magic shall flow through and through.

Boil for about five minutes then allow it to cool. Strain through a coffee filter into a clean glass then use the liquid to top off your bath gel and shake well, repeating the charm again three times as you shake. These are powerful herbs and a little goes a long way. Every time you shower, use the body wash all over you—and make sure to get your face, and in between your toes! It will wash away any negative astral nasties stuck in your aura and leave you shielded and protected for the day! Once you've used part of it, put the reserved body wash from the jar back into the bottle and shake it up again.

Crowning Glory Shampoo & Conditioner

Your hair is your crowning glory. Many cultures believe that hair is a psychic antenna and an expression of spirit and power, so why not use your halo of hair to hold magical power for success and recognition. Pick up a big bottle of your favorite shampoo and conditioner. Using the same method as for the body wash (above), create an infusion of the following herbs, using a pinch of each:

Bay laurel (success and recognition)
Powdered frankincense or rosemary (uplifting vibrations)
Sandalwood (manifesting wishes)
Patchouli (prosperity)
Cinnamon (power)
Cinquefoil (success and receiving favors)

Enchant your brew as it bubbles with this charm:

Success is mine, boil, bubble,
I've got this, it's no trouble,
My crowning glory with magic shall shine
Up the ladder of life I shall climb!

Once the brew cools, strain it though a coffee filter and add some to both your shampoo and conditioner bottle; shake well while repeating the charm again three times for each bottle. Boost it even more with a few drops of jojoba oil for magical success with every shampoo!

Beltane Beauty Moisturizer

Legend has it that dew collected on Beltane morning has the power to maintain youth and beauty. I've been using this modernized version of this ages-old beauty treatment for many years now. One year I even collected enough dew to share with my coven so we could all make Beltane Beauty Moisturizer. I even used a piece of vintage faerie clip art to make custom labels for our magical moisturizer; it looked pretty in our bathrooms and reminded us of our Beltane magic every time we used it. Guys, try an image of a beautiful young Pan or Oberon!

A few days before Beltane, May 1, purchase some good-quality face cream correct for your skin type. (Don't break the bank, but get something decent; even a generic of a good

brand is fine. However, don't use a thick cream because that would make make it difficult to mix in the dew. If you have one you like to use, just put it on after this new moisturizer has been absorbed into the skin, which is the point of this magic!) The night before Beltane, set your alarm to get up right at dawn or before, depending on your schedule. Dawn is the best time to collect morning dew, long before the morning sun begins to evaporate away all that good faerie magic! Swipe a jar or glass through the clover, grass, or any vegetation you can find covered in dew and collect as much as you can. Be sure to thank the faeries when you're done. Here's a favorite way to do so:

> *Respect to the May Queen and the May King,*
> *And all Faerie-kind for the magic you bring,*
> *With beauty and youth, this enchanted morning dew,*
> *Carries blessings of Beltane all the year through!*

Leave a bit of bread with honey outside as an offering to the Fae.

Now add the dew to your bottle of moisturizer and shake well to disperse the magical faerie dew throughout, and apply some to your face. Use it once a week (especially on date night) to boost the magic your skin has already absorbed.

Wipe Away the Day & Wipe on the Magic

Okay, I didn't invent DIY makeup removal/face cleansing wipes, I just made mine magic! These little wipes are really thrifty, cool, and convenient, especially for the busy witch on the go. If you're tired or in a hurry, these can be a life saver, and if you're traveling, just tuck a few into a little zip sandwich bag. This is a basic recipe, but you can alter it depending on your skin type and your planned use.

2 cups water
1 roll of good-quality select-a-size paper towels
1 squirt (2 tablespoons) of a good face wash or baby bath
2 tablespoons coconut oil (purification, protection, repair, and replenish)
Pinch of fresh rosemary (healing, cleansing, youth, supports collagen, fights free radicals)
Pinch of lavender flowers (purification, healing, mild astringent)
Pinch of basil (protection, purification, natural antibacterial and antifungal)
1 drop tea tree oil (cleansing, purification, natural antiseptic)
Clear storage container with a tight-fitting lid that will hold a half roll of paper towels

Using a sharp utility knife, cut the roll of paper towels in half—yes, cut right through the roll. Save one half for your next batch. Boil your water with the rosemary, lavender, and basil just for a few minutes. Allow it to cool until just warm and strain through a coffee filter. Pour the warm witches' brew into the storage container and add the face or baby wash, tea tree and coconut oils, and stir well while you chant:

Making magic beautiful
Activate powers dutiful
By leaf and flower, fruit and tree
Cleansing powers rejuvenate me!

Put your paper towels into the container on end. Let the liquid absorb into the paper towels for a few minutes. Put the lid on and flip it over for a few minutes until the entire roll is wet. Now you can pull out the center tube and discard it. When you grab a magical face wipe, grab from the center and pull one out.

Natural Magic Beauty

Here are a couple quickies made entirely of all-natural ingredients that you can add to your routine. All these ingredients have magical properties in addition to being easy to get and natural—and kinda delicious!

Glowing Passion Face Salsa

¼ cup crushed tomato, liquid squeezed out (bring love, repel negativity)

1 teaspoon lemon juice (removes negativity, invites friendship)

1 teaspoon fresh basil (protection, purification)

Zap it in the food processor and apply to your face (avoid eye area). Leave this skin-brightening formula on for 10 minutes. Wash off with warm water.

Avocado Zen Hydrating Mask

½ avocado (beauty, passion, healing)

1 teaspoon plain yogurt (longevity, spirituality, mood lifting)

Avocado is good for all skin types—it's universal beauty magic! Mash up half of an avocado and mix with yogurt, apply to face, avoiding eyes, for 15 minutes. Wash off with warm water.

∼

These are some fun ways to bring some magic into your beauty routine, but there is one sure-fire formula to appear attractive and confident all the time. Be kind, smile often, nurture your heart, stand up straight, and hold your head up high. No matter what, your inner beauty shining through is the most powerful magic of all!

Spring Cleaning-Hoodoo Style

by Najah Lightfoot

Spring is a time of new beginnings. The dark days of winter are waning and a new beginning is on the horizon. The days are lengthening as Earth puts up signs a new cycle has begun. Tufts of green grass may be showing on your lawn, or you may notice the first blooming crocuses. "Out with the old, in with the new."

Spring ushers in fresh thoughts and new ideas. The darkness of winter has left us eager to stretch and exercise our minds, bodies, and spirits. No wonder spring is time for a thorough housecleaning. And not only the physical homes, but our spiritual and mental homes.

It is known that places and dwellings carry and harbor energy. Your home can also carry and harbor negative energy, which can build and accumulate over time. Not every day is rosy. Family and friends don't get along every day. Unexpected visitors can arrive and bring along their own drama. For these very reasons, a thorough, regular spiritual cleansing is necessary.

On a daily basis, we may light sage and burn candles. Or after a particularly negative episode, we may throw some salt on the floor and sweep negative energy out the door. On a mundane level, we clean our homes by washing the floors and vacuuming the rugs. Some us get down into the nitty-gritty of cleaning, while others may give our homes a once-over and call it good. Everyone has their own way of cleaning house, and I'm not about to tell you to how clean your own home. But would I like to share with you a rite, a time-honored, *intentional* way of spiritually cleansing your home that will wash out stagnant energy, lay down protective energy, and uplift the energy of all who dwell in or visit your home.

The rite takes time, and it takes planning. But all the best magicks take time and planning, do they not? And let's face it, in this world of instant gratification and fast-fast everything, it's good to slow down at times and work your magick. This is magick you put your heart and sweat into. And when you're finished, you'll have the gratification of knowing *you did the work.*

So wrap your head up. Pull up that skirt or roll up those pant legs, and let's get to cleansing your home, hoodoo style.

Planning and Preparation

This rite takes me deep into myself. It opens my mind to my ancestors. I sense them sweeping through each room with me. I see the shacks of the old ones, down on their knees, scrubbing their floors, praying, chanting, knowing the act they are undertaking is to cleanse, protect, and seal their home. In essence, we are keeping the good juju in and the bad juju out.

Timing in magick is essential. One can be very detail-oriented or one can try to generally have a sense of what is going on, astrologically speaking. Since this a spring cleansing rite, try to time the rite to the New Moon that occurs near, on, or after Ostara/Spring Equinox.

This work will require you to wake in the early hours before dawn and be finished by time the sun rises.

You're going to wash your floors, open closet doors, go into the creepy crawly spaces of your home, wash your front and back steps, and bring in good energy once you're finished.

Yes, it's a lot of work. But when you're done, you'll be able to utter one of my favorite phrases from the movie *Poltergeist*—"This house is clean!" There won't be any uninvited or lingering spirits left when you are finished.

〰

We are going to break this work into two sections: items and instructions you will need to cleanse your home, and items and instructions you will need to bring the good juju into your home. May I suggest you familiarize yourself with the instructions and the items needed before beginning the work. Once you begin the work, you won't want to be rushing around or looking for things you may have forgotten.

First things first. In hoodoo, we work with "personal concerns," which consists of items that are loaded with one's DNA that are uniquely yours, such as hair, fingernails, and/or bodily fluids. The cleansing rite you are about to undertake will require your personal concerns in the form of your own urine. Before you gross out or say you can't or aren't willing to use your own urine, let me explain the reason why.

Step back for a moment and think about the animal kingdom. One thing animals are known for is marking their territory. And how do they do that? They do it by leaving their scent. This way any other animals that come across their domain know they have entered into another animal's territory—the scent clearly says, "Hey, this is my territory!"

Your home is your territory, your domain. By using your personal concerns you are putting out the same message: "Hey, this my territory. Watch your step." If you find you are unable to use your own personal concerns, you can skip the step, but the work will not be quite as powerful.

Washing It Down, Washing It Out

On the morning of the rite, when you first awake and go to the bathroom, capture your urine in a cup and set it aside. The first trip to the bathroom is the most powerful one, and this is the personal concern will we use for marking our territory later in the rite.

Do not speak to anyone until the rite is complete. This way, the power is concentrated within yourself. Since you will be working in the dark hours before dawn, this should be easy to accomplish. If you wish, you can notify family members the night before that you will be cleaning the house early in the morning, so you won't freak them out when you sweep through their rooms. Or if your schedule allows, you may choose to wait until your home is empty, so you will not disturb sleeping family members.

After you have collected your personal concerns, put on some clean clothes. Gather the items you will need to cleanse your home. A good practice is to set these items up the night before:

A mop
A bucket
A block of camphor
Benzoin powder
Frankincense (optional)
A bottle of Chinese Wash (easily acquired through spiritual
    supply stores or if so inclined recipes can found online,
    to make your own)
An anointed candle
Charcoal
An incense burner or cauldron (to safely burn the charcoal)

Crumble the camphor and mix it together with the benzoin powder. This mixture makes a good cleansing smoke. You may also choose to add frankincense to the mixture.

Fill your bucket with hot water and pour in approximately one-third cup of Chinese Wash. (**Note:** It is important to *always* dilute Chinese Wash as it is very strong.)

Light your charcoal and your candle and proceed to your first room. You will wash your floors, smoke your rooms and your closets, beginning at the back of the house, making your way to your front door. The process is: wash the floors, smoke the room (by dropping the camphor mixture on the charcoal), set the lighted candle in the room, then proceed to the next room.

When you make your way to your front door, wash your doorstep, then take your dirty bucket of water and throw that water into the street!

Bringing in the Good Juju

Now that your home has been thoroughly cleansed, it's time to bring in the good energy to seal and protect your home. You will need the following items:

Your personal concerns you collected upon rising
A clean broom
Salt
Olive oil or blessing oil
A bell

Fill your bucket with clean hot water. Add your personal concerns to the water. At your front doorstep, with your broom, scrub your front doorstep. Sprinkle some salt on the step.

Carry your bucket to your back door and repeat the process. Any leftover water should be thrown in your backyard or behind your dwelling.

Anoint your doors and windows with the olive or blessing oil. If you have prayers or words of protection that are sacred to you, you can silently repeat them as you work your way through your home.

Once you have anointed your doors and windows with the blessing oil, find the center of your home. You may now speak aloud. I have found these words to be particularly powerful:

> *This house is now cleansed, blessed, and protected!*
> *Blessed be all who enter and dwell here!*

Ring your bell three times. Your work is done.

∽

This rite can be performed at any time. You may find you need to perform it on a monthly basis, or several times a year. The frequency is up to you. Either way, performing a hoodoo house cleansing is a sure way to uplift your spirits and keep your magick strong!

A World of Magick Mirrors

by Stephanie Rose Bird

Looking glass upon the wall
Who is fairest of us all?
"Snow White" by the Brothers Grimm

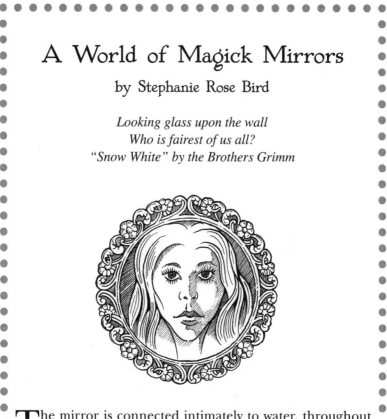

The mirror is connected intimately to water, throughout history, across cultures. It is a tool for clarity, reflection, honesty, truth, divination, and protection. This article asks you to take a closer look into your conception of mirrors and then engage in the magick they hold. We will explore their symbolism and use in folklore, spiritual practices, and fairy tales. In the end, you will find a way to work your own type of magick through this ancient divination tool.

Early Visions of Reflections

We tend to think of mirrors in a fixed way. You buy them or find them, already set up in the place you live or work. They're readymade and widely available. Long ago that was not the case. In fact, many people were taken aback and wondered what was looking back at them when they saw their reflections. Long before mirrors were made, we saw ourselves in other ways. Water, polished stones, and metals were common ways reflections were seen.

These images of ourselves were held in awe. In *The Women's Encyclopedia of Myths and Secrets*, Barbara Walker shares how the ancients believed any reflective surface, solid or liquid, had mystical powers because the reflection is a part of the soul. Hence, soulless beings like werewolves and vampires show no reflection in the mirror.

Reflections in Greek Mythology

In Greek Mythology, the story of Narcissus and Echo invokes a recurring theme noted in various tales. Water is a point of departure for metaphorical as well as physical reflection. Seeing one's self in an object, be it liquid or solid, becomes a way of gaining deeper understanding of the world and your place within it. If our awareness is at its height, we can receive the messages reflections deliver.

Used to feed the ego, as in the case of Narcissus, reflections can turn against us by transforming into what we don't want or by consuming us. Rather than following the behavior of Narcissus, you can use the reflection intuitively and for prophetic visioning. Being that our focus is on magick, we'll want to view reflections as a portals, seeing far past the mundane. We want to see through the mirror, as many people have done since the beginning of time, for divination and witchcraft. First though, it's important to avoid the pitfalls and dangers involved with mirror gazing.

The Toltecs' Smoky Mirror

In *The Four Agreements*, Don Miguel Ruiz takes us into the heart of Toltec wisdom by sharing their concept of the smoky mirror. The smoky mirror aligns somewhat with the Buddhist way of thinking but goes further with the idea of illusion. "Smoky mirror" is how we are trained and conditioned to see the world, through what he calls "domestication."

Domestication is the process of systemically stripping us of the ability to see the world's magick. It begins when we are

children. To the Toltec way of thinking, the smoky mirror is the twisted way we see. It reflects back what we want it to but has nothing to do with reality. Ruiz goes on to tell us that through shielding, we can turn the smoky mirror in on itself to reveal the truth. He gives us hope by teaching how to turn the negative reflections of ourselves depicted in the smoky mirror, implanted by those with evil intentions, back at the perpetrator.

Hathor's Magick Mirror

The essence of the Toltec wisdom shared by Ruiz in *The Four Agreements* regarding mirrors is a notion shared by other cultures, for example the ancient Egyptians. Hathor is a goddess skilled at manipulating the manner in which a mirror can be used for protection.

Hathor is connected to water, which in turn correlates with mirrors and reflection. She is goddess of moisture, the very essence of the universe. Love, fertility, pregnancy, and childbirth fall under her protective wing. A patron of the arts, she loves music and dance. When the Nile River floods, she is behind it. She is most likely the mother of numerous river goddesses around the world.

Her mirror is believed to be constructed of a flattened oval made from either copper or bronze. Copper is symbolic of qualities of the Goddess. It has a handle made from horn or wood. The reflective object she has on her person is reminiscent of a sun disc, which also represents her mystery and power.

Through Hathor's magick mirror, your power as an individual is magnified. It is reflected on one side of it. Other superfluous thoughts planted by friends or enemies, such as those encapsulated in gossip, reflect from the other side. If your power is strong enough, it is quite possible to use Hathor's mirror as a shield. You can aim the negativity of your detractors back at them with the magick mirror.

The Mirror of Oshun

Mirror-toting river goddesses and beings aren't limited to ancient Egypt. They populate the African diaspora. Possessing some of the qualities and attributes of Hathor is the youngest Nigerian orisha, Oshun (O-SHOON). She is one of the Four Pillars or foundations of Santeria.

This orisha's domain is rivers and she is embodied in sweet waters. She is ruler of the element of water, which connects her to the creation of all life. Fertility, love, beauty, sensuality, the arts, witches, and diviners are all under her auspices.

Oshun is filled with all the attributes of magick and womanhood. She is often depicted as a multiracial woman with long, flowing hair. Known as a great weaver of spells, she carries several sacred objects including a fan and drum. One that she's very well known for is her mirror, which she often has strapped to her body under a belt.

Naturally, being of the water, Oshun wanted to get involved with seeing. She had Obatala, another orisha, teach her divination. In turn, she taught her entire village this art for free. There are many telling *caminos* (paths/roads) to connect with her, along with the magick she and her mirror possess. One is *Oshun Ibu Ikole*, Mother of Witches.

A simple way to bring her into your life would be to put out some sweet water—Florida water, rose water, or orange blossom water—on a golden cloth. This would serve as a foundation to an altar. Then, place a mirror you've consecrated on top of it. Next to it set out a copper or orange-glazed earthen bowl of honey. Go to this space to reflect on all that she holds.

Yata-no-Kagami – The Mirror of Yata

The sacred looking glass is a vehicle in which we can travel about the earth. Stories of magickal mirrors proliferate across time and space. Yata-no-Kagami is a sacred mirror and part of the Imperial Regalia of Japan. It is housed in the Shinto shrine of Ise Jingu. This mirror represents wisdom, beauty, and honesty.

It is believed to be a gift from Japan's Sun goddess Amaterasu Omikami. The Emperor was so stricken by its wonders, believing she lives within it, he assigned his daughter to minister as priestess over the shrine.

You might wonder how Amaterasu got into the mirror. This Sun goddess and her maidens reign over a heavenly plain. They are usually busy tending to sacred rice fields. They also like tending to magical animals, weaving, dancing, and having contests. (Contests are prominent in traditional Japanese culture.)

One day her brother, Susanowa, wanted to have a contest with Amaterasu. She agreed to it and he won. His prize was one of her favorite mystical possessions, her necklace. Once he had it, he quickly figured out its magick, and began releasing the five goddesses from it. Amaterasu was incensed because they were her goddesses. Susanowa wasn't finished. He slaughtered and skinned one of her sacred animals, a horse, and then threw the skin into the place she was weaving with her maidens. He also demolished her beloved rice fields.

Devastated, Amaterasu retreated to a cave. Since she is the sun, the kingdom plunged into darkness and everything began to wither and die. People tried everything but nothing would bring her out. Then they engaged the magick mirror. They danced while invoking the energy of the mirror. Then they put the charged mirror in front of the cave in which she hid. Wanting to see what was making all the ruckus she heard, she stuck her head outside the cave. Her eyes got caught on the mirror. Seduced and dazzled, she gazed deeply into it. She was lured outside in order to see the beautiful creature inside it. That creature of course was her.

There was a great celebration. The order of the universe was restored. No longer open to pettiness, jealousy, and competitions, the mirror showed Amaterasu the beauty of her true self. From this story we learn that rather than withdraw from the world when things go wrong, we need to tap into our capacity to see and be who we really are. The object you need to employ for this type of work, which holds the beauty within Amaterasu (the light), is the magick mirror.

~

Obviously, Amaterasu was doing more than simply looking into a glass. She was doing what witches call "scrying." This type of divination occurs when you look deep, using a mirror or other visioning tool as a seer. While scrying, you're looking for symbolic messages and patterns coming through the mirror.

Mirror Meditation

To tap into the mirror magick beloved in so many cultures around the world, try this meditation.

Preparation: You will need to obtain a scrying mirror from a magick (occult) supplier. When you find one, it will most likely be a shiny black color, so do your work under the natural light of Amaterasu (the Sun). You also need a pen. I recommend a quill pen and magickal ink, such as dragon's blood. You'll also need a sturdy journal. Leather-bound works well.

Consecrate the mirror, using the best way on your path. This releases its potential for divination.

When you're ready (this could be in a day or two) and your mind is clearly focused, sit down on Mother Earth where you can see the Sun.

Cradling the scrying mirror in your lap, begin to take slow, measured, deep breaths in and out. Do this until you're in a state of deep relaxation.

Tilt the mirror so it can receive Amaterasu's light.

Begin gazing into it, blinking as little as possible.

Sustain this activity as long as you can.

Look for patterns, people, symbols, shapes, spirits, deities, and guides.

Listen, watch, and try deciphering what is revealed.

Record your observations with the pen and ink in your journal.

Repeat this frequently to sharpen your skills.

Afterwards, spend ample time reflecting on what you've written, focusing on the prophecies your scrying visions hold.

River Song

by Monica Crosson

In the changing light of an early September morning, a low mist clung to the mineral-green waters of the Sauk River. Above the mist, nature was alive and stirring, from the angry chirring of a kingfisher protecting his territory to the soft rattling of alder leaves beginning their slow decline. I looked to my children, who wiped the still-sticky sleep from their eyes, and asked, "Are you ready?"

My boys scrambled for their poles, as if there weren't enough fish in the river for the both of them, then made their way to the bank where my husband, Steve, was already preparing the bait.

My daughter, still young enough to need my help walking across the stony bank, took my hand. "I wanna hear the river sing, Mama."

And so we walked, leaving our boys to their conquest. We looked for interesting-shaped rocks on our way—heart-shaped, moon-shaped, or the ever elusive hag stone, which we would later make into an amulet. Just beyond the willow, there was an eddy shaded by alder and giant black cotton-wood, whose fluffs of cottony seed filled the air.

"Do you think the fairies ride those?" Chloe asked.

"I don't know," I said, "but I would like to think so."

A log rested on that quiet bank, an ancient giant who was taken by heavy rain. Its moss-shrouded remains served as a home to voles and insects and made a nice resting spot for us. We sat and watched as the fog dissipated and exposed the river's familiar curves. "She is lovely, isn't she?" I commented to my little girl, who had gathered small pebbles and had started to toss them—kerplunk, kerplunk, kerplunk.

"Yes, Mama." She smiled.

The tree frogs had grown used to us and began their ser-enade. From our perch, I could spy my husband and boys, their lines like silver flashes in the light of the new sun. Steve stopped every once in a while to help the boys with a cast or to replace lost bait.

I closed my eyes and let the ever-growing sun warm me. My mind drifted—flowing with the current—and I thought back to what it must have been like, before the giants were taken by the mighty saw blades of those first loggers, to a time when this river was truly wild and the salmon was revered as the giver of life by the Sauk-Suiattle people who called these banks home. As I sat, I thought I heard the pounding of drums just above the quivering leaves and the piercing cry of the eagle, beyond the water's lulling rhythm. It was there—steady as a heartbeat and hauntingly beautiful.

"Mama, do you hear it?" my daughter whispered.

My eyes still closed, I asked, "Hear what, Chloe?"

"The river's song. I can hear it, and it's so beautiful."

I opened my eyes. "Yes," I said and gave her a squeeze. "You're right, it is beautiful."

The Element of Water

It was Laura Eiseley who said, "If there is magic on this planet, it is contained in water." Water covers about 70 percent of the Earth's surface and is essential for the human body to function. In addition, for many of us, being near a river, lake, stream, or the ocean invokes a spiritual experience, soothing the body, mind, and soul. Water is moving and changing. Water is cleansing and nourishing to both your body and emotions.

In magick, the element of water is attributed to emotions, intuition, creativity, psychic abilities, transformation, and dreams. The chalice and the cauldron are both tools of water representing wisdom, life, transformation, and regeneration. They also symbolize the womb because, of course, life began in water. Water is feminine. Its direction is west and its colors are blue, turquoise, sea green, and gray. Autumn is its season and its time is twilight. It's also associated with Cancer, Scorpio, and Pisces. Watery people are intuitive and sensitive, and feel more intensely than the rest. They are emotional and nurturing, and like a river, they run deep.

A Spell to Quell Emotions

Life, too, is like the river, as it is always in motion. But from time to time we can emotionally "hit the rocks." This spell is for when you need a little emotional peace.

You will need:

A small stone

A black marker

If you can't be near a natural body of water, you will also
     need a large bowl of water.

Do this on the night of the New Moon. With your marker write (in a word or two) your emotional negativity on your stone. Take the stone to a river, stream, or any body of water (or fill a large bowl with water). Relax and kneel beside the watery edge. Focus on your image in the water. Take your finger and poke it in the liquid, rippling the waters. Then toss the rock into the water and say:

The waters cleanse and the waters calm
My heart and mind from this emotional harm.
As the ripples of discourse spread then cease
Grant me harmony, and with harmony, peace.

Say this over and over again until the ripples have ceased while visualizing yourself within the water, happy and emotionally balanced. When you are done, ground and center. If you used a large bowl, empty the water into the garden as an offering.

Scrying with River Water

Because of water's connection with psychic ability, it can be used as a means of scrying. This needs to be done on the night of a full moon and under a clear sky.

You will need:

A dark bowl

A container of river water (if you can't obtain it from a stream or river, use tap water). If you can position yourself to do your scrying *in* a lake, stream, or river, that would be really great.

A journal and pen/pencil to take notes

Gather your tools, then set up a table (or just make sure you have a nice flat surface available. I use a large, flat stone). If you can do this near the water's edge, that would make it all the better. If not, that's okay; just make sure you are set up where your water can reflect the moon.

Take some time to ground and center yourself. When you are ready to begin scrying, raise the pitcher in one hand, holding it over the bowl. As you do, visualize the wisdom and guidance within the watery bowl. As you pour the water into the bowl, recognize the energy of the moon as it charges the water.

When the bowl is full, position yourself so you can see the moon's light reflected directly into the water. Stare into the water. What do see? You may see images moving, or perhaps even words forming. There may be symbols or just patterns. Remember to use your journal and take notes of absolutely

everything you are seeing. You can spend as much time as you like gazing into the water. It's up to you—it may be just a few minutes, or even an hour. I like to stop when my mind starts to clutter with mundane thoughts.

When you are finished, give the water back to nature. I like to give myself a few days to ponder over my notes. What kind of connections can you make through the symbolism or images you saw?

What Dwells Beneath

Fish have long been revered by our ancient ancestors. Early societies were formed near water. The land was fertile for growing crops and life-giving water for drinking was nearby. Goods and people could be easily transported. Moreover, early people could catch the fish that occupied the rivers. The importance of fish is reflected in many culture's myths and legends.

In Greco-Roman mythology, fish held the symbolic meaning of change and transformation. The fish was the first avatar of Vishnu, and as a guide saved the first man from a great flood. It is one of the Eight Auspicious Symbols used in Buddhism and the symbol of the cosmic philosophy of Tao. In ancient African creation myths, fish deals with fertility and creativity, and in Christian mythology, it is a symbol of abundance and faith as observed in the story of loaves and fishes.

My family fishes our local rivers for salmon and steelhead trout that supply us with most of our protein. We abide by and take seriously the many restrictions on our rivers to ensure the continuation of the species for future generations. Without our "wild and scenic" laws for our rivers and streams, great damage to fish and wildlife habitat could threaten the species.

Also, overfishing and poaching restrictions are very strict in my area to maintain proper escapement levels. The Pacific Northwest natives knew this and it is reflected in their legends. Salmon is a medicine animal for most of the Northwestern tribes, and many rites and ceremonies revolve around honoring the salmon. There are also many taboos and other tribal rules regarding salmon, so as to avoid offending them; special Salmon Dances and First Salmon Ceremonies are celebrated at the beginning of salmon-fishing season throughout the Pacific Northwest.

A Smudging Ritual

If you have someone in your family who is embarking on that river of life, you can perform a simple blessing before they set out on those sometimes turbulent waters.

Smudging has its roots in Native American belief and has been adopted by modern Pagans to use in cleansing rituals. The most commonly used smudge stick is sage, for its ability to dispel negative energy. For this blessing, we will use cedar, which is used to bring good things your way. Cedar is burned while praying either aloud or silently. The prayers rise on the cedar smoke and are carried to the Creator.

You will need:

A Cedar smudge stick

Feather

Abalone shell or small bowl of sand

Light your smudge stick. Use your hands (or traditional feather) to cup the smoke and weave it over the person you are smudging. As you smudge, repeat the prayer (below) or a prayer you have written. This was written for someone experiencing a life-changing event.

I love this popular prayer written by Travis Bowman and have included it because I feel it works well for any smudging blessing. These are the words I used for both of my boys as they started college:

> *Flow like a river dear one. Ever-changing, ever-flowing,*
> *   and growing over time.*
> *I bless your eyes that you may see life's obstacles.*
> *I bless your head that you may be wise like the salmon*
> *   and always know the path that leads to home.*
> *I bless your heart that you always give of yourself freely.*
> *I bless your hands that they mold the lives they touch*
> *   in a positive way.*
> *I bless your feet that they stay steadfast on their course.*
> *Flow like a river dear one.*
> *So mote it be.*

When you are finished, gently extinguish your smudge stick in a small bowl of sand or the abalone shell.

Sacred Salmon

Salmon were also sacred to the ancient Celtic people for their wisdom and forethought; to eat a salmon was to gain immediate knowledge. The salmon was the shaman, the traveler in search of his origin but also of his destiny, and was incorporated into many myths. Gwyrhr, sent by King Arthur to assist Culhwch as his interpreter, questioned a series of wise animals, each one wiser than the previous. The oldest and wisest of all was the salmon of Llyn Llyw. Cúchulainn, an ancient Gaelic hero who was endowed with superhuman qualities, used the hero's salmon leap across the Pupils' Bridge to get to Scáthach's stronghold in order to gain access to Scáthach's advanced knowledge of arms. Eating salmon was believed to enhance knowledge and intellect, and the water of the river itself was believed to enhance second sight. To the ancient Celts, the presence of the salmon at the Winter Solstice identified the site as sacred in nature.

The Salmon of Knowledge

My favorite Salmon legend is "The Salmon of Knowledge." It's the story of Fionn MacCumhail, who when still a young boy was sent to live with Finnegas, a poet who lived on the banks of the river Boyne. According to Druid prophecy, a salmon living in the river had, after eating nine hazelnuts from a magical hazelnut tree, acquired all of the world's knowledge. It was further said that whoever caught and ate the magickal salmon would gain all of its knowledge. Finnegas had been attempting to catch the fish for years. After finally doing so, he instructed his young charge to cook it straight away, but not to taste a morsel.

Fionn set to work, but while turning it on the spit, he burnt his thumb and sucked it to relieve the pain. Upon Finnegas's return, he could see there was something different about Fionn and asked if the boy had partaken of the fish. When Fionn explained what happened, Finnegas replied, "You have tasted the Salmon of Knowledge. The prophecy is fulfilled." He encouraged Fionn to finish eating the fish, which he did and then gained all the world's knowledge and became a great poet, warrior, and leader.

It is said eating a meal of salmon and hazelnuts before meditation will make the messages more clear. Divining rods made from hazel are responsive to subtle energy vibrations and environmental changes and are used to find water and buried treasure. The Hazel Moon offers you an opportunity to connect with your inner reserves of wisdom and intuition and is a good time to practice charms for spirit contact, protection, prosperity, dreams, wisdom-knowledge, intelligence, and inspiration.

Hazel Charms

Hazelnuts grow on the bank of the Sauk River where I live—a place where the veil between the worlds is thin. We sometimes gather them up and make good luck charms out of them. This is a fun one to do with the kids.

You will need:

9 hazelnuts

Black or red colored twine

A nut pick or small drill (0.4 drill bit)

Use a nut pick or drill to bore holes in hazelnuts (help the kids with this part). String them on the twine, making it just long enough to hold the nine nuts with a little bit of space in between. Tie a knot at each end of the nut to hold it in place. As you tie off each end, say three times:

Hazelnuts nine on a string
To this humble home
Good luck please bring

Then hang it up in your home as an amulet of protection for the coming year. My kids would sometimes decorate the hazelnuts with protective rune signs or symbols that were meaningful to them, then string them around their bedrooms.

Lessons in the Song

The song of the river has taught me many things while living these past twenty years near its watery edge. Life, like the river, is constantly moving and changing, but we are all on a similar journey. And though I may not always be happy that everybody is in a different place at any given time, we need to enjoy the journey. Magically it has helped me to increase my psychic awareness, and it has taught me to focus and to see what's just beyond the veil. My kids have grown into young adults, but during fishing season we always spend at least one misty September morning together exploring its watery edges and fishing its clear emerald waters.

~

I watch my husband and our boys as their lines flash in the ever-growing light. But now it's the boys who are giving Steve tips and sometimes helping him tie a lure on his line. When my daughter isn't joining in on their fun, she still walks with me. We steady each other so as not to trip on the stony bank and we look for interesting rocks. Though a teenager, she still gets excited when she finds a hag stone. Her eyes sparkle as she announces, "I will make my next amulet for you, Mom."

The river is constantly shifting and changing the water's edge. The eddies and shady nooks of yesterday have changed, some vanishing completely, but there are always new niches and areas to explore. We sit on a sandy bank under the shade of a big-leaf maple. There is a pool of water there that is perfect for the occasional dip. The sounds are the same as we quiet our minds—the rush of water, the quiver of tired alder and cottonwood leaves beginning their decline, and the kingfisher, who lets us know our presence is not particularly favored.

I close my eyes and once again reach back to a time when only the echo of an eagle's cry could be heard through the primeval cedar that dominated this area. There were no roads; only the river and I can hear that ancient drumbeat. Then my daughter leans in. "Do you hear the river's song, Mama?" she whispers.

"Yes, my sweet girl, I do. It is beautiful."

For Further Study

Ancient Wisdom. "Tree Lore: (Sacred Trees.)" http://www.ancient-wisdom.co.uk/treelore.htm.

Coppens, Phillip. "Newgrange: Empowering the Salmon of Wisdom." *Phillip Coppens* (website). http://www.philipcoppens.com/newgrange.html.

First People: The Legends. "Native American Legends: Legend of the Lost Salmon." http://www.firstpeople.us/FP-Html-Legends/Legend-Of-The-Lost-Salmon-Yakima.html.

Old Man Krampus

by Emyme

First of all, allow me to affirm my belief in Santa Claus as a spirit of generosity and good throughout the world. I have never seen the man in corporeal form, but I have seen the physical representation of his positive and compassionate soul. I'm a believer. However, in the spirit of artistic license, some of the following may appear as if I do not believe. Let me repeat—I believe.

~

A generous saint, a kind toymaker, a jolly old elf—three of the most endearing and enduring images of Saint Nicholas, Kris Kringle, Santa Claus. Yuletide, what many call Christmas time, is a happy and giving holiday; an observance and preparation for the return to the light. From the end of November to December 24, and beyond, family and friends gather. Grand meals are enjoyed and gifts are exchanged. Festivals and community celebrations abound. Naturally, the other side of light and goodwill is dark and evil. For every saint there is a sinner. This is where we say hello to Krampus.

The idea that Santa Claus is "making a list" has shown to be not enough to keep some children out of mischief throughout the year. Additionally, and until recently, the general public has been reluctant to lay the dispensation of severe punishment at the feet of Santa Claus. Krampus is but one of the varied bad/evil personages invented to keep children inclined to poor behavior in line. His origins go back to the time of gods and goddesses, superstition, and earth-based beliefs. When Christianity came to be—and grew and flourished—it is easy to see how the punishing tone of the church would embrace the idea of penalties for behavior they deemed "bad." Some of the other names for this phenomenon are: Knecht Ruprecht, Certa, Perchten, Schmutzli, and Klaubauf. All come from the same general pool of fearful imagination over which Krampus dominates.

Krampus: Methods or Madness?

Krampus's physical being may take several forms. Most common is the part man, part beast (goat, ram, or other cloven-footed animal) seen in numerous illustrations. Large, curved horns and demonic expression aside, perhaps the most disturbing part of his visage is the lolling, bright-red tongue. He has been known to wear no clothing, due to his furry appearance. Alternately he is portrayed with trousers, in Santa Claus's red suit, or the bishop's robes of Saint Nicholas. On his back, Krampus carries a sack, similar to Santa Claus's bag of toys, or a basket full of birch sticks or switches. He may go about anytime from December 19 to Christmas Eve, traveling with Santa Claus. More often he is known to travel the world on December 5, the "Eve" if you will, of Saint Nicholas' Day: December 6.

Krampus's methodology may be considered by some to be rather severe. Bad children receive no mere lump of coal from this fellow. Legend has it the first form of punishment is a beating with those birch switches. As previously mentioned, many characterizations of Krampus show him carrying a large, sometimes lidded, basket on his back full of the pliable, stinging branches. In the way that parents act on behalf of Santa Claus by leaving gifts under the Christmas tree, this punishment is quite easily accomplished by parental figures. It is not unreasonable to imagine that during less-enlightened times, church leaders encouraged parents to blind-fold their less-than-angelic offspring, herd them to a dark room, and level various degrees of "beatings." Older siblings, those no longer believing in Saint Nicholas, may have been recruited for this task, or perhaps other relatives, or even those same church leaders. A more unpleasant thought is the children may have been brought together for a Saint Nicholas celebration, or Holy communion, or final Confession before Yule, and those bad children were taken away to be chastised, all in the name of Krampus.

It may be assumed that, for many children, only one disciplinary action was sufficient to ensure years of obedient behavior. A second punishment by Krampus was prescribed for those more incorrigible. When the beatings did not accomplish the desired level of obedience, children were said to be taken away in the basket or a sack. Again, it is not outside the realm of possibility children actually were placed in sacks, or large baskets with lids, and carted off. Offspring would have been "allowed" to "escape" or would be "rescued" by parents before Krampus made off with them completely. It's pretty likely that these escapees would have been frightened enough to change their ways. Relating the experience to an awestruck audience of their peers helped ensure those contemplating some mischief would think twice.

The ultimate penalty dispensed by Krampus is said to be spiriting children away forever, to the underworld, for whatever nefarious ends we can only guess. His nasty, drooping tongue suggests the horror of cannibalism. Following this mythology to the darkest place, it is probable this part of the legend arose from actual events. Children do indeed succumb to illness and die, are killed by accident, or under unspeakable circumstances become the victims of heinous crimes or are abducted never to be seen again. Tragically, this has happened throughout history. The early church, in all its fire-and-brimstone teachings and preachings, may have seized on these heartbreaking catastrophes as a means to keep the newly indoctrinated in line. Any of those events occurring around Yuletide might be used as a deterrent by well-meaning parents: "You had better behave or you may end up dead/you may be taken away like little John Doe."

~

While there have been times when Krampus appears to have been almost dormant, bits and pieces of his legend are recorded and have been mixed and blended for well over 4,000 years. Remote European, most especially Germanic, tribes untouched by Christianity due to geography held onto old traditions and celebrations as late as the fourth century BCE. The Brothers Grimm brought previously oral peasant folklore to the masses with their publications of fairy tales in the early 1800s. Farther north, Hans Christian Andersen compiled his magickal stories. Creatures and characters with a love of punishment similar to Krampus appear in these and other eighteenth and nineteenth century narratives. Varying degrees of harsh and violent images abound. At one point in history it became a popular custom to send and receive Krampus cards and postcards. Safe to say, it was around that time his ability to strike fear and curb recalcitrant tots began to wane. In modern times, he has become something of a camp figure. Krampus is experiencing a resurgence in popularity in the twenty-first century, explainable by modern fascination with the macabre and

horrible. Due to the overcommercialization of the Christmas/Yule holiday, Krampus figures begin to show up around Halloween/Samhain. Examples of Krampus in popular culture can be found in the following American television shows: *Supernatural*, 2007; *The Colbert Report*, 2009; *Grimm*, and *American Dad*, 2013. Krampus-nacht (Krampus's Night) events are increasingly popular the world over. Internet searches offer more than a half million hits, and he enjoys websites totally devoted to his legend, one being www.krampus.com. At least one craft brewery in upstate New York has a seasonal lager named for the nefarious critter.

A much less threatening cousin of Krampus is Pelznickel or Belsnickel. He appears several weeks prior to December 25, clad in furs, not actually having fur. His blustery threatening of the children with switches is seen as humorous. At festivals he will chase children between the stalls until the tide is turned and children chase him out of town. In the United States, this tradition may have been blurred with Krampus as immigrants from many sections of Eastern Europe settled across the country.

❧

Poorly educated and superstitious minds look for reasons. Myths and legends, orations and fairy tales are created to explain what cannot be understood. Much of the demonizing of earth-based religions and belief systems may be laid at the church altar. This is not meant to be a condemnation of how poorly Pagans have been treated through the centuries, but just one more example of how the church fathers found, and continue to create, bad out of good. Early Christianity appropriated Pagan celebrations and Wiccan practices. Beliefs that could not be so easily changed to suit the church became sinful. In the same way that healers and herbalists were condemned, and as witch became synonymous with evil, so Krampus came to be. The ancient legends of a benign bully evolved into a brutish being with a taste for the flesh of children. In these more enlightened times Krampus still thrives, possibly keeping youngsters in line as the clownish "bad cop" to Santa Claus's "good cop." Both were once used as deterrents to unwelcome, delinquent behavior. Only one was turned into a friend.

Unlock Your Inner Spirituality with the Magical Power of Water

by Lynn Smythe

Invoke the power of water when working spells and rituals dealing with love, friendship, healing, peace, divination, intuition, dream work, and psychic awareness. Learn how to unlock your inner spirituality using the magical power of water. The correspondences associated with the element water are dusk, west, fall, taste, female energy, and moon energy. Invoking the magical power of water causes an emotional awakening and spiritual purification of your body, mind, and soul.

Water Personality Types and Animal Totems

My sign is Scorpio, one of the zodiac's three water signs along with Pisces and Cancer. I've embraced the element, as a resident of south Florida for over twenty years who lives a short distance from the ocean. I have a dolphin tattoo on my right shoulder and a scorpion tattoo on my left ankle. Other animal totems you can include in your magical practices when working with the water element include fish, sharks, whales, seals, toads, frogs, and turtles.

I am lucky to live by a small pond, home to a variety of aquatic life. We also get occasional visitors from J. W. Corbett Wildlife Management Area such as water moccasins, baby gators, and a particularly feisty otter that likes to help himself to our pet koi. On any given day, I can choose to work with one of these magnificent creatures as my own personal animal totem. I love living next to a 60,000-acre wildlife refuge and working with the gifts of nature!

Water Colors, Gemstones, and Symbols

Water manifests as a variety of colors including gray, green, blue, and white. Certain colors lend themselves to specific rituals. You can use food coloring to change your water to any shade of the rainbow. Use dark blue for rituals dealing with loyalty, success, and expansion of occult powers. Light blue is the perfect shade for inspiration, truth, harmony, inner peace, and communication. Silver is a great color for meditation and developing psychic powers. Use white when working spells for purity, truth, and spiritual awareness.

If using water isn't an option, simply substitute one of the many gemstones associated with the water element. Water gemstones include aquamarine, aventurine, blue topaz, chrysocolla, moonstone, and opal. And don't forget the gifts from the sea including shells, coral, and pearls.

A cup is the magical tool associated with water. The suit of Cups in tarot cards refers to relationships, emotions, feelings, and connections. A reversed Cup card signals sorrow, melancholy, indifferent emotions, or an overemotional state of mind.

Cups aren't the only symbol used to portray this suit; chalices, cauldrons, or goblets—really any vessel that will hold liquid, such as an abalone shell or small saucer—can symbolize water.

Predict the Future with Water

Hydromancy, or water scrying, is a form of divination, or fortune-telling. Water scrying predicts or interprets past, present, and future events. Most any body of water, either moving or stationary, including wells, rivers, ponds, and lakes, can be used for hydromancy rituals.

A Tibetan singing bowl or mortar and pestle set would make a perfect scrying vessel, but any bowl or saucer will suffice. Fill your bowl with water and gaze upon the surface. Use your fingers, a small branch, or a magic wand to trace circles in the water around the edge of the bowl. Observe the motions of the water and record your interpretation of the symbols you see in a journal or small notebook for predictions of what may happen in the future.

Skipping rocks across a pond and interpreting the motions of the rippling water is another form of water fortune-telling. A form of botanical hydromancy is to throw a handful of leaves into a moving body of water and interpret their patterns of movement.

Water Rituals and Water as Creator

Water is a very powerful force and sometimes, instead of creating life, is a deadly taker of life. Whirlpools, water spouts, tempests, monsoons, tidal waves, and tsunamis are some of the most destructive forms of water.

However, water is the perfect element to invoke during rituals for fertility, renewal, rebirth, and transformation because of its many magical curative properties, including the power to heal. According to legend, particularly potent waters such as springs, wells, and the Fountain of Youth were capable of bestowing the power of immortality. All you had to do to enjoy the magical powers was to either bathe in or drink the water from the fountain, and enjoy eternal youth.

Wicca and other Pagan traditions use water in a variety of ceremonies. Magically blessed water is also called consecrated or holy water by certain religions. Create your own magical water by mixing ½ teaspoon of salt with about 1 cup of water. Some people feel that rainwater mixed with sea salt is more potent than tap water mixed with iodized salt, but it's okay to use whatever products you have on hand. If you live near the beach, you could collect a bit of seawater, which is naturally filled with salt.

Holy water banishes evil spirits and eliminates negative energy from your magical workspace. Use your blessed water as a spiritual cleansing before starting your ritual work.

Moonlight Water Purification Ceremony

The moon influences all water bodies on the earth. The monthly cycle of the moon phases causes an ebb and flow of tides in oceans, seas, and large lakes. You can create magical

water imbued with the energy of the moon, and use it as your own special form of consecrated water. Use your purified moon water to wash away any negative energy before casting a circle for spell work.

Refer to an almanac to learn what phase the moon is in on any given day. The full moon is a perfect time to work abundance spells while the waning moon is better suited to banishing spells.

Add a bit of water to a small container such as a glass or ceramic bowl. Place the bowl outdoors in a sheltered place, so small animals such as the neighbor's cat can't disturb it. Let the bowl of water soak up the rays of the moonlight, either overnight or at least for a few hours.

Recite the following charm while decanting your moon-purified water into a clean container:

Beautiful mother moon,
We hope to see you soon,
Imbue our water with your silvery rays of light,
Shine down your energy and lend our spell some might.

Fresh Water Direct from Nature

Some people think that moving water from streams, lakes, and rivers is more spiritually alive than tap water or water collected from a nonmoving source such as a pond, pool, or canal. Nowadays, that assertion is debatable.

I remember collecting fresh mountain springwater when I was a preteen and teenager living in the Adirondack Mountains of upstate New York. We never worried about pretreating the water before drinking it, as we thought it was pure and all natural.

Unfortunately, freshwater is not as safe as it once was. Storm-water runoff, sewage discharge, and contamination from fertilizers makes much of our fresh water supply unfit for human consumption. Common freshwater contaminants include Giardia, E. coli, brain-eating amoeba, and flesh-eating bacteria.

You must devise other means of obtaining safe drinking water. It's okay to collect water used for ritualistic purposes, and not for drinking, from just about anywhere. Treating water by boiling, bleaching, or iodine tablets leaves a product that is bland and inert with a funny aftertaste sometimes. Using a filter, such as a ceramic cartridge, to cleanse the water is about as close as you'll get to the real thing.

If you think tap water is lacking in spiritual energy, try collecting your own water the next time it rains. I like to collect rainwater as it falls from the sky, but you need some sort of basic filtering system to strain out any dirt and debris. I used to have a large rain barrel set up under a downspout gutter at my house. I took a large piece of plastic window screening and placed it across the top of the barrel to keep larger bits of debris from falling into the barrel.

There was a small spigot toward the bottom of the barrel for pouring off the desired quantity of water into a watering can. My houseplants loved a drink of fresh rainwater. Prior to using the water for ritual work, I strained it through cheesecloth to remove the finer bits of dirt and sand. I also mixed the cleansed water with a bit of sea salt to create my personal stash of blessed water. I think it's time to set up a rain barrel at my new house and start collecting the magical element of water!

The Hidden Moon: Magical Workings for the Void-of-Course Periods

by Diana Rajchel

Magic workers learn early about the relevance of moon phases to their work. In simple terms, the waxing phase signifies a time for spells of gain, and the waning phase is a time for spells of wane. Magic workers delving deeper into astrology eventually discover the moon's influence affects more than what kind of spell to do. As the moon transits through the signs of the zodiac each month, it regulates more than the tides of the sea; it also manages the ebb and flow of our attention, our subconscious minds, and our capacity to act on instinct.

Every few days, this lunar energy takes a pause in the stories it tells our dreaming minds. Astrologers call this lunar pause "moon void-of-course," which means it does not have any aspects to any planet used to make astrological predictions until it reaches the next astrological sign. For example, even though Venus may appear nearby, the moon in Aries does not interact with it, and since the moon mediates the influence of all the other planets in the solar system ... no one feels much of anything until the moon goes direct again in Taurus.

These void-of-course rest periods seem to serve the collective consciousness by giving the universe a chance to pause and consider what has happened in the preceding days. This status can last anywhere from a few minutes to up to two days at a time. Magic workers often find out the hard way that a void-of-course moon comes with a troubling effect: anything you try to make happen also goes into some mysterious lunar void. Often described often as the "nothing will happen" effect, this is really the best time to tell people the things they don't want to hear. It will register, but with the moon out of aspect with other planets, its ability to form a strong pull on emotions just won't happen. It also comes with some annoying effects. More items get lost in plain sight during a moon void-of-course, so that water bottle you set right in that place is still right there, but for some reason your eyes just glance over it until the moon goes direct again. During this time, people often miss or are late for appointments, and Mercury retrograde–level misunderstandings can happen (although they can correct much faster since void-of-course never lasts longer than a couple days). Normally prompt and organized people find themselves procrastinating. Any project you try to start, any date you try to make, any promise you intend to keep will be a nonstarter if you begin during the moon's void-of-course period. The good news is that without the moon tugging on your emotional life, you will likely take these inconveniences in stride.

This lunar period really is the best time to break up with all but the most ardent of drama queens and kings. It is also the closest to a safe time to tell your boss what you did

that lost the company a few thousand dollars. Perhaps offer your difficult neighbor compensation for the mailbox you ran over at this time. If you must break a lease, tell your landlord during a void-of-course moon. Essensially, anyone wishing to minimize consequences for mistakes should especially make note of these periods.

On the other hand, if you need something to happen *now*, a void-of-course moon can make life especially frustrating, even more if you have a short amount of time to make energy happen *now*. Conventional wisdom for magic workers is to take a break during the void-of-course moon. Use the time to meditate, pray, and maybe do some introspective journaling since you won't start a new emotional phase until the void-of-course period has ended.

As in most magical scenarios, often what appears an absolute simply requires some rethinking. The moon's void-of-course period definitely offers distinct possibilities for magical work. Think of this as you would if you worked in retail: some work can only be finished during slow periods, and those happen in waves. These lunar rest periods are the best time to work magic that you really do not want or need others to know about—the type that does not have visible results. Especially good workings to do at this time include invisibility work, magic to put a dead stop to something (usually a magical attack or a social injustice), to influence someone's unconscious, to wrap up a project that has gone on too long, and to work magic on yourself. Please note that protection magic works at any time you choose, in part because with the best protection magic, *nothing happens.*

Let's look at three examples of hidden-moon magic: invisibility, dead-stop work, and working magic on yourself.

Invisibility

As the late magician Donald Michael Kraig pointed out, many people confuse invisibility for translucence. Invisibility workings make the magician (or an object the magician chooses) unnoticeable. This is often used by people who

wish to cross through crowded areas without suffering street harassment, ignore desperate students who didn't study, or simply avoid one specific person. In this case, the moon's void-of-course "nothing happens" energy works by making sure that the invisibility worker does not register on the consciousness of nearby viewers.

To work an invisibility spell on your person during a void-of-course moon, make a tea from the following herbs and add it to a bath (or pour over yourself in the shower): chicory, poppy seeds, and fern leaves. As you soak in the bath, pour some of the water over your head, picturing the herbs sinking into your aura. Picture yourself walking down a busy street, while absolutely no one notices you—his or her eyes simply pass over you as though you are not there.

Address a prayer to the Egyptian goddess Aumaunet, the "hidden one" of her own cosmology:

Hail Amaunet,
present at the birth of the universe,
who reigns eternal!

Make me as hidden as the moon,
Unseen, unheard, untouched
Until I desire to be seen.
So mote it be!

If you need to switch invisibility on and off throughout the day, keep a penny in a jar that soaks in the herb solution. Carry it in your shoe when you need invisibility and remove it from your person when finished.

Dead-Stop Work

There are times in life when you just need to put a stop to any nonsense. Whether you find yourself embroiled in a witch war (hey, they happen) or you want to prevent nuclear dumping in your neighborhood, void-of-course magic is the track to take.

To put a stop to an ongoing situation, gather the following: an apple sliced crosswise, camphor, a half-dozen walnuts, and any papers, flyers, and whatnot that relate to the situation. Meditate until you find a word that summarizes the problem. Carve that word into the bottom half of the apple's flesh with a paring knife. On a plate, set the papers relating to the problem down, along with the bottom half of the apple. Around the edges, push in the camphor (near the seeds) and the walnuts (on the outer edges). Visualize the apple working like a "make it stop" grenade. Once you feel the full power of that visualization, bring the top half of the apple down on top of it. Bury the apple and papers away from your home.

Work Magic on Yourself

There is an argument that all spells cast ultimately are on the magician first, whether by changing his or her perspective or by altering his or her physical experience with the external world. Since the void-of-course moon is also a short rest period for your emotional life, this is a good time to examine your personal emotional difficulties and apply magic to help heal the most severe issues. The example given is for obsessiveness, especially stemming from an infatuation. This type of work also applies well to anger management/rage, troubling memories, and the negative thoughts that accompany social anxiety.

Create a tea from garlic leaves, angelica root, and licorice. Allow to steep for twelve minutes and then strain, reserving the liquid. Stir in a tablespoon of coconut oil. Bless the mixture, instructing the herbs and oil to cure you of your pain by stopping the repetitive, unproductive thoughts.

Rub the mixture on your hair, and leave on for about twenty minutes. Rinse out, and shampoo as normal. Repeat this at every void-of-course moon until relieved.

~

Several smartphone apps and websites now offer information and charts regarding moon void-of-course. *Llewellyn's Witches' Calendar* and *Datebook* also offer moon information, so when you plan a working, make note of those periods and adjust your work accordingly. Understanding how the moon's influential absence can work for you can free you from a great deal of frustration in your magical work.

For Further Reading

Kraig, Donald Michael. "Can You See Me Now?" Llewellyn (blog). September 6, 2013. http://www.llewellyn.com/blog/2013/09/can-you-see-me-now/

Gem Elixirs

by Charlie Rainbow Wolf

I've always been very conscious of my body and its systems, and I try to be as proactive in my own vitality as I possibly can. I'm not perfect—I can enjoy a gourmet donut along with the best of them! I can, though, usually tell if there is something out of whack. One of my favorite ways to bring things into balance is with crystals and gemstones.

When I'm doing this type of balancing work for others, I can lay out the stones on them, using different crystals on various pressure points. That's harder to do when I want to use stones to treat myself, so several years ago I started working with gem elixirs in order to ingest the healing properties of the gemstones. It was hit-and-miss for a while, but now I've got a method that works, and I feel very comfortable using it for my own balancing and teaching others how to do the same.

To get the most out of using gem elixirs, first you have to understand how they work. It's all done through vibrational healing. Each stone vibrates on a different frequency, and that gives the stone its own unique signature. We also vibrate with our own unique energy signature. Stress, illness, and other challenges in life can disrupt that vibration, but herbs, stones, and other items that resonate on the appropriate frequency can help to restore the natural balance.

The Elixirs

It sounds easy enough, but there's more to it than throwing a rock in some water and then drinking it.

For one, many healing stones will not react kindly to getting wet—selenite, for example. Some also may be harmful to the system. Many stones contain traces of aluminum, copper, or even arsenic and other toxins. The best way to create a gemstone elixir is to allow the energizing properties of the sun to be the catalyst for activating the water.

One of the simplest ways to make a gem elixir involves a good-quality clear glass, a glass test tube, the stone, and a sunny windowsill. Place the stone in the test tube, place the test tube in the glass of water, and place the glass of water in the sunny windowsill. Let the sun charge the water with the stone's energies, and you've got a gemstone elixir. I usually charge the water for about three days around a full moon, but there is no hard-and-fast rule. This is a very safe method because no toxins or impurities can leach into the water.

It would be very easy to get caught up in the minutiae such as choosing the purest glass, the best water, and so on. Remember that your intent is the strongest influence, not the glass or the test tube. I use a high-quality glass (my favorite container is a very old canning jar that belonged to a family member, but that has more to do with the antiquity of the jar than anything else), and reverse-osmosis or distilled water.

Your crystal will have been many places and handled by many people before you start using it to make an elixir, so you will want to cleanse it. If you have a favorite way of cleansing and charging ritual tools, by all means use it. Just remember that every stone reacts differently, and what may work for one stone—washing in running water, for example—could be detrimental to another one. I keep things as uncomplicated as possible, usually putting my stones in the light of the moon for three days to cleanse them and then under my pillow for the rest of the month to attune them to me. Another method is putting the stone in the test tube and then sinking the test tube in sea salt. There's no right or wrong way; do what works for you. However, I have found it best to cleanse one stone at a time. It seems to keep the energies clearer.

The Stones

There are many ways to select the right stones when making gem elixirs. I initially chose my stones by dowsing over them. Kinesiology is another method. If you are used to letting your psyche guide you, then tap into your intuition. Or, you could simply follow the more time-honored approach of matching your need to the traditional meaning of the stone. This is what we're going to be exploring here, taking a look at some popular stones and the chakras with which they resonate.

Hematite

Although tumbled hematite is usually a metallic pewter in color, it is has a high iron content and is often red in its raw and unpolished state. It is a grounding stone that helps strengthen the body, making it a great stone to use when under stress. Hematite can help prevent the body from absorbing negative energies and also help it to rid itself of those energies.

Hematite resonates with the root chakra. This energy center at the base of the spine not only helps you to stay balanced and grounded, it also affects libido and sexual energy. A lot of people overlook this area, preferring to work instead with the chakras that are higher and more spiritual. However, if this chakra is out of balance, it will be hard to bring the others into balance. I recommend starting here and working up, rather than the other way around.

Carnelian

Carnelian is a lovely semi-opaque, flame-red stone. It should look warm and feel inviting. Carnelian's energy is one of courage and action. Its vibration enhances motivation and action, allowing you to manifest your heart's desires. This stone can also come to your aid when making life-changing decisions so that you move into your new path with determination and ambition.

Carnelian's energy works well with the second—or sacral—chakra, which involves the organs around the navel, including the female reproductive system. This is where feelings reside, which is why you get "butterflies" in your stomach when nervous or why you may get a "gut feeling" about something. Carnelian helps bring this area into balance so that both the physical and the emotional body can be healthy, while also stimulating creativity.

Citrine

Citrine is actually a variety of quartz. It's incredibly similar to amethyst—in fact, much of what is being sold on the market today is not natural citrine at all, but rather a form of heat-treated amethyst. The heat-treated stones don't have quite the same energy as the natural citrines, so when obtaining stones for your gem elixirs, try to get the natural ones. Citrines help you lose your fear and anxieties so that you can celebrate the good things that are coming your way.

Citrine's energy works with the third chakra, the solar plexus, which is the seat of your will and determination. Found in the abdominal area, it governs the stomach and intestines, as well as the liver and the spleen. This area needs to be in balance for you to be certain that you have good digestion and liver function. Citrine can assist in a metaphoric way when it comes to absorbing information and ideas by getting these systems to function harmoniously and helping you to develop your willpower.

Rose Quartz

Rose quartz is—obviously—another form of quartz. This is the stone most associated with love. This isn't the "I love you, do you love me, how much do you love me, will you always love me," type of love that often comes to mind when considering relationships. Rose quartz offers a very compassionate and universal type of love—the love that assures you that you're okay just as you are. It is one of the most gentle stones to work with, and it does a marvelous job helping to heal the heart chakra and the chakras above it.

Rose quartz is a powerful heart chakra stone because of the vibration of universal love with which it resonates. This is the fourth or middle energy center, and it divides the lower chakras from the upper ones. It is concerned with love, in all of the spiritual senses of the word, as well as with compassion, kindness, and truth. This chakra can be found in the center of the chest, where the heart lies. It influences the heart, the respiratory organs, the thymus, and the circulatory system. It's interesting to watch people when this chakra is out of balance. Many times they will round or hunch their shoulders, as if trying to protect their heart from emotional pain.

Sodalite

Sodalite, with its lovely blue and white coloring, is a cleansing and calming stone. Reminiscent of lapis, it is a stone that can help you open up to your own intuition and psychic abilities, clairvoyance, and other metaphysical talents. It helps create a channel where information from your higher self can find its way into your conscious mind. Sodalite can be a hard taskmaster. It asks you to live up to being the best that you

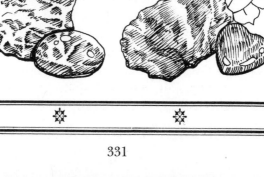

can be, and it will help you to unlearn everything that other teachers taught you so that your own truths can be uncovered and celebrated.

Sodalite is one of the stones associated with the throat chakra, around the thyroid area. This is the center where honesty, integrity, and clear communication of your thoughts and ideas reside. Very often when this chakra is blocked, people talk, but never feel as though they are being heard. This chakra is associated with speaking, but also with listening. Many people listen not to hear the other person, but to think about what they are going to say next. Using cleansing sodalite when working with this chakra can help restore the balance between speaking and listening.

Amethyst

Amethyst, yet another form of quartz, is considered a very high and spiritual stone. It is no coincidence that the Pope's ring is amethyst. Amethyst comes in many forms, from the twinkling druse to the large, single points to the cut-and-polished gemstones in jewelry. Amethyst stones help to quiet the mind, so that communication with spirit is easier. It is a protective stone, as well as a communicative stone. Its soothing energies make it an excellent companion for meditative work.

Amethyst is associated with the third eye chakra, the energy center around the ears, eyes, nose, and brain. It is here that the "sixth sense" is said to be found. If you were interested in developing your psychic talents, you might choose to stimulate this area. This chakra is also good to work with if you are seeking visions and vivid dreams.

Clear Quartz Crystal

Of all the stones I work with, this has to be my favorite. It comes in so many terminations (points at the natural end of the stone) and with so many inclusions. Each one is different—just like the whorls on the tips of our fingers are unique. Quartz is easy to obtain and comes in many different forms, from tumbled stones to single natural points to clusters, and more. Quartz is an excellent amplifier, which makes it a wonderful stone to use with the crown chakra.

The crown chakra is located just over the top of the head—as if you were wearing a crown. Spiritual energy comes into the body here while this chakra also draws energy up through the other chakras, making the crown a focal point for energy. This chakra is all about knowing, as in the word *gnosis*. It relates to spirituality, selflessness, and the higher self. Working with this energy creates a bridge to infinity, and by bringing this area into balance, you can reach your fullest potential.

Storing the Elixirs

You now know how to make the elixirs and which stones to use to resonate with each chakra, so let's look at how to actually use the elixirs. The sunlight will help the water absorb the energies of the gemstones very well, but that energy will fade if not stored correctly. I recommend two things. The first is to store the gem elixirs—carefully labeled—in a sealed glass vial or bottle, in a cool place. I prefer blue bottles, but green and amber are just as suitable. Even a clear bottle can be used if it is wrapped with light-proof paper, which can help identify the elixirs, as they can be wrapped in paper that matches the color of the stones used. Another thing you can do is to put a drop or two of brandy into each vial of elixir—a ratio of 1 part brandy to 10 parts elixir is good. If you do all of this, the elixir should keep well for at least a month. Gem elixirs are easy enough to make, so there's no reason why long-term storage should be necessary.

Using the Elixirs

The most popular way of using gem elixirs is to take them internally, and if they are prepared using the safe method recommended earlier, there is no reason why they cannot be imbibed. That's not the only way that they can be used, though. They can be misted through a room to clear energies, added to a cleansing or a ritual bath, sprayed onto the skin, applied as a warm or cool compress, and more. I strongly advise that you always start small and work up to a larger dose. Once the gem elixir has been taken internally, you can't remove it like you could if you were wearing that stone as a piece of jewelry. If you err on the side of caution and let the stones teach you, you could find that working with gem elixirs opens up a whole new world for you when it comes to balancing your chakras and communicating with your higher self.